THEORY FOR SOCIAL WORK PRACTICE

Theory FOR SOCIAL WORK PRACTICE

RUTH ELIZABETH SMALLEY

COLUMBIA UNIVERSITY PRESS

NEW YORK AND LONDON

Ruth Elizabeth Smalley was formerly Dean of the School of
Social Work at the University of Pennsylvania in Philadelphia.

Copyright © 1967 Columbia University Press

First printing 1967
Third printing 1971

ISBN 0-231-02769-9
Library of Congress Catalog Number 67-14290

Printed in the United States of America

TO

the memory of my Mother and Father,

AND TO THE MANY OTHERS—

FAMILY, FRIENDS, COLLEAGUES, AND STUDENTS—

WHOSE LIVES HAVE SO ENRICHED MY OWN

PREFACE

SOCIAL WORK, old as a cause and in purpose and purview, new in this century as a profession, has been subject to swings of interest and concern to its practitioners and the citizens and officials who support its programs. A major swing has been from cause, or zealous purpose, to function, or assumed programmatic responsbility of society,* and, currently, back to cause. To understand the oscillation, to evaluate its significance, and to find our own center for present-day operation within it require a brief look at history.

The roots of social work are in man's earliest concern for his fellow man and for his group, his society. All the major religions early identified as virtue care for the widow, the orphan, the poor, the sick, and the disadvantaged, and charged their believers to practice that virtue. Programs of care for persons needing succor were developed and conducted by religious individuals and religious groups over the centuries. Such efforts were followed and accompanied by the activities of lay persons motivated by humanitarian concerns, and by the gradual assumption of responsibility by government for the well-being of all its members. The passing of the Poor Law of England, in 1601, the antecedent of this country's public programs of financial assistance, constituted a codification of existing laws in this area and, in this

---

* Porter Lee, *Social Work as Cause and Function and Other Papers*. The relation of cause to function in social work is developed with clarity and vigor in this prescient work.

sense, marked a turning point in a government's assumption of responsibility for one kind of human need.

The scope of the efforts of today's social workers has broadened to include programs for the alleviation of psychological as well as physical distress, as found in an economic social and cultural cross-section of the population, and has come to include prevention as well as alleviation of social ills, through the development of appropriate social policy and social services. Social work practice reflects increasingly the democratic ethic in identifying social welfare as a "right" of all rather than a "gift" of the privileged to the underprivileged. Yet social workers still identify themselves with the long tradition of concern for human need and social stress. Their focus continues to be on man's relationship to others and to his society, and on society's relationship to an individual or group.

Whether the programs within which they work are designed to serve individuals, groups, or communities, the thrust of their effort is to release human power in individuals for personal fulfillment and social good, and to release social power for the creation of the kind of society that makes social self-realization most nearly possible for all people.

Preoccupied as the predecessors of today's social workers were with cause, fired by concern for the disadvantaged or suffering, dedicated to efforts in behalf of others, it was not until early in the twentieth century that serious attention was given to *method*, to analyzing and describing the way certain social services, notably the services of the charity organization societies, could be made available so that they might hold the greatest promise of achieving their purposes, as assumed programmatic responsibilities of society. It was Mary Richmond, in this country, who ushered in the era of concern with method, and it was the focus on the individual person and his family which led to the development of the method of casework, the first of the social work methods to be analyzed and taught. Only gradually, and much later, did social workers engaged in working with groups through settlement and neighborhood houses and young peoples' organizations, both sectarian and nonsectarian, address themselves to the same degree to "method." And in our own day, the segment of the profession concerned with work with communities, either through community organization or community development, is just now struggling to identify a method that rests on a theory for practice.

The early concern with method, first stated in any comprehensive way in Mary Richmond's *Social Diagnosis,** grew out of the necessity to improve the effectiveness of a social welfare program. The program was designed to help with social problems experienced by individuals and families. The focus of the program was primarily on the outer or external circumstances of the individual client or family, and the nature of the method employed reflects that focus.

Social work method was revolutionized by the influx of psychological knowledge after the First World War, and by the impact of Freudian psychoanalysis and the development of other psychologies which followed it.

Virginia Robinson, in *A Changing Psychology in Social Casework,*† was one of the first social work writers to identify the portent of the new psychological insights for what could be truly a social work method. Subsequent contributions by such writers as Hamilton, Hollis, Towle, and, to some degree, Perlman, pointed up the use of psychoanalytic theory for understanding the individuals served by social workers and for the treatment engaged in. This was a period of great enrichment of social work method, but it served also to create some problems for the profession. In making psychoanalytic theory their own, for understanding and treatment, a great body of social workers took over not only certain insights and methods of psychoanalysis, or adaptations of methods, but to some extent its purpose as well. The older social work purpose had inhered in the programs which were being administered and had served to unite social workers in working toward the goal of effecting greater opportunity for

* Mary Richmond, *Social Diagnosis.*
† Virginia P. Robinson, *A Changing Psychology in Social Casework.*

the economically and socially disadvantaged, and strengthening
individuals to use social opportunities. The newer one, more individual than social in focus, was based on a psychology of emotional illness and had as its goal the curing or alleviating of such
illness. The social purpose of the *program* within which the
social worker functioned became secondary to the purpose of individual psychotherapy.

Functional social work developed in the School of Social
Work at the University of Pennsylvania, under the leadership of
Virginia Robinson and Jessie Taft. They had taken much from
the philosophy and teachings of Mead and Dewey and later from
Otto Rank, one of Freud's earlier followers, once described as
"the Crown Prince of the Early Psychoanalytic Movement."
Functional social work differed in two respects from Diagnostic
social work, as it came to be called. It differed in psychological
base since it operated not from a psychology of illness but from a
psychology of growth with an emphasis on the creative potential
of man and on the place of social and cultural factors in his development. It put the client rather than the worker at the center
of the social work relationship, with the worker constrained to
lend herself to the client's growth purpose for himself, rather
than to evaluate his degree and kind of sickness and do what
would make him well according to her, or whatever, norms. But
it differed in another essential too, and this had nothing to do
with Rank or his psychology or any psychology. It differed in
continuing to define a purpose for social work that was social
rather than individual and that found its specific definition
within the function of some social agency or program established
and maintained by society or some significant section of it in the
interest of society as a whole as well as in the interest of the individual served.*

The preoccupation with psychological method, then, which

---

* Jessie Taft, "The Relation of Function to Process in Social Casework," introduction
to *Journal of Social Work Process,* Vol. I, No. 1 (1937), pp. 1–18. Reprinted in *Jessie
Taft, Therapist and Social Work Educator,* edited by Virginia P. Robinson. It was in this
article that the concept of agency function in its relation to social casework method as
leading to a social casework process was first developed in some detail.

seemed, to some degree, to deflect one large segment of the profession from social purpose and from concern with social problems, did not operate in the same way for the functional group. This group continued to be concerned with the social problems with which social agencies were set up to deal. The method used, a method based on relationship and making full use of dynamic psychology, was designed to make those programs most usable by the clientele served, in their own interest, and in the interest of society too.

The devaluation and lack of attention to method, particularly the method of social casework, so evident in the professional literature of the mid-1960s, appear to stem in part from a recognition that the kind of method being devalued is designed to achieve a purpose important in itself, but foreign to the proper purpose of social work as it has come to be understood and supported by "society." It stems also from lack of understanding of the way attention to method, that is, a kind of method which, in its very nature, is relevant to its social task, is essential to the achievement of broad social purpose, as that purpose finds expression in specific agency purpose, and to the implementation of social policy, as that policy finds expression in social welfare programs.

In repudiating what appears to some social actionists among social workers as a narrow and "clinical" concern with individuals in favor of affecting social policy on a large scale, and addressing itself to social problems such as poverty, mental retardation, delinquency, social work is in danger of taking unto itself a too total responsibility for the cause and cure of social problems in a way that ignores their complexity, the many factors that enter into their genesis, and the many professional disciplines as well as the will of the body politic which must enter into their resolution or alleviation. Social work is in danger also of failing to make its proper, distinctive, and appropriate contribution to the alleviation and prevention of social ills through participating in the formulation of social policy, the development and modification of social welfare programs, *and* through the use of its distinctive methods conceived as ways of implementing social agency programs.

It is my purpose in writing this book to develop a theory for social work practice, which in its base and nature is effective for the accomplishment of social welfare purposes as they are manifest in social agency programs and in community "patterns" of programs.

After describing the present purpose and purview of social work and identifying its major fields for practice, I shall identify the methods, the use of which lead to the processes through which social work presently operates. I shall then develop a psychological base for social work practice whatever the process skill or field of practice; a social base located in social agency or program purpose; and a process base rooted in an understanding of process as a psycho-social phenomenon underlying all social work practice. There will follow an identification of some principles of practice which derive from the psychological-social-process bases established, as they are applicable in social work processes both primary and secondary. Illustrative process record material for each of the major primary processes, that is, social casework, social group work, community organization, will be presented and discussed to point up the generic principles used, as exemplified in the recorded material, and to identify some principles of practice specific to the particular process employed. There will be brief consideration of some implications of what has been developed for social work education.

The task is formidable. It will be clear immediately that I shall not attempt to present or analyze the several process skills in depth or detail; each requires its own book. I merely want to establish a frame of reference within which all the processes of social work may be viewed, secondary as well as primary, and to develop a unifying base in theory from which each may be developed, in its distinctive difference, while retaining the characteristics which mark it a process in social work appropriate and effective for realizing a social work purpose.

Let me add that I see social work practice, requiring a process skill and operating from certain generic principles, just as effective for producing change *within* social agencies, and within the pattern of social agencies, as it is for administering programs which presently exist. I see the essentials of such skill as applicable, also, to the kind of participation in social policy-making which is peculiarly appropriate for social work. In short, I propose to develop certain characteristics of a method, which in use becomes a process skill, appropriate for the effective achievement of social work purposes. For I believe that social work as a profession will stand or fall not alone on whether it continues to be true to the purposes which are traditionally its own, but on its continuous refinement and development of the method or methods through which it achieves its purposes.

The method I propose to develop involves the worker's use of certain basic principles, as he participates in a relationship process, directed toward a defined social purpose. The professional skill which the use of such a method requires is peculiarly suited, in its very nature, for the realization of social work ends.

This kind of social work method will differ, in some respects, from what is conceived by others as method appropriate for social work practice. I choose to present a method theory, or theory for practice,* which, in its essence, is consistent, which has been developed over a considerable period of time, which has proved effective at every level of practice, in widely diverse fields, and as engaged in by a considerable body of practitioners. It is my hope that others will continue to develop different theories and conceptual schemes for social work practice, and that together we may contribute toward the evolution of something in social work method which, while it may never be as unitary as the values and broad purposes we share, may yet move us closer toward a

---

* I am using the word "theory" not in the strictly scientific sense of a closely drawn hypothesis which can be tested and proved or disproved but more loosely, in the dictionary sense of a "plan for action," or scheme for practice, resting on the use of a set of identified principles which are related to each other and which derive from common bases in relevant knowledge.

commonly accepted theory for practice than we are at present.

My point of view in this connection is similar to that expressed by Jerome Frank, writing on the art-science of healing (Persuasion and Healing, pp. 232–33):

Our survey has suggested that much, if not all, of the effectiveness of different forms of psychotherapy may be due to those practices that all have in common, rather than to those that distinguish them from each other. This does not necessarily mean that all therapies are interchangeable. It may well turn out, when types of patients and effects of therapy are better understood, that certain approaches are better for some types of patients than for others, and that they differ in certain of their effects, which have not yet been specified. Until these questions are clarified, the advance of both knowledge and practice is probably better served by members of different schools defending their own positions, while being tolerant of other schools, than by being uncritically eclectic. For the therapist's ability to help his patient depends partly on his self-confidence, and this in turn depends on mastery of a particular conceptual scheme and its accompanying techniques. Since the leading theories of psychotherapy represent alternative rather than incompatible formulations, it is unlikely that any of them is completely wrong. As an eminent philosopher wisely said: "A clash of doctrines is not a disaster—it is an opportunity." The activity stimulated by the clash of psychotherapeutic doctrines will eventually yield sufficient information either to prove that they are to all practical purposes identical or to clarify and substantiate differences between them.

It is in a spirit, then, not of defending, but of defining, a point of view that I write—with the intent not of competition with other points of view, but of contribution to a profession which unites all social workers.

RUTH ELIZABETH SMALLEY

University of Pennsylvania
Philadelphia, Pennsylvania
December, 1966

ACKNOWLEDGMENTS

ALTHOUGH I refer to social work theory which has been identified as "functional," trace its origin to the School of Social Work of the University of Pennslyvania, which I have served as Dean, and make extensive reference to and use of the writings of two who contributed vitally and centrally to its origin and development, Virginia P. Robinson and Jessie Taft, I want to take full responsibility for what I develop here as theory, as my own statement. It is my assumption that faculty, past and present, would be in essential accord with the central thrust of my thesis, but I cannot speak and do not wish to speak for anyone but myself in this writing. My debt is great to the early faculty of the School of Social Work of the University of Pennslyvania, especially to Jessie Taft, Virginia Robinson, and Kenneth Pray, and to the others, too, who worked with them to develop a theory for social work practice, alive and socially responsible, in fresh new ways.

I am deeply indebted to current faculty, also, especially to Rosa Wessel, Harold Lewis, Richard Lodge, Helen U. Phillips, Eleanor Ryder, and Tybel Bloom, whose consultation and writing I have freely sought and searched, and to other faculty as well whose penetrating thought and devoted practice inspired me and gave substance and direction to my efforts. I am indebted to Evelyn Butler, the School's librarian and to her able staff, for their invaluable assistance in locating reference material. Appreciation is expressed to colleagues who have no connection with the "Pennsylvania School," whose points of view differ in some respects from my own. Their conviction and their scholarly and professional contribution have provided important grist for the mill of my own grinding.

Much appreciated is the record material contributed by Barbara Friedman, Rachel Breslau, Harry Citron, and Carol Bauer, with the permission of the agencies within which they practiced.*

I am deeply grateful to Mildred Tate for her careful preparation of the manuscript from scribbled notes to final copy, and to my administrative assistant, Maxine Evons, who sustained me through crowded days. Finally, I have a word of appreciation for my friend Margaret Robinson, who endured the stress of the long pull with generous patience and unfailing strength.

R.E.S.

* The work of Friedman (M.S.W. 1963) and Breslau (M.S.W. 1962) appears in M.S.W. Theses, School of Social Work, University of Pennsylvania. The work of Citron (Advanced Curriculum Certificate 1955) in an advanced curriculum project, School of Social Work, University of Pennsylvania. Bauer's work was drawn from a record used for teaching in the School of Applied Social Sciences, Western Reserve University. Appreciation is expressed to that School's Dean, Herman Stein, for permission to use it here.

CONTENTS

THEORY FOR SOCIAL WORK PRACTICE

1 PURPOSE AND PURVIEW FOR SOCIAL WORK PRACTICE

THE UNDERLYING purpose of all social work effort is to release human power in individuals for personal fulfillment and social good, and to release social power for the creation of the kinds of society, social institutions, and social policy which make self-realization most possible for all men. Two values which are primary in such a purpose are respect for the worth and dignity of every individual and concern that he have the opportunity to realize his potential as an individually fulfilled, socially contributive person.

Many factors contribute to the difficulty of finding a base for unity in identifying social work as a professional practice. Social work addresses itself to a variety of problems and takes place in a variety of fields. It is institutionalized in agencies and programs under diverse auspices and with diverse sources of support. It serves persons varying widely in social condition and personal characteristics. The very processes through which it is carried on, as they are directed to individuals, groups, or communities or to the facilitation and administration of programs of social welfare, differ necessarily in significant ways. Such diversity discourages and may even appear to defy the finding of an underlying unity that can establish social work as one profession, rooted in commonly held values and in a commonly accepted body of knowledge, with a single broad concern or purpose. Yet social work requires use of a method for the achievement of that purpose

which can be identified, taught, and learned as, in certain respects, a generic social work method, whatever its special character in specific situations or types of situations. Certainly such
diversity makes it difficult to identify boundaries or, to put it
positively, to establish a purview for social work practice. Speaking more than a quarter of a century ago, Kenneth L. M. Pray [1]
identified social work as

a normal constructive social instrument . . . a necessary part of the
structure of a civilized, well-planned society because it is directed to
helping individuals meet the problems of their constantly shifting relations with one another and with the whole society, and to helping the
whole society, at the same time, adjust its demands upon its members
and its services to them in accordance with the real needs of the individuals that compose and determine its life.

Such a concept avoids the bothersome, because unreal, division
of social work's province into the trilogy of "Restoration, Prevention, and Provision," as suggested by Boehm [2] and Boehm's later
equally inconclusive and divisive scheme of "Social Habilitation
and Social Restoration." Yet it includes, within a positive frame
of reference, all those purposes. Pray's concept is embodied in a
view of social work that is concerned with social welfare programs and processes for releasing individual power for personal
fulfillment and social good, and social power for the fullest possible socially responsible self-realization of all of society's individuals.

Social work is based on a recognition that in our complex society, with its often conflicting demands and its uneven provision
of opportunity for differing individuals, there are inevitable
stresses as individuals, groups of individuals, and whole communities seek to find a meaningful and productive place for themselves within the scheme of things. This is a seeking which can
never be finally achieved. Life does not stand still, neither the life
of society with its social institutions, its customs and values, its
demands and expectations of its "parts" nor the life of any individual, group, or community with its changing needs, aspirations, and capacities.

Into a world characterized by continuous change in the relationship between man and his society, and by continuous change in each of the parts to that relationship, comes social work. The central concern of social work is that the relationship should be a progressively productive one for the individuals who make up society, through promotion of their well-being and provision of opportunity for their realization of potential, and for society as a whole, through the continuous development of the values, customs, and institutions which further such well-being and self-realization for all its people.

Helen Witmer [3] early identified the social focus and essential nature of social work when she described as its "prime function" "to give assistance to individuals in regard to difficulties they encounter in their use of an organized group's services, or in their own performance as a member of an organized group," adding that "by this work not only are individuals aided but the adequate functioning of social institutions is facilitated and human needs are thereby more effectively met." She concluded: "In a sense then, social work is an institution that serves other institutions. . . . This interdependency of institutions is . . . characteristic of the total social structure, but it is only social work that has the specific task of rendering the work of other institutions more effective."

Karl de Schweinitz, [4] more recently, brought clarity into the often confused picture of social work as differentiated from the social services and from social welfare through formulating the following definitions in the course of teaching a class in the history of social work:

Social Welfare: the well-being of people everywhere in their personal daily lives, in particular the fullest possible opportunity for spiritual expression and satisfying human relationships at home and abroad, for health, education, pleasant housing, interesting employment, recreation, cultural development, social security, and an income adequate to these and other essentials.

The Social Services: The instrumentalities through which men translate into action their sense of obligation to contribute to the well-

being of others and to the development of those phases of social welfare which contribute to that well-being.

Social Work: The body of knowledge, skill, and ethics, professionally
employed in the administration of the social services and in the development of programs for social welfare.

A concept of social work as the professional administration
and development of social services limits its purview to no one
kind of person, to no one class, or group, to no one category of
social problem, nor to the use of any one method in the sense of
work with individuals, groups, or communities.

In summary, social work is characterized by its special concern
with man's social relationships and opportunities, in essence with
the relationship between man and his society, and by its responsibility for the furthering of a relationship that will be progressively productive for both. It is characterized, furthermore, by its
responsibility to operate from its own defined values and to employ its distinctive body of knowledge and its distinctive methods for practice, or operating skills, as they are continuously developed by the profession for the most effective discharge of its
purpose, however microscopically represented in a specific program of social service.

Social work is an institutionalized profession. It achieves its
purpose through the administration, development, and modification of programs of social service; and it is the program of service, not the independently determined activities of individual
social workers, which society supports through United Fund contribution or other like giving, or through tax monies. It is the
program of service which society not only supports, in its own
interest as well as in the interest of the clientele served, but also
controls, both through financial contribution and through the
direction given by boards of directors as representative of society's stake in the operation a particular program. It has been well
said that social agencies are the "agents" of society.[5] Professional
social workers are employed to administer programs of social
service, because the administration of such programs constitutes
the particular purpose of social work as a profession, and because

the knowledge and skill specific to social work is required for the most effective operation of social service programs. Social workers have a responsibility to contribute their professional wisdom, indeed to give informed leadership, to the shaping and changing of social service programs, to community patterns of social service programs, and to social policy as it relates to the development and operation of programs of social service. But their primary task remains the provision of a service which society, or groups of persons representing the interest and stake of "society," has identified as important, and which society supports. The general direction of the program or service, whether it continues to exist at all, and if so in what form, will be determined by its source of support, "The public." If social workers cut themselves off from society and see the agency or program whose service they are administering as somehow a let or a hindrance to what they, as social workers, really want to do, are prepared to do, and should be doing, they may well be denying the essential nature and purpose of their profession and failing to realize the richness of the contribution they alone, as a profession, can and are responsible to make.*

The purview for social work practice in the sense of "extent, sphere, and scope," which has here been developed, is based on a concept of both a unifying *purpose* for practice and a unifying *form* for practice, that is, the institutionalized form of the social agency. Such a purview not only encompasses the present activities of social work but also anticipates others yet to be.

Yet social work, as a single profession, developed in no logical, neat, and tidy way. Programs of service arose in somewhat haphazard fashion in this country as elsewhere, in accordance with the concern of individuals or groups of individuals with a particular social problem or category of persons, for example, homeless

---

* The dilemma for the private practice of social work, with support of individual practitioners by individual persons through payment of fee, lies in its appearing to wipe out society's stake in a social service, society's ultimate responsibility for its direction, and the social worker's responsibility to society as well as to the individual, not only for a method of helping but also for a program of service, with the helping method inextricably linked to the service.

children, handicapped children or adults, the mentally ill, the poor. Activities which can be thought of as the beginning of social work as we know it today were motivated by humanitarian concerns as well as by society's self-interest. The identification of a commonness or unity in what was in many respects diverse and disparate effort was recognized in this country in the creation in 1878 of a Conference of Charities and Corrections,[6] which in that year separated itself from the American Social Science Association, established itself as a distinct body, and provided a forum for the discussion of common problems and interests by individuals and groups engaged in a wide range of social welfare activities. Still later the Milford Conference[7] made an historic contribution to the development of social work as a single profession through its identification of the "generic" in social casework practice.

As the first schools of social work were developed at the turn of the century and preparation was given for practice in diverse fields, social work's identity as a single embryonic profession was given further impetus. Yet its origin in a variety of what often felt like quite unrelated programs of service, utilizing a variety of methods, influenced its nature and development in important ways, including the character of its early educational programs. The first schools of social work were organized within social agencies as a means of training staff to do a specific job, to practice in a specific field. Even after schools of social work were transferred to and, later, originated in universities, quite frequently there were separate curricula for the preparation of workers for practice in specific fields. As individual fields for practice and methods of practice developed to a point of identifying themselves as "social work" and as requiring a "social work" body of knowledge, they sought inclusion of preparation of workers for their particular areas within the developing schools of social work. In many instances, while students and faculty organizationally constituted single schools, in reality they were a collection of "little schools" in family social work, child welfare, medical social work, psychiatric social work, group work operating under a single aegis, with separate curricula, and a minimum of educational experiences common to all students. The 1950s, and 1960s have witnessed a rapid development of programs of social work education as "generic programs" in the sense of their constituting core curricula to be required, for the most part, of all students with differentiation in curricula being confined almost entirely to method as taught in class and field rather than to field of practice. At the time of this writing, there is some experimentation with teaching, if not a *single* method, two or more methods in a single practice class or sequence. The role of the Council on Social Work Education in the growth, improvement, and unification of social work education cannot be overestimated; it will be elaborated on in subsequent chapters.[8]

Another instance of the effect of social work's beginning as a variety of disparate programs was the early form of membership organization for social workers. At different points in history, social workers organized into groups related sometimes to a field of practice, for example, psychiatric or medical, sometimes to a method for practice, social group work, and later social work research. The "generic" membership organization for all practicing social workers, The American Association of Social Workers, was organized in 1921. It included on its rolls, in addition to persons otherwise unaffiliated with a social work membership organization, some, but by no means all, of the social workers organized in their respective particularized membership organizations, each with its own education or other requirements for membership, national and local structure, staff, and program.

Programs of the several organizations were varied, according to the particular interests of their members, with several determining the content of education for their fields and even carrying the actual accrediting responsibility for that part of an educational program which prepared for practice in their "field."[9] Inevitably there was duplication of program and effort in the several organizations and fragmentation in the development of social work as a whole profession, and in its impact on and relations with the community.

It was not until 1955, through the creation of the National Association of Social Workers, that the profession found a commonness in values, purpose, program, and practice methods sufficient to permit a single organization, requiring for membership a single educational base. The earlier development in 1952 of the educational organization, the present Council on Social Work Education, outgrowth of its own several predecessor groups, had laid the base in educational program and in procedure for central development of curricula and accreditation of schools of social work, which made "graduation from an accredited graduate School of Social Work" [10] possible as an accepted requirement for membership in the new professional membership organization.

Yet social workers continued to practice in rather widely divergent fields. Some forms of organization, other than individual membership organizations, based on specified educational requirements for membership, such as the Family Service Association of America, The Child Welfare League, the American Public Welfare Association, continued, to support and further social work practice in their particular fields in addition to discharging other functions.

Governmental agencies, operating for the most part under the aegis of the Department of Health, Education and Welfare, have given direction and support to social work practice and to education for social work practice, in addition to carrying other responsibilities. These agencies include the Children's Bureau and the Division of Family Services within the Department of Welfare, the National Institutes of Health, the Vocational Rehabilitation Administration, and, operating as an independent governmental agency, the Veteran's Administration. Some have worked through federal structure alone, some through federal, state, and local structure. To some extent the categorization of the social work program administered or furthered has reinforced fragmentation of the total social work effort. On the other hand, such categorization has contributed its own richness and has often provided leadership in advancing the total effort. Organizations such as the National Social Welfare Assembly have furthered the cooperation of agencies and organizations as they participated in the formulation of social welfare policy and the accomplishment of social action goals.

Clearly distinctive fields of practice for social work appropriate to its broad encompassing purpose as earlier developed have been and can be variously defined. Within the National Association of Social Workers, the original establishment of "sections" represented the then current locus or field for practice of those members who had previously had some formal organization and wanted to continue a working relationship with colleagues in their own field within the new single organization, indeed required such opportunity as a condition of "merging"! As a consequence the following sections constituted parts of the National Association of Social Workers at the time of its establishment: [11] medical social work, psychiatric social work, school social work, social group work, social work research. In addition, a committee on community organization recognized the need for association of those members whose interest and activity were in this field of practice. While members of the predecessor organizations were blanketed into membership in the new organization, and to section membership within it, sections were empowered to make specific requirements in education or experience above the base for association membership for subsequent membership in a particular section. Provision was made for the organization of sections at both the national and local chapter levels.

The group which drew up the original organizational plan was aware that the creation of the designated sections made no comparable organizational provision for the great body of social workers who, taken together, constituted the bulk of the association's total membership. They were notably workers in the family and children's fields, in the burgeoning departments of public assistance, and in the field of corrections.

Meanwhile, the Council on Social Work Education, organized just three years earlier, newly faced with the responsibility for curriculum development and accreditation of the educational preparation of all social workers whatever their field or method of practice, sought to discharge that responsibility by eliciting from individuals and organized groups in all the generally recognized fields a statement of the knowledge and skill considered requisite for social work practice. This necessarily led to the identification of fields of practice whose participation would be essential if the whole of social work practice was to be covered in planning the nature and content of social work education as it prepared for practice.

Major fields of practice for social work identified by the working group called into being by the Council [12] were listed as "among others": child welfare, correctional work, family welfare, medical and psychiatric service, public assistance, public education, public health, recreation and informal education. Agreement was reached by the working committee that specialization in social work education, later to be identified as concentration, should henceforth be by method or process rather than by field of practice, since the nature of the process used was conceived to be more significant than that of the field in its influence on the character of practice and consequent requirement of specialized knowledge and skill. Primary processes in direct service were identified as social casework and social group work. Other "secondary or enabling" processes identified were community organization, administration, supervision, consultation, teaching, and research.

This identification of fields of practice provided a useful classification and led to the development of materials solicited from the various fields which moved forward and enriched social work education as a whole through contributing to the identification of what was common in knowledge and skill. It served as well to identify what was specific in knowledge and skill in practice in a particular field, to be learned either within or following the basic formal educational program, or in some combination of both. Omitted in the classification of fields for practice, made by the Ad Hoc Committee, was community planning and development, although community organization was identified in the listing of social work processes.

A subsequent reorganization of the National Association of Social Workers resulted in the abolition of sections and the establishment, instead, of councils, a looser form of organization within the newly created Division of Practice and Knowledge of the Association. The councils made no specific requirement for affiliation other than interest and purported to cover the special interests and probable loci for operation of the great bulk of the nearly thirty thousand association members. The councils, established in 1962 as part of the planned reorganization of the Association, were: [13] schools, medical and health services, mental health and psychiatric services, correctional services, community planning and development, family and children's services, group services, social work research, and social work administration. The establishment of a commission on practice and of commissions on the three practice methods of social casework, social group work, and community organization sought to provide structure for the development of social work practice as a whole and through the processes which constituted its primary methods.[14]

It is immediately apparent that the newly established councils included research and administration, which constitute methods rather than fields for practice, applicable in any field. But certain members of the Association who were convinced that a council form or organization was best for their "province" achieved a triumph of conviction over logic in these instances. The combining of the family and childrens' fields was responsive to the current focus on the family whatever the social work service and recognized the extent to which service to children in their own homes and work with parent-child relationships characterized both family and childrens' agencies, as well as the increasing number of multiple-service agencies.

However, it is also apparent that the establishment of a Council on Family and Children Services failed to offer organizational opportunity for workers engaged in such a specific field as child placement and adoptions to work together on what is distinctive to this particular field of practice, including the special kind of relation to own family which is involved. Neither did it provide organizational opportunity for workers serving families, when child placement is not involved, to identify and develop what is peculiarly theirs and what, developed through separate effort, could be enriching for the total field. Even more grave is the identification of the Family and Children's Council as the appropriate locus for social workers engaged in the public assistance program, now known as the Family Service Program under public auspices. Once again, this development has the laudatory purpose of recognizing the public assistance or family service program as being one of service to families and children, so clearly established in the enactment of the 1962 Amendment to the Social Security Act. However, it ignores the fact that, for the present at least, a grant for maintenance assistance is one of the conditions of eligibility for such service in the great majority of settings. The very real difference this fact introduces is a difference which calls for special attention to the development of what is specific in knowledge and skill to that practice field as well as the application of what is generic to it as to all fields for practice.

There is reference in the literature to the growing edge of social work and to the fact that some loci of practice do not seem to fit any of the present fields of practice as identified in the present council structure of the NASW, and that some represent new or atypical developments such as private practice, practice within industry, or unions, or housing projects.

So it is that social work developed as separate programs of service or fields of practice and as separate methods for practice, and only gradually moved toward recognition and definition of itself as a single profession concerned both with the development of programs of social service and their implementation through professional method skills. This move toward identification of itself as a single profession has been reflected in social work's forms of membership organization and through the changing character of its educational programs, yet there remains continuing recognition in both membership organization and educational programs of difference introduced by field of practice and by method of practice, for which provision must be made.

For purposes of this writing, the *purview* of social work or the fields for social work practice will be identified as follows: family service under public auspice (with a money grant for assistance constituting eligibility for service in the great majority of instances); family service (under private auspice); service to children, to include child placement in foster homes and institutions, adoptions, service to children in their own homes, and children's protective services; corrections; medical social work; psychiatric social work; school social work; group service; community planning and development.

This classification is made with no intent of casting "purview for social work practice" in concrete to stand for all time, or of establishing a scheme of fields useful for all purposes. It provides a form for examining the present scope of social work practice and for developing some general principles for its practice, whatever the specific program. It is suggested that practice within "unincluded" fields such as housing developments or industry can be considered as falling under an "other" heading, and that the same principles of practice to be developed will be found applicable within them as within the listed fields.

It is apparent that in some instances social work is a subsidiary service within an institution which has its own purpose and uses social work in order that its own purpose may be more fully realized (for example, hospitals, clinics, courts, and schools use social work in this way). In other instances social work is employed to administer a service which can be identified in a narrower sense as a social service (for example, family counseling service and children's protective service may be identified in this way). In still other instances the situation is less clear, as in the use of social work within a settlement or neighborhood house, or in public family service programs which administer financial assistance. It should be emphasized that despite the common knowledge and skill required for social work practice whatever the field, the *particular* field within which it is practiced introduces elements of difference which must be understood and taken into account if social work is to make its full contribution in that field. This point will be developed further in Chapter 4.

SUMMARY

Social work, in the present as in the past, addresses itself to a variety of social problems and is practiced under a variety of auspices. Its major fields for practice at the present time have been identified as family service under public auspice; family service under private auspice; children's service; medical and health service; psychiatric service; correctional service; school social work; group service; and community planning and development. It constitutes a single profession first of all through its unifying primary purpose, however manifest in a specific program, of helping individuals meet their constantly changing relationships with each other and with society as a whole, and of helping society better serve its members.

In a society which values the dignity and the difference, and appreciates the interdependence, of its members, its specific concern is the relationship between the individual and society, with recognition of the responsibilities of individual and society to each other in their mutual interest. Stated another way, its province is the development, modification, and administration of programs of social service which further a progressively constructive relationship between the individual and society.

Social work has been described as an institutionalized profession in the sense that it is practiced within some social institution or agency and has the immediate end of using its distinctive knowledge and skill to assure the fullest possible realization of agency purpose in the interest of both the clientele served and society as a whole. Its purview is seen as derived both from its unifying purpose for practice and its unifying form for practice, the institutionalized form of the social agency. Its varied origin and uneven development in its several fields have been reflected in its forms for membership organization and in its educational programs. Differences in its practice arising from the specific agency function being discharged have been viewed as significant for the enrichment of the profession as a whole as well as for its effective contribution in the particular instance. But not withstanding its continuing operation in diverse fields of practice, social work has been seen as characterized by progressive identification of itself as a single profession, with commonly held values, manifest in an over-riding commonly accepted purpose and requiring a commonly accepted educational base for the development of the knowledge and skill requisite for its practice.[15]

As has been said, social work constitutes a single profession first of all through its unifying primary purpose, however diverse its programs. An equally compelling requirement if it is to constitute a single profession is a unifying method or professional skill for realization of purpose. Yet, just as varied fields for practice have complicated and sometimes obscured the recognition of social work's unifying purpose, so have differences in method delayed the recognition of what can be common and identifying as social work method, whatever the differences which rightly and necessarily continue to inhere in the several methods commonly used for the accomplishment of social work ends. It is to this problem that Chapter 2 is addressed.

2 SOCIAL WORK PROCESSES

JUST AS the years have seen the emergence of "fields of practice" for social workers, so have methods for social work practice evolved, and in much the same rather ragged and haphazard yet "contributive-to-a-whole" fashion. Throughout this century social work literature has given an increasing amount of attention to method, more properly to the nature and characteristics of the specific *methods* through which social work purposes are carried out.

It is important at the outset of this discussion to define method, process, and skill as they will be used in this book. *Method,* in the sense of "a general or established way or order of doing anything,"[1] refers to the social worker's part, or to what the social worker is responsible for doing, in manner and timing as well as in content, in the how as well as the what, in order to discharge his functional role and responsibility as a social worker in a specific situation. *Process* in the sense of "a course of operations, a forward movement . . . produced by a special method,"[2] refers to the nature of the interacting flow which results from the use of a specific method. The use of the casework method leads to the casework process in which worker and client are mutually engaged. So with each of the social work methods. The use of each by the worker in relationship with the "other" leads to a characteristic process marked by engagement in movement toward a mutually affirmed purpose as that purpose finds expression in a specific program or service. *Skill* in the sense of "the familiar knowledge of any science (or) art . . . as shown by dexterity in execution or performance" [3] refers to the social worker's capacity to *use* a method in order to *further* a process directed toward the accomplishment of a social work purpose as that purpose finds expression in a specific program or service.

While this concept of social work method sees as central the engagement of some other or others in a relationship process toward a social work end, it includes all that is done "in behalf of" the other outside the face-to-face contact in the sense that whatever is done is related clearly and consciously by the social worker to what is eventuating through the relationship process, and in the sense that the same values and, to some extent, the same skill are operative in the extra-client situations.

The primary methods for the practice of social work, methods which reach the clientele directly, have come to be identified as social casework, social group work, and community organization. Secondary methods, or processes which facilitate an agency's operation and service without touching the clientele directly but require for their discharge a social work skill taught as such in accredited schools of social work, have been identified as supervision (one aspect of administration); administration (the process through which the agency's operation as a whole is carried out); research; and teaching or education for social work. It is immediately clear that each of the processes identified as "secondary" is employed in a wide variety of undertakings and is in no sense limited as process or skill to social work programs or purposes. However, such a method may be thought of as resulting in a social work process or a process in social work when it is used within a social agency auspice to accomplish a social work end. In such situations, in addition to the very considerable body of knowledge and skill required for its use in any setting, the method calls for the learned and conscious application of certain principles equally applicable to all social work processes. As a consequence there should be provision for its development as skill within the curricula of the profession's schools. It can readily be seen that any of the processes of social work may be used in any field of practice, if "education" as process is broadened to include programs of undergraduate social welfare sequences and staff development in social agencies and not limited to graduate professional education within schools or universities.

As pointed out in Chapter 1, a significant development in social work in recent years has been the identification of primary method (casework, group work, community organization) as more "differentiating" for practice than field (medical, childrens', etc.). As a consequence of that identification, or perhaps as evidence of it, concentrations in schools of social work are by method or process rather than by field of practice as was once the case. And even though concentrations by method exist in schools, common curricula are required of all students, whatever their concentration, with the differentiating element in the educational experience limited primarily to the methods of practice sequence and to the method used in the field placement.*

Although the 1962 Curriculum Policy Statement of the Council on Social Work Education [4] identifies a concentration in a specific method as desirable for every student, there is ferment in the mid-1960s because of the recognition that all social workers serve individuals, groups, and communities. As a consequence, there is experimentation in some quarters on the practice of a single social work method or, in social work education, on the teaching of a single social work method or several methods in a single practice class, with relevant modification of the field assignment. In this chapter what is specific for the several social work processes, both primary and secondary, will be considered. This study makes their differentiation useful for practice and recommends concentration in a single method in the basic (master's degree) program of professional education. At the same time certain common characteristics or principles for practice

---

* Parenthetical note should be made that in some schools a kind of emphasis in a field of practice is still possible and is available within today's generic curricula through the provision of field placement, locus for research and thesis, and specialized seminars in a given field, as well as through the planned inclusion in the commonly required courses of content with special relevance for a particular field.

which mark all social work processes as processes in social work will be identified; indeed it is the focus of this book to identify them.

As these generic principles are mastered for the development of skill in any one of the processes, they become transferable and usable in any other, whether primary or secondary. But their use does not constitute the whole of the process, each of which has its distinct characteristics growing out of its distinctive purpose, configuration of relationships, and consequent demand on the worker's use of himself in the particular situation. To deny the differences in the processes seems as impoverishing for social work practice as to deny the differences introduced by field of practice, differences which, as we have seen, need not obscure but can enrich the over-riding social work or social welfare purpose, whatever the specific program. Indeed one of the generic principles for practice to be presented is the consistent use of the focus and purpose that inheres *both* in a specific field for practice as represented by an agency function *and* in the specific method being employed.

SOCIAL CASEWORK

The earliest social work method to be identified as such was social casework. It was conceived as an individualized method for administering a social agency's service. The agency in question was the Charity Organization Society, the forerunner of today's family service agencies under private auspice, and it is Mary Richmond who is generally credited with the first thorough-going development of social casework as method. Although the one-to-one relationship between worker and client was emphasized as central in social casework, the family focus was never absent, even in the earliest writings, in the sense of an appreciation of the significance of the family to the individual, the place of the individual in his family, and the importance of family relationships for individual development and well-being. The family as *focus* for a service, a central social work concern of the

1950s and 1960s, was described in some detail by Jessie Taft and by Robert Gomberg, writing in 1944 in *The Journal of Social Work Process.*[5] Here the emphasis was on the way a focus on the family could serve as a dynamic in the helping process.

As early as 1899 Mary Richmond identified relationship or, at least, worker capacity for sensitive appreciation of another's feelings, as fundamental in casework:

Friendly visiting means intimate and continuous knowledge of and sympathy with a poor family's joys, sorrows, opinions, feelings, and entire outlook upon life. The visitor that has this is unlikely to blunder either about relief or any detail; without it he's almost certain, in any charitable relations with members of the family, to blunder seriously.[6]

In subsequent writing[7] Richmond specified the purpose of casework as being to effect better adjustments between individuals and their social environment. It is significant that in this same writing she identified other methods or "forms of social work" as group work, social reform, and social research, and counseled that "the caseworker should know something of all forms—the more knowledge he has of all the better—and should carry through his special task in such a way as to advance all the types of social work enumerated."[8]

In referring to the specific purpose of social casework, she said: "Examples of social casework show that by direct and indirect insights, and direct and indirect action upon the minds of clients their social relations can be improved and their personalities developed."[9] She found the test of social casework to be "growth in personality" as measured against such questions as: "Does the personality of its clients change and change in the right direction? Are energy and initiative released that are in the direction of higher and better wants and saner social relations?"[10] It was in this work that she wrote:

Human beings are not dependent and domestic animals. This fact of man's difference from other animals establishes the need of his participation in making and carrying out plans for his welfare. Individuals have wills and purposes of their own and are not fitted to play a passive part in the world; they deteriorate when they do.[11]

Her *Social Diagnosis,* first published in 1917, with its exhaustive presentation of the nature of social evidence required by the caseworker and the processes leading to its admission and use as a basis for treatment, stressed the importance of sources of information *about* the client other than the client himself (although he is not ignored). It developed also a content and form for diagnosis in a way that missed the intuitive spark and feel for the heart of social casework as a process in human relationship, so beautifully set forth in both her earlier and later works, to which reference has been made. The effort to be "scientific" gave the effect of deadening the spirit.

Richmond's formal definition of social casework is familiar to every social worker versed in his profession's history: "Social Casework consists of those processes which develop personality through adjustment consciously effected individual by individual between men and their social environment." [12]

The purpose of the casework relationship as Richmond saw it was clearly one of reform. Yet her interesting question, "Are energy and initiative released that are in the direction of higher and better wants and saner social relations?," speaks to her intuitive awareness that the sources for change lay in the client himself, and his own wanting, and that the intent of the worker was to release the wanting and the energy and initiative for its realization in socially desirable ways. She referred also to the method of social casework as leading to those *processes* which develop personality, and she appeared to glimpse the existence of a "process" in its qualities of interaction, engagement, and flow, purpose or end, which could lead to client change and growth, a concept which has since been developed with more sophistication.

Richmond worked on social casework only as it was developed and used in the charity organization societies. "The function of the agency" she appeared to equate with the purpose of the method, which was easy to do because of the particular focus and scope of family agency programs. This purpose (of both agency and method) she sees as inhering in her own person and in the person of every worker.

It remained for the historic Milford Conference,[13] in which Mary Richmond participated, to establish social casework as a "definite entity" and to conclude that "the outstanding fact is that the problems of social casework and the equipment of the social caseworker are fundamentally the same for all fields." In thus establishing the "generic" in casework method for use in practice in all fields, it is significant that the conference did not deny the difference introduced by a specific field. After the monumental work of this illustrious pioneer, and of her colleagues and contemporaries, social casework has been variously defined and developed over the years.

Almena Dawley, long Associate Director of the Philadelphia Child Guidance Clinic, early emphasized the understanding of human behavior as the essential part of the caseworker's task.[14] Virginia Robinson, for many years Vice Dean of the School of Social Work of the University of Pennsylvania, was one of the first writers to stress the significance of the relationship for the casework helping process:

If the history of social casework teaches anything it teaches this one thing outstandingly, that only in this field of the individuals' reaction patterns and in the possibility of therapeutic change in these patterns, through responsible self-conscious relationships, can there be any possibility of a legitimate professional casework field.[15]

If casework accepts squarely this responsibility for relationship, it has a field for research, for experiment, demanding the most untiring scientific accuracy and the most sincere, unceasing self-discipline.[16]

Jessie Taft added the concept of agency function, a more sharply defined concept of process, and the portent, for method, of their relationship in the development of skill in her epochal article "The Relation of Function to Process in Social Casework."

There is one area and only one in which outer and inner, worker and client, agency and social need can come together effectively; only one area that offers to social workers the possibility of development into a profession—and that is the area of the helping process itself.[17]

And, again, she wrote: "There is no escape . . . from . . . the necessity to establish ourslvees firmly not merely on the basis of social need, but on a foundation of professional skill." [18]

Taft, in establishing the impossibility of basing the helping process (of social casework) on an understanding of need alone ("something that can never be known exactly or worked on directly"), suggested that

we limit our study of needs to the generally recognized categories (of social services) as they emerge out of the larger social problems and leave to the individual the freedom as well as the responsibility of testing out his peculiar needs against the relatively stable function of a particular agency. There remains to us a large and comparatively unexplored area for future development, an area in which to learn how to maintain our functions intelligently and skillfully and how to isolate whatever can be isolated from the particular situation in terms of the law, the nature of the general pattern of the helping process.[19]

Anita Faatz [20] refined and further developed the concept of social casework as an individual helping process given form and direction by social agency function. Prior and subsequent to that writing, in addition to the continued publications of Taft and Robinson, numerous articles in professional journals (notably by Aptekar, Dawley, Faith, Marcus, Pray, Smalley, and Wessel) identified, described, and illustrated social casework as the "functional school of thought" was developing it.

Meanwhile the impact of Freudian psychoanalysis on the practice of social work in this country and primarily, in the early years, on the practice of social casework had resulted in another development in social casework method commonly referred to as the diagnostic method in contra-distinction to the functional method, to which reference had just been made. The functional method was developed, originally, in what is now the School of Social Work of the University of Pennsylvania and in the Philadelphia community of social workers. The diagnostic method, as method, was perhaps first developed in its purest form in what is now the Columbia University School of Social Work and in the community of social workers in New York City. The profound insights developed by Freud and the analysts who were his colleagues and those who followed enriched all of social work, just as they revolutionized the practice of psychiatry.

However, a substantial body of the profession, in taking over psychological understanding in the specific form developed by Freud, were influenced by its somewhat mechanistic, deterministic view of man which saw him as pretty much prey to the dark forces of an unconscious, on the one hand, and the harsh restrictive influence of internalized parental dicta in the early years of growth, on the other. It was only in the middle 1900s that the Freudian analytic group, through its emphasis on ego psychology, reflected a more optimistic view of man which conceived him to be creator of himself as well as creature.

It is this view, first developed for psychotherapy by Otto Rank, a disciple of Freud, and later corroborated and elsewhere developed by a considerable body of writers and scientists in a variety of disciplines, which contributed to the thinking of the "functional school" from its beginning. This influence followed from Rank's serving on the faculty of the Pennsylvania School of Social Work and from his having been a dynamic influence in the lives of Taft, Robinson, and the community of social workers in Philadelphia. As was earlier suggested, in taking over the Freudian interpretation of human nature, the diagnostic group identified to some extent both with the purpose of psychoanalysis and with adaptations of its methods, with a resultant acceptance of responsibility to "diagnose a pathological condition" and to "treat it." This was close in spirit to Mary Richmond's emphasis on diagnosis of a social problem and assumption of responsibility for its treatment, with the substitution of a medical or quasi-medical "internal" focus for a more purely social "external" focus. The significance of the purpose of the agency and of the social service being administered became secondary to the purpose of treatment of socio-pathological conditions in individual clients. Indeed the agency's service was sometimes referred to as a "tool" in treatment.

To summarize, and all too briefly to do the "schism" justice, differences between the diagnostic and functional schools of thought, reflected in the practice and teaching of social casework as method, were related to three kinds of understanding. (1) *Understanding of the nature of man.* The diagnostic school worked from a psychology of illness, with the worker feeling responsible to diagnose and treat a pathological condition, and with the center for change residing in the worker. The functional group worked from a psychology of growth and saw the center for change as existing not in the worker but in the client, with the worker's method consisting of engaging in a relationship process which released the client's own power for choice and growth. The functional group used the term "helping" in referring to its method, the diagnostic group "treating," or treatment. The functional group's view of human nature also took into account to a greater extent than did the diagnostic group in the early years of its development the effect of social and cultural forces in human development. This was due in part to Rank's emphasis on these forces, and in part to other influences. (2) *Understanding of the purpose of social work.* The diagnostic group saw it as the effecting of a healthy personal and social condition in the clientele served, with the specific purpose of the agency not only secondary but also sometimes in a curious way parallel to, or detached from, or even in opposition to the purpose of the worker. The functional group saw the purpose of the agency as representing a partial or concrete instance of social work's overall purpose and as giving form and direction to the worker's practice, with casework method constituting not a form of social treatment of individuals but a method for administering a specific social service in such a way, and with such psychological understanding of the helping process, that the agency service had the best possible chance of being used for individual and social welfare. (3) *Understanding of the concept of process itself.* This concept was not developed in the diagnostic group, some of whom have referred to social work method as a "repertoire of interventive acts" (apparently acts of the worker). The functional school developed the concept of social casework as a *help-ing process* through which an agency's service was made available, with the principles in social work method having to do with the initiating, sustaining, and terminating of a *process* in human relationship.

These three points will be further developed in Chapters 4, 5, 6, and 7, which will establish the base for social work practice from which principles of practice, to be presented in Chapter 8, are derived. They are introduced here only to point up differences which characterized the development of social casework in the 1920s and 1930s, differences which are being minimized as "diagnostics" and "functionalists" have learned from each other but still exist, at each end of a spectrum, in recognizable form.

Gordon Hamilton was among the early leaders in the development of social casework as method, in the diagnostic tradition. She wrote:

Casework is concerned with the release of resources in the immediate environment and capacities in the individual which may give him a fuller and more satisfying life both economic and personal. . . . The caseworker deals with persons and situations one by one. . . . The great social movements can serve us only if the individual is not repressed and forgotten. As between social action and social casework there can be no "either-or," but always a two-way process.[21]

Hamilton, a pioneer in establishing a knowledge base for practice, developed a concept of social casework based on "study-diagnosis-treatment" as constituting the order of the process engaged in, with recognition that treatment begins with diagnosis and diagnosis is continuously modified in the course of the treatment. She classified treatment roughly as direct and indirect, stressed the significance of a direct experiencing of relationship, and differentiated casework from psychotherapy by the level on which it operates in regard to psychic conflicts, and through the directing of attention upon social rather than psychopathological processes.

While Hamilton referred to a goal of social casework as releas-

ing capacities in the individual, the context of her writing sometimes seems to suggest that she sees this accomplished for the
most part through the worker's remaining at the center, diagnosing what is wrong, with a minimum of client participation
and engagement in definition of problem. The order of the process is the worker's order of study-diagnosis-treatment, not the
order that inheres in the interacting process itself, with the
worker responsible for putting in what initiates and sustains it.
The relation of the purpose of the particular social agency to the
method used is not seen as central in the nature of the method
itself.

Florence Hollis [22] brings together and carries forward the
thinking of her earlier writings in establishing casework as a
psycho-social treatment method. She recognizes both internal
psychological and external social causes of dysfunctioning and
sees the purpose of casework as being to "enable the individual to
meet his needs more fully and to function more adequately in his
social relationships." [23] She describes categories of casework treatment appropriate to various categories of psycho-social problems,
or kinds of psycho-social dysfunction manifested by clients, as
established through diagnosis for which the worker is responsible.

The significance of agency function for casework helping, and
as affecting the nature of the process through which help is
given, and the nature of the helping process itself as a process
characterized by certain common principles, whatever the "personality diagnosis" of the client served, are not developed.

Helen Perlman [24] defines casework as "a process used by certain human welfare agencies to help individuals to cope more
effectively with their problems in social functioning." This concept of social casework as method sees its relationship to a social
agency and identifies some elements of a process of engagement
of the client in the work undertaken, with more room for the
client in the process than is suggested in some of the more strictly diagnostic writing. Although the social agency may be seen

more as constituting a place, a "setting," for operation than as constituting a dynamic and giving form, focus, and direction to the helping process, the significance of the agency as the form for social work practice is consistently appreciated by Perlman. The engagement of the client still seems to be something that seeks to enlist the client in the worker's plan. "On setting forth in their work together, the caseworker may share with the client what the hoped for goal might be and what the general direction is." [25]

A different emphasis and indeed a different psychology would have been involved had the statement included helping the *client* share with the *worker* the *client's* hoped-for goal, with the worker clarifying each step of the way. Could the agency be party to such a goal, and if so under what conditions? Or what other, perhaps related, goals *could* the agency be party to, if the client were interested to pursue them? Or where in the community might he pursue his chosen goal if it was not appropriate to the particular agency with which he was presently engaged? It should be noted, however, that at other points in her writing Perlman identifies the significance of the client's working to achieve his own ends and overcome his own difficulty.

Felix P. Biestek, in *The Casework Relationship,*[26] an integrative work both scholarly and spiritual in quality, advances an understanding of casework as method for furthering the self-determination of individuals in respect to their use of social services.

What can be taken from all this is that social casework is generally accepted by the profession of social work as one of its primary methods for the accomplishment of its purposes—the first of the methods to be developed theoretically. There would probably be agreement that it constitutes an individualized form of helping people cope with problems in social functioning, involving, as central, the use of a worker-client relationship. There would not be agreement at the time of this writing on the essential nature of the process involved and the respective roles of worker and client in it, or on the relation of specific social agency purpose to the casework process.

As was earlier suggested, much has been written in the 1950s and 1960s of "family-centered casework," whatever the agency service, and much has been done with multi-client interviews, interviews with families as families, with married couples, with parent and child seen together. In carrying on this kind of joint or multiple client interviewing, something can undoubtedly be learned from group work method and process to make the helping more effective. Indeed much has been learned, and its value has been demonstrated in practice. But a substantial body of social work remains which focuses on helping through a one-to-one relationship from which much has been learned also.

The use of a "one-to-one" relationship to induce change in another's use of himself in social relationships and situations continues to be a kind of helping configuration which has some uniqueness as well as commonness with all other social work processes. It seems important to continue to identify and develop that uniqueness in order that the wealth of what is known of one-to-one helping may not be lost through too quick and easy an embracing of a single social work method. Such a move, in practice and education, could detract from the continued development of casework as a process in its own right and from the enrichment its understanding can bring to each and to all of the other social work methods.*

For the purpose of this writing, social casework will be defined as a method for engaging a client, through a relationship process

---

* The emphasis on family-centered casework, first introduced with psychological penetration by Traft and developed in the early writings of Robert Gomberg, has been given fresh emphasis in recent years and perhaps some new vocabulary, through the closer rapprochement of social work and sociology. Perhaps it is time, while welcoming the enrichment this development is bringing, to keep alert to the significance of the individual as a person in his own right, and as more than the sum of his "roles" as father, husband, worker, etc. And perhaps the continuance of social casework as method, essentially one-to-one in its operation, can serve to call attention to the individual in all his individuality at the same time that it seeks to help him find a way to be what he is in constructive relationship to, and in large part *through* his relation to, the groups, large and small, of which he is a part.

essentially one-to-one, in the use of a social service toward his own and the general social welfare.

SOCIAL GROUP WORK

Social casework was first developed as a method, as we have seen, through the writings of Mary Richmond and the training programs of the early charity organization societies. It was carried forward, refined, and modified by workers in a wide variety of programs and conceptualized by individual writers and by groups of social caseworkers through their several papers, publications, and organizations. Social group work as method had its beginnings in the early social settlements and was later employed and conceptualized for use in neighborhood houses and in youth-serving agencies, including organizations concerned primarily with "recreation and informal education." Only comparatively recently has the group work method been used in all the major fields for social work practice, and some of its skill coveted by social caseworkers, particularly in their work with families and small groups, in agencies where casework has been the most commonly used method. As was earlier noted, social group work was identified as a method in social work by Mary Richmond, writing in 1917, but it was not until the late 1920s and early 1930s that it was generally accepted as a primary method for the practice of social work. An organized course, called Group Service Work, was first offered in the School of Applied Social Sciences of Western Reserve University. Much of its theoretical base was drawn from an early sociometric study of group adjustment.[27] A course for the training of workers for settlement houses was developed at about the same time at Northwestern University, with a theoretical base laid primarily in theories of play developed by anthropologists and sociologists.

In 1935 a separate section on social group work was established as part of the National Conference of Social Work, and in the same year the editors of the Social Work Year Book included a heading on social group work.

The year 1936 witnessed the establishment of the National Association for the Study of Group Work. It was to become, a decade later, the American Association of Group Workers, one of the predecessors of the National Association of Social Workers (1955), whose members were to constitute a section of the new association until its reorganization in 1963 substituted councils (including a council on group work) for the earlier organizational form.

Throughout the early years of the development of group work it was not always clear whether a *field* for practice or a *method* of practice was meant by the term "social group work." There was loose reference to "group work agencies" or "casework agencies" until the clarifying work of the Council on Social Work Education and various committees and groups of the professional membership organization established group-serving agencies as a field for practice (see Chapter 1) and group work as one of the primary methods of social work.

Because the primary concern of those agencies in which group work originated as method was broad social reform, or service to groups of persons seeking experiences in recreation or education rather than service to individuals and families experiencing personal and social problems, as was true for casework, group work method from the first drew heavily on sociological and educational theory, and particularly on theory on the small group process. Grace Coyle wrote:

As group workers began in the 1920s and 1930s to define their functions and to examine their practice by a study of group records there evolved certain agreed upon concepts and at least a rudimentary theory which drew upon the theoretical sources available at that time for its understanding of the behavior of groups. When group work began to be taught in the Schools of Social Work (1925–1935) the theory of individual behavior taught was already in its psychoanalytic stage. It therefore became necessary to integrate an advanced and highly developed personality theory already focused on treatment purposes, especially on emotional problems, with a relatively rudimentary small group theory and with agencies geared to recreation and informal education rather than individualized treatment.[28]

Subsequent years saw intensive research in both sociology and social psychology on the dynamics of group behavior, all of which
had an influence on the development of group work theory. The
impact of psychoanalytic theory on social casework practice and
the education of students for the practice of group work as well
as for casework within single schools of social work resulted in a
rethinking of the purpose of group serving agencies and of
group work as method.

Some practitioners of group work adopted a purpose of treatment of behavior or emotional problems comparable to the purpose affirmed by the diagnostic school for social casework as
method. Group therapy became a form of group work practice
although some writers sought consistently to differentiate social
group work as a method in social work from group therapy in
which, with no defined unifying theoretical base for practice,
psychiatrists, social workers, psychologists, and educators became
engaged in a variety of settings.

Just as early courses in social casework in professional schools
of social work and early writings on social casework were preoccupied with the dynamics of individual behavior rather than
with casework as method, or as an individualized helping process
in social work, so early courses and writings on group work focused on the dynamics of group behavior rather than on group
work as method, or as a social work process of helping through
the medium of group relationships.

Coyle makes reference in the work cited to the "concept of
role" as defining the various roles of the social worker as group
worker, administrator, community organization worker. She
writes also of the necessity for understanding the interplay of social relationships which make up the group—the interpersonal
reactions between the members and the relation of each to the
group as a whole. In an earlier work she refers to the agency
function and its defined objectives as the framework within
which any group leader will work.[29] This is her summation of
group work as method leading to process:

In the concrete act of the practitioner these steps, the inspection of the
situation, the recognition of factors by means of concepts, the classifica-

tion into recognized types, the bringing to bear of the available and appropriate generalizations of types of problems and of possible solutions (treatment) constitute the intellectual functions for direct practice.[30]

This is a concept akin to Hollis' concept of casework as method with treatment focus but is at variance with values and theory as developed by Coyle in this and in other of her writings. They seemed to see the group as the center for its own change and the change of its members, with the social group worker lending himself to the group's accomplishments of its purposes within the framework of agency purpose. It appears to reflect the impact of the psychoanalytic influence in social casework on Coyle's own concept of social group work. Subsequent writing saw her recapture and further develop her earlier understanding of the power in the group for its own movement. Wilson and Ryland wrote of the purpose of group work:

Most social agencies serving groups have two purposes in common: (1) to help individuals use groups to further their development into emotionally balanced, intellectually free and physically fit persons; (2) to help groups achieve ends desirable in an economic, political, and social democracy.[31]

Social group work method designed to carry out these purposes of group-serving agencies is defined in some detail in this book by Wilson and Ryland, with the part of the worker described in the following way: ". . . he stimulates, clarifies, implements, teaches, expedites, limits and permits as the occasion demands." [32] What is lacking in their book which has contributed much to the field is a unifying sense of process directed toward an end determined by agency function, with the separate "activities" of the worker finding their place in relation to the purpose and process which sustain and give direction to the group relationships.

Helen U. Phillips, writing in *Essentials of Social Group Work Skill*, summarized her position in the following way:

The uniqueness of social group work stems from the purpose of this segment of the profession—to help people use group experiences for their self-growth toward social ends. The distinguishing characteristic of the group work method, therefore, lies in its emphasis on group relations, its inevitable identification with the interacting process between group members, consciously stimulated and directed by a worker.[33]

Phillips' book develops the nature of the social group work skill necessary for achieving "group work purpose" and sees as central in that purpose the development of responsible behavior. She identifies as one component of social group work skill, using the agency function within which the particular group work service is being offered.*

Group work, as understood here, is a method for engaging a group as a whole and its several members, in relationship processes with the worker and each other to facilitate use of group experience for achieving individual and group purposes, within the purpose of an agency or service program.

The purpose of the agency or program may be the provision of group experience in recreation and informal education. It may be any other social agency or social service purpose whose realization is possible through a process of relationships within a group or as a group.

What differentiates social group work from social casework as *method* is not its *purpose* for individuals (which, in both cases, is to further capacity for personal fulfillment and social functioning) but (1) its *additional* purpose, which in group-serving agencies is to further the group's accomplishment of a social purpose, as a group, and (2) the configuration of relationships through which its purpose is realized—with all the complexity of relation of group members to each other, to the group as a whole, and to the worker and the worker's relation in turn to each and to all. In both casework and group work a relationship, of which the worker is a part, is the medium through which the process is carried on. In both the worker is responsible for his

---

* Among the contributors to a substantial literature on social group work method, in addition to persons whose works have been cited, are Margaret Hartford, Clara Kaiser, Gisele Konopka, Richard Lodge, Helen Northern, William Schwartz, Mary Lou Somers, Robert Vinter—a far from definitive list.

part in the process. In both an agency service is being made available whose purpose is one manifestation of an embracing social work of social welfare purpose. It is noteworthy that in a one-to-one casework relationship, the worker is not part of the "social situation" which is the focus of concern. In group work, he is, since he is part of the life of the group.

COMMUNITY ORGANIZATION PROCESS

Community organization is the last of the three primary methods to be identified, conceptualized, and analyzed by the profession in the way that has been true for casework and group work. There has been, and is, some failure to differentiate between community organization as method and community organization as field of practice. Yet activities and programs generally accepted as falling under this heading have characterized social work from its beginning. Indeed the organization of charity was the first focus of the charity organization societies within which, as has been noted, the social casework method was later developed as method.* Community organization in social work has been defined as "the process by which people of communities, as individual citizens or as representatives of groups, join together to determine social welfare needs and mobilize their resources." [34] Before the implications of this definition are considered, other definitions and concepts of community organization are introduced, and the community organization process is placed as one of the three primary processes of social work, it may be well to differentiate it from "community development," another field which has been calling on the professional knowledge and skill of social workers in recent years, particularly in the two fields for practice of underdeveloped countries and urban redevelopment.

The term "community development," according to one source,[35] like "community organization" is referred to as a process of citizen participation, but in its more general usage it

* For an interesting account of this development see Katherine A. Kendall, "Social Service," in *Encyclopaedia Britannica,* revised 1964.

refers to a kind of program concerned with simultaneous improvement of all phases of community life. Many processes are involved, and various methods are used to influence these processes in the direction of program goals. The goals themselves are of two kinds: (1) Technical goals, that is, those concerned with scientific and industrial development, education, agriculture, housing, health and sanitation, and so forth. The attainment of these goals requires the assistance of experts (frequently people from outside the community) in each field to plan, to advise, to consult, to teach, or to perform the necessary tasks in which they have special skills. (2) Social goals, that is, those concerned with human relationships and with the development of participation of the local residents in the planning, administration, execution, and evaluation of the community development program.

Experience has taught that a community development program, if it is to be successful, must take into account both these sets of goals. Elaborate technical assistance programs have been known to grind to a halt with great waste of materials, equipment, and technical help because the planners failed to take into account the personal needs and values of local residents. Even worse perhaps are the programs focused on citizen participation in problem identification, diagnosis, and plans for action without the help of experts, equipment, and materials in the areas needed. These tend to result in frustration, despair, and sometimes civil violence.

It will be clear that social work has a contribution to make to community development through the use of all its processes as they implement programs focused on community welfare. A special value of the group work process as it is employed in group service agencies is the assistance it gives to individuals in learning to work and play together in small face-to-face groups as a basis for becoming able, through group action, to identify social problems and work together toward their resolution.

Community organization, in contradistinction to community development, to restate in a slightly different form the definition proposed at the beginning of this section, is that process through which individuals and organizations develop and maintain relationships within which they can work together toward the selection and achievement of mutually acceptable social goals. These goals have been identified either as integrative or change-focused. Integrative goals are concerned primarily with coordination of planning and activity of a wide diversity of interests. Because of the diversity of interest and the necessity to involve all interests in a process of coordination, the achievement of this kind of community organization is likely to be in the direction of establishing and maintaining an equilibrium, a sort of preservation of the status quo, with change occurring gradually in a manner approved by all participants. Change-focused goals are more likely to be goals selected by a more homogenous special interest group seeking to acquire enough influence to effect the change desired.

What has been omitted from the foregoing descriptions has been the role of the worker, which identifies community organization as a method in social work and requires the use of certain generic methodological principles leading to a "community organization process," which is a process in social work. As this writer sees it, a community organization worker would operate from the values which actuate all social workers as a professional group, and as they are continuously developed, stated, and restated through the professional membership organization. He would be operating under the aegis of an organization which had a community mandate to engage in community organization process in various spheres of action, toward the achievement of either an integrative or a change-focused goal. And he would be employing the special knowledge and skill which characterize the social worker whatever his process, that is, a skill in the use of a relationship process to free individual and social power for the achievement of a social good.

Much controversy has raged about the nature of the community organization process as a process in social work. The early writings of Dunham and McMillan, the classic "Three Papers on Community Organization," [36] edited by Donald S. Howard and published by the American Association of Social Workers in 1947, W. I. Newstetter's contribution of the concept of "intergroup" work as characterizing community organization, the later writings of Murray Ross and others,* the papers developed in connection with the Curriculum Study under the auspices of the Council on Social Work Education,[37] as well as studies underway at the time of this writing testify to the current lack of agreement of practitioners in the field on the purpose and nature of community organization either as a method in social work or as a field for social work practice.

A unifying definition of social work as framework for his definition of community organization as a social work method was early proposed by Kenneth Pray and is consistent with this writer's present view:

Social work is the effort specifically and directly applied in the pursuit of a social welfare purpose to facilitate the process by which people are assisted and enabled to use these instrumentalities (social welfare enterprises) or any other social relations open to them for the more effectual fulfillment of their own social well-being within the framework of a stable society.[38]

Pray placed Community Organization as a process in social work in the following words:

Community organization practice is social work practice . . . its practitioners can share in the development of a single profession of social work, on three conditions: first, if their primary concern and objectives relate always to the development and guidance of the process by which people find satisfying and fruitful social relationships, and not to the attainment of specific preconceived products or forms of relationship; second, if these objectives are sought consistently through the realization of a democratic philosophy and faith which respects the right and the responsibility of communities as of individuals to create their own satisfying relationships, and to use those relationships to their chosen end; and finally, if the basic processes, methods, and skills that are demanded and employed in practice are those that inhere in the worker's

---

* In addition to persons whose works are cited in this text, contributors to practice theory for community organization include Arnold Gurin, Robert Morris, Meyer Schwartz, Thomas Sheerard, Violet Sieder, and John Turner, among others.

capacity to initiate and sustain a helping not a controlling relationship with individuals and groups.[39]

Whether the worker is engaged in community organization in the sense of furthering the collaborative effort of social agencies and institutions to serve a community, or community development in the sense of furthering a community's identification of a purpose of social improvement and movement to realize it, his task as here presented is to lend himself, his professional knowledge, and skill to the community for its achievement of its own purpose within the encompassing purpose represented in his agency function.

Lewis speaks cogently to this point in identifying community organization process as a helping process applied in the formation of social welfare policy:

Community social workers are aware of the competing social norms and individual values that enter into policy formulation and execution. The force with which norms and values are expressed in the shaping of policy is in proportion to the power generated by individuals and groups seeking to incorporate their philosophies into formal and informal authority carrying coercive sanctions. The community social worker is concerned not only with knowing and understanding the structure, organization, history and practice of social welfare institutions and the norms that guide the use of power by competing community interests, but with developing increasing skill in work with human elements in the exercise of power-shaping social welfare policy.[40]

He concludes:

Community organization is viewed as a helping process precisely because it contains a heavy element of discovery necessary to the formation of social welfare policy. The community social worker practices his art using such scientific knowledge as may be available to him, to facilitate and sustain this helping process. Facts that are created in the initiation, development sustaining and termination of the process may play as important or a more important role in guiding his practice decisions as those "given" by prior events and study efforts. It is for this reason that theory most germane to the community social worker's practice relates to the use of his own self as an agency representative, to the process to which he applies his method of work, to the behavior of individuals and groups as participants in this process and to the problems in relationship effecting the process. To these areas he can and does make original contributions because his practice uncovers and creates new facts not otherwise available. In the study of such facts he may well organize his work in accordance with a problem-solving model. Their creation, however, is a testimony to his skill in practicing the helping art.[40]

Difference has been expressed in recent literature as to whether a community organization worker is "directive" or is an "enabler." [41] Leedy, in commenting upon the position advanced by Rothman writes: "His clearly enunciated principles that the final decision rests with the community and that the practitioner has the responsibility to bring his professional knowledge and judgement into the process in a substantive way are basic to the community organization method." Friedlander, in the same issue of *Social Work*, wants to return the notion of "the enabling role to the obscurity it deserves" and "look more deeply at the several roles of the community organization practitioner."

What is not grasped in the latter point of view is the essential nature of a community organization process that makes it a social work process and precludes the use of assorted techniques in assorted situations without any identifiable and unifying skill within which the "techniques" can find their place.

It is not only that the "community must make the final decision" as a matter of ethical right but also that only as the community makes the final decision will it stick and constitute growth and forward social movement on the part of the community as a whole. It is the nature of the social work process itself which furthers the community's becoming increasingly able to make and act on community decisions. Once this tenet is grasped and adhered to, the worker may "intervene" in a variety of ways, authoritatively (if he carries a real authority), as representative of a social purpose or goal which inheres in his agency purpose, as stimulator of thought and action, through making available facts and figures or through calling on and enlisting experts in various fields. Whatever he does is geared not only to a respect for the community as an entity but also to a belief in a community's capacity to act in its own behalf. Method so understood requires the use of an identifiable skill effective in furthering such action, which in turn is based both on knowledge of the "other" being served, in this instance a community, and on knowledge of what constitutes an effective use of the self to further responsible action of that "other" toward a social work purpose.

Pray's concept of community organization as a process in social work is based on this assumption. He identifies as the central objective of social work practice "to facilitate the process of social adjustment of individual people through the development and constructive use of social relationships within which they can find their own fulfillment and can discharge adequately their social responsibilities . . . the objective is not to make over either the environment or the people involved in it, but rather to introduce and sustain a process of dealing with the problems of social relationships and social adjustment" [42] through which (the author adds) people or groups in communities may "make over" themselves on the basis of their own choice. This is in line with Frederick Allen's much quoted statement, "No one can change another person—but people can change."

In summary, then, community organization process, like casework and group work process, serves a helping not a controlling function. The outcome rests with others not the worker, although the worker is fully and solely responsible for his part in that process. The core of the process is the disciplined use of the self in direct relationship with individuals and groups, with sensitive awareness of what is happening to everybody affected in the process and of the way the social worker's own participation is affecting the feeling, interest, and participation of all concerned persons.

The process of community organization differs from the processes of social casework or social group work in its specific purpose, as stated in this section; in the configuration of relationships through which it is carried on, with all the complexity of interacting individuals and groups; and in the consequent distinctive role of the worker responsible for his part in a process which involves in appropriate ways all related to the focal undertaking.

Community organization is here defined as a method for engaging a community as a whole and its several parts—groups, organizations, and individuals—in relationship processes with the worker and with each other toward the achievement of a purpose of community welfare within the purpose of a sponsoring agency.

These then may be identified as the three primary methods through which social work achieves its purposes: *social casework,* with its focus on initiating and sustaining a process through which an individual is helped to use a social service for his own fulfillment as an individual who is social; *social group work,* with its focus on initiating and sustaining a process through which small groups of individuals make use of a program of social service for their own development as individuals and for the achievement of some common social purpose; and *community organization,* with its focus on initiating and sustaining a process through which a community makes use of some program for social planning, coordination, or community development, for the better identification of its welfare needs and the coordination, modification, or development of resources for meeting them.

All the primary processes fall within the definition of social work practice, developed by the Practice Commission of the National Association of Social Workers, under the chairmanship of Harriet Bartlett.

Social work practice like the practice of all professions is recognized by a constellation of value, purpose, sanction, knowledge, and method. No part alone is characteristic of social work practice nor is any part described here unique to social work practice. It is the particular content and configuration of this constellation which makes it social work practice and distinguishes it from other professions.[43]

All the primary processes of social work seek to realize values held by the profession as those values are embodied in the purposes of specific social welfare programs or services, and as they are embodied in the nature of the methods used to develop or administer those services. The method in each instance consists in the worker's use of himself in a disciplined relationship process, whether with individuals, groups or communities (through relationships with the individuals and groups who comprise them), to the end that the purpose of the particular program or service being administered may achieve its fullest possible realization in individual and social welfare.

3 SECONDARY SOCIAL WORK PROCESSES

BEFORE presenting certain bases for social work practice and certain principles which characterize all of its methods, as herein defined, it is necessary to place the secondary or facilitating processes of social work: supervision, administration, research, and teaching of social work, within the same general context which has just been developed.

SUPERVISION

Supervision is sometimes considered to be one aspect of administration and so not identified as a social work process in its own right. Its focus, however, as it is here understood, is on the individual worker in the agency and on the facilitation of his giving the agency's service in a way that is increasingly effective and helpful for the clientele served, responsible and contributive to the agency's functioning and growth and rewarding and developing for himself. Its *focus* is not on the operation of the agency as a whole . . . as is true for the process of administration, although its conduct is essential to the effective operation of the whole. Like all the other methods and processes of social work, supervision has developed its own internal controversies and produced its own literature. As social work evolved as a profession there was growing concern among some of its members that the continued use of supervision would "keep workers dependent," and the point of view was often presented that social work would never be a profession so long as supervision of workers continued a characteristic part of agency operation. There was even the suggestion that supervision (and administration) was "undemocratic." Various somewhat bizarre proposals were made and experiments undertaken in which workers were free to seek supervision when they wanted it and from whom they wanted it. Within such operations, the source of supervision might shift from day to day and case to case, with a different person being sought for "consultative help" by an individual worker according to his personal preference and the nature of the problem for which he was seeking consultation. Recent years have seen increased use of the group method of supervision, and there has been much effort directed toward defining levels of practice proficiency, with different frequency and foci for supervision planned in accordance with the level of proficiency reached by the worker.

Supervision as process is used widely in business, industry, and many fields of human endeavor in the sense of "overseeing the work of another with responsibility for its quality." Within the professions it has had a different development where service is offered largely by the individual practitioner (like medicine and law) and where service is largely institutionalized, like social work. The large-scale programs of public welfare which developed in the 1930s made a special demand for supervision of staff, largely untrained, if the purpose of the agency was to be realized in a way that was accountable to the public supporting it, helpful to the clientele served, and rewarding, as task, to the worker.

Supervision is necessary in social work, first of all, because what the public is supporting, in each instance, is not the private practice of a group of professional social workers but a specific welfare service. It becomes the responsibility of agency administration to institute and sustain a pattern and a process of supervision which assure a program and quality of service which both the supporting and using community can trust. It is sometimes argued that the fact that the workers are professional social workers (that is, MSW graduates of accredited schools of social work or, more recently, members of the Academy of Certified Social Workers) is sufficient guarantee of quality of service. But this would be true only if the service being offered were an individualized practice for which "the profession" took full responsibility rather than the provision of an agency service, accountable *as such* to the supporting community.

The community is supporting programs of child placement, or of family service, or public assistance; or a social institution (for example, public school or hospital) is engaging social service to help it realize, more fully, its own purpose as school or hospital. To be accountable for a service calls for the continuous shaping, defining, and redefining of its purpose and nature as it meets or fails to meet the needs for which it was established. Supervision, in the sense of a sustained relationship process with persons making the service available, not only releases increased skill in giving the service, worker by worker, which is as rewarding to the worker himself as it is to the clientele served, but it also provides a channel through which the agency's service, according to fixed policy and procedure, may be made available in a sufficiently "standard" way that it can be counted on by supporting and using community alike as "agency-service". Equally important, it provides a channel for the individual worker to make available his individual experience and judgment for the modification of agency service and agency policy, as changing conditions warrant. This point has been well developed by Eisenberg.[1]

Social work has done more than any other single profession to raise supervision to the level of a professional process in its own right. Other professions and fields of effort have recognized this fact and borrowed from it in the development of their own supervisory processes. Its development as a relationship process, within the profession of social work, has undoubtedly been due to social work's dealing with human problems through institutionalized forms of service, and evolving relationship processes for doing so. It was inevitable that what had been learned in the helping processes of casework and, later, group work should be transferred to the helping relationship of supervision of workers engaged in those processes, but with a purpose and focus which were appropriate for its particular task and differentiated it, as process, from any of the primary processes in social work. For supervision to accomplish its purpose has a teaching, evaluating, and administrative function as well as a helping one.

Virginia Robinson wrote in 1950 of the contribution to supervision as a process that had been made by its being used in the field work of students, as a central part of their professional education as social workers:

The stimulus of the professional school and the authority inherent in its teaching function were necessary to lift supervision out of complete identification with casework and the worker, and enable it to take over the authority and responsibility it must accept in order to fulfill its teaching function. . . . It has not fully accepted the authority which belongs to its function deriving from its relation to administration and to the agency as a whole.[2]

Robinson's two books on supervision [3] are unequaled in social work literature in clarifying the nature of professional supervision in social work, particularly as it is used in field work, in social casework, as part of social work education. She herself identifies the distinctive contribution of each book in the following way:

In my book published in 1936, I defined supervision as "an educational process in which a person with a certain equipment of knowledge and skill takes responsibility for training a person with less equipment. In the field of social casework this teaching process is carried by a succession of conference discussions between the supervisor and the student." To this definition of 1936, a decade of training experience in the use of functional supervision has contributed one revolutionary change. It has clarified the significance of a time structure with a beginning, focus, and ending, and its utilization for the movement of a relationship process. This difference between a succession of conference discussions and a time structured process is crucial.[4]

It is this particular distinction, that is, the concept of supervision as a time-structured process, which makes it possible to work on supervision *as process*, as it shifts in frequency and focus for workers of varied education and experience. But it is its administrative responsibility, as well as its responsibility to keep the agency's service individualized and alive for clientele and to be a vehicle for the creative expression of each individual worker rather than a mere mechanical delivery of a service, which assures it a continuing and essential place in social service administration.

Among the writers who have contributed significantly to the understanding and development of supervision as a process in social work are Grace Marcus and Charlotte Towle. Marcus, speaking of the necessity of a worker's acceptance of "professional interdependence," writes:

The growth of a profession's store of knowledge and skill and its tortuous advance out of its limitations rest on the active intercommunication of its members and on their working together in responsible relationships under the discipline of a shared purpose. This holds for the caseworker in a professionally oriented agency, however experienced and mature she may be.[5]

Towle notes the distinctive helping aspect of supervision without confusing it with a purpose of therapy, or social casework in a service agency, and identifies it as a part of supervision's "threefold function of teaching, helping, and administering." [6]

What makes supervision in social welfare agencies a social work method is the fact that it is concerned with initiating and sustaining a relationship process, as an aspect of agency administration designed to further the achievement of a social agency purpose, with its focus on the immediate purveyors of that service, that is, those engaged in a primary social work process, or in large agencies on the supervisors of those workers. It is suggested that the same generic principles of social work practice which are later to be developed are as applicable to supervision in all its distinctiveness, in purpose and as process, as they are to the other processes under consideration.

ADMINISTRATION

Administration in social work with its responsibility for the total operation of a service or agency, in common with its sister processes, has produced its own literature and generated its own differences in points of view. Like casework, it has sometimes been viewed as a "repertoire of acts," as requiring a variety of seemingly unrelated knowledge and skills, or the use of "a little casework, a little group work, a little community organization" while calling for personal qualities considered as "given" and not subject to development, certainly not to development as a planned part of social work education. Such views fail to recognize that a difference in purpose and focus for a relationship process in social work so alters it that it becomes a process in its own right, rather than a patchwork or amalgam with its own distinctive characteristics, at the same time that it may be characterized by principles which make it properly a social work process, for which preparation may appropriately be given within the profession's schools.

There appears to be general agreement, as reflected in the literature with the "proposition" stated by Spencer, that

social work administration is a social work function, involving the making of judgments and the use of professional knowledge and skill which, while not wholly peculiar to social work, nevertheless differ considerably from the knowledge and skill required in business administration.[7]

There also appears to be general agreement that preparation for the practice of administration is an appropriate function for a school of social work. What is not so clearly grasped or perhaps agreed upon is the essential nature of its difference as practiced in social work, from its use in other fields, the generic principles whose conscious use identify it as a process in social work, and the nature of the differences which distinguish it from other social work processes.

Certainly distinctive knowledge and skill, more frequently

taught in schools of business administration than in schools of social work, are needed by social workers as by all administrators. But unless they find their place in relation to a comprehended and motivating purpose, which includes both the purpose of the social work program or service being administered and the purpose of administration as a method, involving the initiating and sustaining of a wide variety of human relationship processes toward the achievement of a shared goal, administration as process in social work fails to realize its potential or make use of the profession's own knowledge and skill to the extent possible. Kenneth Pray wrote in this connection:

Research, administration, planning and interpretation are frequently assumed to be concerned only with facts, with ideas rather than with people; they are made to appear as products of some sort of occult private operation apart from any process that goes on in relationship with others. Sometimes they are made to assume such importance in the total equipment and activity of the community organizer: [one might substitute administrator or researcher] as to overshadow the primary social work process, method, and skill of using onself in direct personal and group relations. They are even thought to require an utterly different kind of person, subject to a different kind of discipline.[8]

A fragmented view of administration as a constellation of activities rather than a unitary process is characteristic of its description as POSDCORB, a term which served to suggest a course outline for many a course in administration in schools of social work and elsewhere in the early years of this century.

It was Lewis Merriam who wrote of the administrator:

Some genius has invented a new word to describe him. The word is made from first letters of the major classes of duties he performs. It is POSDCORB:

P   is for Planning
O   is for Organizing
S   is for Staffing
D   is for Directing
CO is for Coordinating
R   is for Reporting
B   is for Budgeting

While acknowledging that these duties are indeed important parts of the administrator's responsibility, Merriam concludes:

The most important thing that has been omitted from that fascinating word POSDCORB is knowledge of a subject matter. You have to plan something, you have to organize something, you have to direct something. . . . Intimate knowledge of the subject with which an administrative agency is primarily concerned is indispensable to the effective intelligent administration of that agency.[9]

Robinson,[10] in a paper presented at a conference called by the American Association of Social Workers in 1937, affirmed the position taken by Merriam, worked on how an "intimate knowledge" of subject matter could be secured by the social work administrator, and went on to identify administration as a distinctive process requiring both knowledge and skill. Speaking of it as skill, Robinson wrote: "As I am presenting it here it is as truly professional as casework skill, while it differs from it as characteristically as teaching or supervisory skill differs from casework skill and from administrative skill." Robinson identified the essential difference of administration from other processes in social work as lying in its scope: "The administrator is seen to embody or to represent the function of the agency more completely than any individual worker. He actually *is* the agency." She emphasized its greater, or wider, range of skill requirement, with its need for flexible capacity to change from one use of self to another (in carrying responsibility to clientele, to staff, and to community) and spoke to the characteristic time form within which it moves. "The skill of the caseworker, the supervisor or administrator can be judged by his understanding and control of his own time form."

Robinson took issue with the use of the term *enabler* to describe the administrator's function because it failed to bring out the values which inhere in its leadership aspects. "The physiological concept of organized pattern evolving around a gradient, determined by the dominance of a head end, applies here." She identified the fact that administrative skill is expressed in a series of functional relationships, in individual group and intergroup conferences, in the formulation of policies and plans, in the expression of decisive opinions and the laying down of final judgments, and defined as administration's overriding purpose "the responsibility for sustaining the function of the agency, keeping it clearly defined to the public while never permitting it to become too harsh to clients or dead or stereotyped to the staff." She characterized it as requiring strength to remain firm in emphasizing the good of the whole against the pressures and special pleadings of the parts.

The essential point in this analysis, as yet unsurpassed in the literature of administration as a process in social work, is that skill as well as substantive knowledge are identified as required for its conduct—skill seen as "a fundamental use of the self in a set of situations determined by function with techniques falling into a position of secondary importance, taking care of themselves . . . once skill is established." The skill required of the administrator is informed by his administrative purpose. It functions through the initiation and sustaining of processes involving relationships with people, singly and in groups. Administration, too, requires a "use of the self in a certain set of situations determined by function," moves within a characteristic time form, and operates from generic principles common to all processes in social work, while retaining its distinctiveness as process.

In these midcentury years social work administrators have shown an increased interest in their particular skills and processes. This interest is evident not only in the coverage of skill as a topic in professional journals but also in its place in social work conferences and meetings, and in the insistence of social work administrators on a "council" form of organization within the National Association of Social Workers which can provide some structure for their consideration of common concerns.

SOCIAL WORK RESEARCH

Research, in the sense of "diligent, protracted investigation for the purpose of adding to human knowledge; studious inquiry," has received increasing emphasis not only as a proper but as a necessary function for social work and social workers. Concomitantly in social work education considerable attention has been given to the preparation of social workers with a "methods concentration" in research, rather than in social casework, social group work, or any of the other possible methods for concentration.

From the beginning, the focus of social work was on action, action to effect social change and action to effect change in individuals, or in groups of individuals. Social workers, in the course of their engagement in social action or in the administration of social services, learned much about social welfare programs, their effectiveness or lack of effectiveness; about social work methods, their usefulness or lack of usefulness in achieving the purposes for which they were designed; and about people, the way they grow and change within their physical and social environments, how they respond to opportunity and lack of opportunity, to beneficence and to stress, physical, psychological, and social. But such knowledge was empirically come by, rather than deliberately sought through the use of scientific research method. It was a concomitant of giving a social service and remained either unformulated and the private possession of those who had amassed it, or it was put forth in conferences or in professional papers as an individual or group record of experience, a "clinical hunch."

Until the twentieth century was well under way, whenever social workers or social agencies wanted a serious study undertaken of some phenomenon related to social work practice, it was customary to call on researchers who had been trained in disciplines other than social work, most frequently in psychology or sociology, to "do the research." Much knowledge of great value to social work has been and continues to be developed by non-social-work researchers using rigorous scientific methods in the conduct of their social work studies. However, they sometimes suffer from two handicaps: first, from a lack of knowledge of certain of the phenomena they are studying, for example, social work programs and methods of practice; and second, from the lack of

understanding of and skill in the use of a method of working
with people, which in its conscious employment of certain principles can be identified as a social work method.*

As schools of social work increasingly took responsibility for
research as a content area to be required of all graduate social
work students, and as a possible methods concentration for some,
it became necessary to consider what the research component of
the basic professional master's degree program should be, what
should comprise a methods concentration in research for the social worker, and where in the educational continuum it should
fall.

Samuel Mencher, writing on the research method in social
work education, as a contribution to the curriculum study [11] of
1959, identified a dual objective for the research sequence: (1)
laying the foundation for critical thinking by including the principles and elements which underlie problem solving generally,
and (2) applying critical thinking attitudes and abilities to the
content of social work research. He identified four major content
areas for the research sequence in schools of social work as scientific method, problem solving through research, research in social
work, and statistics.

Mencher does not address himself to the question of whether
the social work researcher or, to be explicit, the social worker
who is a researcher should share with all other social workers
not only a commitment to social work values and purposes, and
a body of social work knowledge, but also a helping skill in
working with people *as a researcher*.

Wrote Virginia Robinson in the paper on administration to
which reference has been made:

The limitation in research (as an adequate basis in training for administration) is that it does not necessarily provide the discipline and
development of learning to relate oneself to people. Supervision might

---

* It goes without saying that social work profits enormously and will continue to profit
from research carried on in related fields as it has relevance for social work. Reference is
made here, however, to social work research, research related to social work programs,
policies, and service, having as its goal the development of knowledge useful for social
work practice.

make up for this lack if the research field understood the use of the supervisory process.[10]

What Robinson referred to was a supervisory process that takes responsibility for helping the supervisee engage others through the medium of a relationship process in working toward a shared goal.

Harold Lewis, in "Research Analysis as a (Social) Agency Function,"[12] identifies research conducted within a social agency as a "helping process," sanctioned by the agency. He adds: "In addition to problem solving skills (the researcher) must have skill in human relationships, since his services are generally transmitted through such relationships." Lewis identifies a process which moves within its own time form, with the researcher taking responsibility for each of its phases, the beginning or request for research service, the middle with its continuous engagement of the "clientele" in participation in the research process, and the ending phase or presentation of findings and recommendations in such a way that they have the best possible chance of being used by the agency staff. Attention is given to the kind of feelings the function of the researcher engenders, referred to as the clientele's difficulty in seeking, asking for, and using research help, and to the researcher's responsibility to be aware of and responsive to those feelings throughout the conduct of the research process, without in any sense abandoning his commitment to the conduct of a research study that in design and method is appropriate to the problem being researched. Lewis concludes: "[The researcher] is committed to the goals of science, the ethics of research practice, *and to the helping research function* that alone justifies his presence in the agency."

Social work research, as here conceived, is seen to have a service function, service to the field and profession of social work, and when carried on within a particular field of practice or social agency, to that particular field of practice or social agency, in addition to its function of advancing knowledge.

Identification of social work research as one of the helping processes of social work in no way modifies its requirement of its practitioners of a highly developed and extensive body of knowledge and skill which it shares with research in any field. Such identification, however, does make applicable to it, as a process involving relationships with individuals and groups, the same basis for practice, the same generic principles of practice, which are to be developed for all the social work methods.

A relevant question for the field is: Does and should the social work researcher take as much responsibility for the disciplined use of himself in a set of situations determined by function, in this instance the research function, as he does for his technical competence as a researcher? And a further question is: Is he really a social worker, through possession of skill in a relationship process directed toward a social purpose, and for which he holds himself responsible, unless he does? There is an assumption here with which there will not be full accord. It is that to be a social worker requires not only commitment to the values and purposes of social work, and possession of a specified body of knowledge for functioning within a social agency, but also skill in the use of a method, which for all its uniqueness has characteristics in common with all social work method, and is taught as such within the profession's schools.

SOCIAL WORK EDUCATION

Education, like supervision, administration, and research, constitutes a field and process not unique to social work. Yet, as is the case with each of the processes described, social work education requires a common base in knowledge of people, affirmation of purpose as determinant in role and program, commitment to process, and the use of certain principles inherent in all of the processes in social work, without any minimizing of their distinctiveness. Other educators, or more properly educators engaged in other fields, may work from the same bases and principles knowingly or not knowingly. The distinction is that a social worker, who identifies himself as such by education and experience, is obliged to operate from them knowingly and with willed commitment in such a way as to enhance his effectiveness as social work educator.

Much has been written on social work education in the 1950s and 1960s, stimulated, in part, by the active and effective Council on Social Work Education and other professional organizations related to education for social work. The Hollis-Taylor report [13] constituted an important experience in social work education's study of itself at a crucial period. The curriculum study of the late 1950s,[14] again under the aegis of the Council on Social Work Education, and with Werner Boehm as editor, constituted a second comprehensive and intensive evaluation of education for social work.

Subsequent conferences on various aspects and phases of social work education, held under a variety of auspices, have continued to engage the participation and to stimulate the practice and writing of social work educators throughout the country. In harmony with the spirit of the times, there has been great emphasis on "knowledge building," on developing and delineating the knowledge required by the prospective social worker and suggesting forms for its organization and presentation at various educational levels. Less attention has been given to method * in social work education, to the process through which the educational experience is made available. The quest for knowledge, development of new knowledge, selection and organizing of knowledge must go forward continuously for social work education to be the effective social instrument it should and can be. The concern of this particular writing, however, is not with knowledge content in social work education but with establishing the thesis that there is a process through which it is transmitted that again can make conscious use of generic principles of social work practice, for its more effective discharge.

It is the thesis of the writer, as stated elsewhere,[15] that graduate educational programs in social work have certain common

---

* At the present writing, a consultant on teaching methods, Marguerite Pohek, on the staff of the Council on Social Work Education, is giving vigorous leadership throughout the field to consideration of method in social work education.

characteristics, not only in their content but also in the method through which content is transmitted. Any such program may be viewed as a process, an experience characterized by duration in time, which has a beginning, a middle, and an end. It involves, every step of the way, each student's finding and affirming his own commitment to learn what he is learning in order to become what he wants to be—a social worker. In other words, the entire program is designed to release in the individual student, and in all students, power to become social workers. There is something in the nature of the educational experience itself, in its engagement of the student to use the school for his own chosen ends, which is similar to the very process he will be using as a social worker. For he will be seeking to engage individuals, groups, and communities in using social work services or programs for their chosen ends, even though, as in certain protective or other services, the original initiative or decision for intervention comes from the outside and may not be the client's own until he is helped to make it so.

There are psychological principles governing the way an individual can be helped to find a goal and work toward it with increasing commitment to the use of his own powers which are as true for a program of social work education as for a program of social work. As the student engages in an educational experience that helps him through his relationships with teachers, supervisors, and classmates, as well as through his acquisition of knowledge content, to become a social worker, he gains the ability to engage in the same kind of psychological relationship process with individual cients, groups, or communities seeking to use the services he is making available.

To summarize, social work education which seeks to produce social workers qualified to practice social work, as here presented, focuses not only on educational content but always and consistently on educational structures and processes, as well, that conduce to the student's use of what is taught for responsible effective social work practice. Such educational programs are designed to graduate social workers ready to enter immediately on practice, but stimulated and committed, too, to continue their professional development throughout their working lives. The social work educator is responsible for "the use of himself in a set of situations determined by function" as truly as the social worker engaged in any of the other processes of social work. Educational method in social work, whether used in a graduate professional school of social work, an undergraduate program in social welfare, or staff development programs in social agencies, in addition to requiring the special knowledge and skills of an educator, can be identified as leading to a process in social work only as it *also* embodies conscious knowing use of certain generic principles which characterize any and all methods in social work.

SUMMARY

In Chapters 2 and 3 primary methods in the practice of social work have been identified as social casework, social group work, and community organization. Their use leads to the respective processes. There has been recognition that all social workers engaged in direct relationship with clientele work with individuals, groups, and communities. But it has been suggested that there are differences in social work processes essentially one to one, those involving small groups and those involving communities. These differences inhere in the specific purpose of the method employed, the configuration of relationships involved, and the consequent role of the worker, as well as in the purpose of the programs or services being administered. At the same time each of the primary methods has been viewed as holding a purpose of initiating and sustaining a process of human relationships designed to further an individual, group, or community's use of a social service or program in its own and society's interest. It is this likeness which makes possible the establishment of a common base for practice and the development of certain principles of practice equally applicable to all methods in social work, without denying, minimizing, or distorting their uniqueness.

Secondary, or facilitating, methods in social work have been identified as supervision, administration, research, and teaching. There was recognition that the processes resulting from the use of these methods were in no sense peculiar to social work, and that, particularly for administration, research, and education, substantial knowledge and skill not specific to social work, and more highly developed elsewhere, are necessary for their conduct. Each of these methods was seen as informed and characterized by its distinctive purpose, and hence as distinctive in nature. Yet each was viewed, when used to accomplish social work purpose within a social work program or service, as involving the initiation and sustaining of characteristic processes and patterns of relationship toward the achievement of a social agency or social institution's goal.

As was true for the primary processes, this was seen as leading to a requirement for establishing some common base and generic principles for practice with recognition of the necessity of each process's continued development of its unique character, and the acquisition of the *specific* knowledge and skill essential for its effective discharge.

Since all social work processes, both primary and secondary, operating in any of the fields of practice have been established as working through human relationships, and as involving the worker's use of himself to further or release capacities and power for action in others, a base in understanding of human growth and human nature is required and will be the first of the "bases" to be developed. Is there any basis, in what is known about the growth, development, and nature of the human being, for believing that it is possible for a professional social worker, using any of the social work methods and through the medium of human relationship, to release power for growth and development and constructive, responsible social relationships?

4 A PSYCHOLOGICAL BASE FOR SOCIAL WORK PRACTICE, I

ALL the processes of social work, primary and secondary, require the use of the worker's self in relationship with others; in other words, they call for skill in a human relationship process directed toward some specific social purpose within a general encompassing purpose appropriate for social work. An understanding of human nature, of the process of human growth, and of the way human relationship is used and can be used for growth is therefore essential for practice in any field and through any process. Such an understanding can constitute a psychological base for practice. Furthermore, since social work processes are used with individuals, groups, and communities, an understanding not only of the individual but also of the group and the community, as distinct phenomena, is necessary. Such understanding is needed in especial depth by workers whose focus is on work with group or community, but by all social workers as well, since the very nature of social work, whatever the process or field, requires it.

What will be developed here as a concept of "human nature" and human growth will necessarily constitute a point of view rather than an exhaustive theoretical treatment, as it takes its place as part of a conceptual base for a theory of social work practice. Any psychology of human nature and growth is applicable to worker and client alike. There is no room for a client psychology and a worker psychology in the sense of a different theory of human nature and growth being applicable to each party to a social work, or any, relationship. The same "psychology" applies to both. However, as will be subsequently developed, the fact of *being* the worker or *being* the client or group served creates its own psychology, which must be understood and taken into account by the worker whatever his field or process. Always, professional responsibility requires the social worker to be aware of and responsible for his own part in the process, just as he is aware of and responsive to the "other's" part.

HUMAN GROWTH AS PURPOSE

The last thirty years have seen increasing emphasis on growth as purpose, as motivated from within and subject to continuous self-direction and control. A feeling for the power of the thrust that inheres in each fertilized ovum is strikingly conveyed in the writing of George W. Corner,[1] embryologist. The growth of the embryo from 1 cell to 200 billion cells, during a period of 9 months, from 15 ten-millionth of a single gram to 3,250 grams, staggers the imagination. The orderly course of embryological development and the capacity of the embryo to deal, within its own limits, with unfavorable enviromental circumstance in its inexorable move toward realization of its purpose of growth suggest an inner direction, force, and flexibility which can be assumed not to cease at birth but to continue to characterize man's biological and psychological capacity for coping and creating throughout his life.

Dr. Corner's description of embryonic life, so scientific in its use of fact, so poetic in its expression, lays a base for understanding (1) the nature of human growth in its purposiveness and orderly progression, (2) respective roles for the environment and endowment in their interaction, on the course of growth, and (3) the origin and nature of difference as between man and other species, and as between man and man.

Corner's feeling for the purpose and struggle which characterize growth, both physical and spiritual, is conveyed in the following quotation:

How then shall I speak of the spirit, but humbly employing such vision as may be granted to an embryologist? I declare my conviction that the spirit of man, all that makes him man rather than beast and carries him onward with hope and sacrifice, comes not as a highborn tenant from afar, but as a latent potentiality of the body. It too is received as a germ, an opportunity, something to develop. The spirit, with the body, must grow and differentiate, organizing its inner self as it grows, strengthening itself by contact with the world, earning its title to glory by struggle and achievement.[2]

Corner refers to the power of choice and decision and exercise of the will as rooted in man's biology:

We are led . . . by the evidence of comparative anatomy to ponder upon the freeedom of the will, or at least freedom of action, which we have because our bodies are versatile, untrammeled by specialization for extreme but particular skill, and capable of any task the mind may imagine. . . . The scope of the human mind, the freedom of human decision, are bound up inextricably with the generalization of the body.[3]

Edmund Sinnot,[4] biologist, writing of the biology of purpose, speaks of living things as "seekers and creators" and of striving for goals as the essence of all life, adding that in man these goals have risen to heights before undreamed of, and suggesting that man can set them even higher at his will. He refers to the organizing, goal-seeking quality in life, of life as regulating, purposeful, ascending, of each human being as "an organized and organizing center, a vortex pulling in matter and energy and knitting them into precise patterns," [5] and as capable of creating new patterns never known before. Sinnot does not deny or minimize the effect of the environment on the life of the organism. Indeed, he writes that the exact character of the organism will depend in some measure on the environment within which it develops. "In all these cases the genetic constitution of the organism is not changed, but the way in which this expresses itself in development is very different depending on the conditions under which development takes place." [6]

Sinnot's essential thesis is stated in the following words:

The insistent tendency among living things for bodily development to reach and maintain, as a means or goal, an organized living system of a definite kind, and the equally persistent directiveness or goal seeking that is the essential feature of behavior, and thus finally the basis of all mental activity, are fundamentally the same thing—merely two aspects of the basic regulatory character all living stuff displays. Regulation implies something to regulate *to,* a norm or goal. The goal in embryonic life may be regarded as a series of stages that lead to a mature and properly functioning individual, and the goal in psychic life as a purpose or series of purposes, simple and unconscious in primitive instinct, but rising in the mind of man to far higher levels. [7]

Sinnot's hypothesis that living organisms move toward definite goals both in their bodily development and their behavior provides a unified conception not only of man's nature but also of his relation to others and to the universe. [8]

Not only embryologists and biologists but also psychologists, anthropologists, psychiatrists, psychoanalysts, educators, and philosophers are placing increasing emphasis on the place of purpose in life, on the human capacity for choice and decision-making, on the power of rationality. Gordon Allport writes:

Up to now the behavioral scientists have not provided us with a picture of man capable of creating or living in a democracy. These sciences have, in large part, imitated the billiard ball model of physics, now of course outmoded. They have delivered into our hands a psychology of an "empty organism" pushed by drives and molded by environmental circumstance. What is small and partial, what is external and mechanical, what is early, what is peripheral and opportunistic—have received the chief attention of psychological system builders. But the theory of democracy requires also that man possess a measure of rationality, a portion of freedom, a generic conscience, propriate ideals and unique value. . . . [9]

He concludes that the emerging figure of man appears endowed with a sufficient margin of reason, antonomy, and choice to profit from living in a free society and adds: "The portrait, however, does not discard the darker portion of truth discovered by the youthful psychology of the recent past. The truth stands and it will ever remain the duty of psychology to correct idealistic exuberance."

Maslow's concept of self-actualization, Karen Horney's view of man's inner strivings as positive, and the individual as a continually growing person, Lecky's development of a theory of unity and consistency of the self, as well as the contributions of Angyal, Fromm, Goldstein, Rank, and others have been brought together by Clark Moustakas in "The Self-Explorations in Personal Growth." [10] Moustakas, in his preface, describes his book as stressing the positive, healthy, growing potentials of the individual, as pointing to the essential quality of intrinsic (human) nature and its expression in uniqueness and variation, in differences, as presenting the individual self as unified, consistent, as being and becoming.

Of particular significance for readers wishing to explore further the psychological base on which the theory for social work practice being developed in this book is based in the work of Helen Merrell Lynd "On Shame and the Search for Identity." [11] Lynd presents a psychology of potential abundance to replace a psychology based upon an economics of scarcity, which, she contends, characterized the period when Freudian psychology developed. She writes, in opposition to a "compensating" theory of personality:

Accurately as a theory of compensation accounts for many aspects of personality development, particularly in our contemporary society, there are other aspects that cannot be accomodated within it.

Human beings . . . have capacities for being spontaneously active and creatively interested in other persons, and in the non-personal world, that find only meager expression in what we call human behavior or human nature in our society. In this perspective, goals, instead of being only specific objects to release tension, become expanding purposes in which the whole personality may be involved. Wonder, curiosity, interest, thought, sympathy, trust, love are all seen as characteristic human attributes, not simply as secondary derived aims. Reality

becomes something capable of yielding knowledge, interest, and fulfillment instead of being mainly a threat to be coped with. A whole philosophy of society and of history is expressed in the widely current use
of the phrase "coping with reality" which implies that society and
reality are felt as difficulties or dangers by the individual, something to
be warded off, coped with, at great sacrifice adjusted to. A psychology
of potential abundance may replace a psychology based upon an economics of scarcity.[12]

In this connection Lynd's footnote to the foregoing statement
is important: "Questioning the concept of reality as something to
be coped with does not imply that reality can ever exclude conflict or that conflict is necessarily 'dysfunctional.' It implies only
that society and reality can be something other than threats to
human beings." Lynd's references to literature and to scientific
and philosophic writings in the development of her thesis are
particularly illuminating.[13]

To summarize, there is growing recognition by scientists in diverse fields, philosophers, and educators, as well as by professional persons, including social workers, whose recognition derives from their own experience as well as from theory that man
is properly conceived as the center of his own life, capable of
acting upon as well as being acted on, creator (of himself) as
well as creature, able to use circumstance, including human relationships, to achieve his own purpose, including the purpose of
the continuous creation of himself. This is not to deny the irra-
tional, the unconscious, the powerful potentially crippling effects
as well as supporting effects of life experiences, particularly early
experiences and relationships within the immediate family. It is
essential to any worker in the field of human relations to know
the limits imposed by endowment and by circumstance on human development, the hazards to which every developing
human being is subject at every point in his existence from conception forward.

However, it is possible also to establish a frame of reference
which sees the push toward life, health, and fulfillment as primary in human beings, and the human being as capable through-

out his life of modifying both himself and his environment in accordance with his own changing purposes, within the limitations and opportunities of his own capacity and his own environment. This view sees man as capable of using human relationships (including relationship with a social worker) both to find and to strengthen his own purpose for himself and to move toward its realization.

HUMAN GROWTH AS PROCESS

Social work, practiced by human beings, in relationship with other human beings, requires not only the use of a concept of man as purposive and of purpose as biologically established, but also an appreciation of difference as characterizing human beings, despite the likeness which derives from their common humanity. It is to the *purpose* of the individual, group, or community that the social worker relates. He lends himself, his professional knowledge and skill, the resources of the agency he represents, and his *own* purpose as it inheres in his agency's function, his particular method, himself as a professional social worker, to the "other's" accomplishment of a purpose, clarified and affirmed through the helping process itself.

But for that help to be most effective, the individual, group, or community served must be understood in its uniqueness and difference as well as in the characteristics it shares with others of its kind. The difference of the individual person inheres, in part, in genetic endowment, but also in the fact that the individual is a process, moves in time, has a series of experiences which affect the self he becomes. So, too, the difference of each group and community inheres not only in its composition, at any point in time, but also in its history since its continuing life is constantly affecting its nature, just as it is affecting "the outside."

Each individual, each bearer and sharer of the human condition, began with the first stirring of life on earth and, before that time, as part of the mystery of life's origin. He constitutes an expression of life force which has been unbroken since life began.

More narrowly, he is the product of a multitude of ancestors over thousands of years. Most recently he is the product of what may be thought of as his "immediate ancestors" whose traditions, customs, and characteristics, known through living relationship or as passed along through family recounting, influence his development, as do the genes he has inherited, and the immediate circumstances and relationships which constitute his present environment.

So similar, to the strongest microscope, is each tiny fertilized ovum which constitutes a living human being's beginning as an individual self, yet each is already teeming with *difference,* both biological and cultural.

As embryonic life pursues its orderly course, the purpose of creation of a human self is consistently at work, and is idiosyncratically at work, since differences in rate and quality of growth have been noted in foetal life. The new individual, in some respects a parasitic growth within the mother's body, suspended in fluid, unable to perform independently the functions of respiration, digestion, circulation, is yet quite unlike the true parasite, for it carries from the moment of conception the tremendous task and potential for creating its own structure, evolving complex differentiated systems of organs, until that moment when independent life becomes physiologically possible, and eventuates through birth.

Throughout his first nine months each individual is realizing his biological purpose to become a human and distinctive self and is using his genetic resources as well as the resources available to him in his immediate environment to accomplish that purpose. Lacks, failures, inadequacies in that first environment, as in all later ones, can alter and even stop the course of development, just as richness and suitability of the environment for growth can further it. Genetic endowment sets certain limits to the nature of the development which can take place, but it offers opportunities for development also.

The significance of birth in the life of an individual has been variously appreciated. Otto Rank's emphasis on its importance for subsequent psychological development, as developed in *The Trauma of Birth*,[14] marked his break with certain tenets of established Freudian psychology. Rank emphasized the development of life fear and death fear, out of the birth experience, and saw all individuals as expressing and experiencing in varying and changing degrees these two fears throughout life: the fear of not living, of not experiencing, not realizing potential, which can be thought of as death fear; and the fear of separation of independent existence outside the womb, and so of any kind of separation or differentiation as a person, which may be thought of as life fear.*

Whatever the significance of birth and the effect of its nature in the specific instance on the course of individual development no one can deny that it constitutes a profound alteration in the life situation of the embryo, now infant. Throughout the first two years of life each individual continues his growth and development, with different and changing capacities for using human relationships and other aspects of the environment, and with changing relationships and environments available for his use. The comfort of closeness to the mother, or person who takes physical care, replaces the "primal intrauterine pleasure" and supports the infant as neural and sensory development gradually make possible increasingly independent functioning. Nursing, enjoying the use of the mouth in sucking, learning to drink from a cup and to manage feeding himself, however awkwardly, development of the capacity to crawl about, to stand erect, to walk and run, to be "clean and dry" in accordance with society's prescription constitute opportunities as well as potential hazards for the infant's gradual sense of himself as a separate person, capable of some measure of control over his destiny, and capable as well of yielding to a larger whole without a damaging loss of self-esteem. Central in this early period of life, wherein the infant has left the chemical exchange system of the womb for the social

* The central intent of Rankian therapy is to free the individual to *use* an experience of relationship for the "claiming" of his own difference and to *leave* the relationship for the discovery, affirmation, and furtherance of his capacity for "independent living." This point will be developed further later in this chapter.

exchange system of society, as his gradually increasing capacities meet the opportunities and limitations of his culture, is his relationship to members of his immediate family: first of all, his mother, or mother surrogate, and later his father, brothers or sisters, and the larger family of aunts, uncles, cousins, and grandparents.

Jahoda [15] writes that the maturing organism continues to unfold, not by developing new organs but by a prescribed sequence of locomotor, sensory, and social capacities. Each stage becomes a crisis because of a change in perspective. Different capacities use different opportunities to become full-grown components of the ever new configuration that is the growing personality.

Erikson [16] describes three components of the developing personality in the early years of life as "balances" each individual achieves: (1) trust and mistrust, (2) autonomy and sense of shame or doubt, (3) initiative and guilt. He writes of the importance, during the first year of life, of the development of trust in the self and its capacities, and in others. This is the incorporative stage, the "taking in" by mouth and eye stage. All important is the urge to "get"—to get what is given, to get someone to do for him. Only later is it possible for the child to identify with the giver.

What Erikson describes as the second oral stage, the active incorporative stage, characteristic of the second half of the first year is marked by its own crises: physiologic, as the infant seeks to incorporate and appropriate, more aggressively, as through the use of his teeth, than in the first six months of sucking; psychological, as he becomes aware of himself as a person separate from his mother; and environmental, as his mother gradually turns away from an almost continuous care of him to some of her former and usual pursuits. His growth task is to continue sucking without biting and, above all, to maintain a "feeling" balance essentially trustful, when mother goes away, is not there when he needs or wants her, and yet to develop enough *mistrust* of his every want's being immediately satisfied from the outside that he is stimulated to continue the development of increased autonomy and self-reliance.

The second component—autonomy versus shame and doubt— is emphasized in the experience of toilet training as the infant learns to hold on and let go through self-control without the loss of self-esteem based in a sense of omnipotence and "letting fly" as instinct and impulse direct. It is muscular maturation that sets the stage for holding on and letting go at will, makes it physiologically possible, and so establishes the principle of law and order in the infant's life as something which can be self-affirmed without loss of self-valuing. Here as in the oral incorporative period, the attitude of the mother can help or hinder. Too little assistance to the baby in being clean and dry, as he is physically able, contributes to what may be a continuing strong impulsiveness, a feeling of outside requirement as unduly thwarting to self-expression. Too early and rigorous training may result either in too ready acquiescence to routine with loss of sense of self as significant and strong, or to a constant fighting of rules as unjust.

The third component, resulting from the development of a balance between initiative and guilt, evolves as the infant, convinced that he is a separate person, asks himself what kind of person he is going to be. With the use of language his imagination expands. With the use of his legs, not only to move about but to get him where he wants to go, he enters on an "intrusive stage." To what degree will he venture? To what degree dare he venture to be a person separate and different from parents without suffering undue guilt and constriction of activity and thought. Allen develops this point, in detail, as he writes of the dilemma of growth for both mother and child:

The dilemma for the mother can be formulated in this way: How can she direct and guide the life she has created toward a personally and socially acceptable goal and yet allow the emergence of a separate and different self? How can she give all that she must without engulfing the child and making him no more than the product of her own will for whom she could continue to feel full responsibility? How can she encourage creativeness in the product of her creation?[17]

The growth dilemma for the child he describes as . . . "How does he acquire the courage to be a self different and separate from the self that created him?" Allen makes the point that any child is a product of forces which operate entirely outside himself, but that life which obtains its start through the operation of external forces continues only through the gradual taking over of responsibility for direction and the achievement of its own integrity. He emphasizes that "a child is an active participant in his own growth, and a dilemma exists for him irrespective of, although greatly influenced and exaggerated by, the adult's attempt to solve his own part of the difficulty."[18]

The preschool years witness a changing relationship to the mother, increased interest in the father on the part of both boys and girls, in other children in the family, and in the neighborhood or nursery school if that is part of the child's experience. The world is expanding, the child's capacities are developing; he has increasingly more power to use enlarged opportunities for his growth as a separate but related (social) person.

The Oedipal conflict is variously interpreted by psychologists, psychiatrists, and others. The traditional Freudian view of it was challenged by Rank,[19] who saw the myth as pointing to the danger of "knowing," of too great self-consciousness, which can interfere with willing, rather than as an illustration of sexual desire on the part of the child for the parent of the opposite sex, consequent rivalry with the parent of the same sex, and resultant castration fear in the boy and "grief" (sense of inferiority and being punished) in the girl.

Erikson[20] sees the Oedipal crisis for children which precedes the school years as involving a taking in by boys and girls that they are not as big and strong and capable as the parents and can never have the kind of relationship with father or mother, as the case may be for a boy or girl, that the parents have with each other, with the ensuing query, "Do I dare to venture at all?" Is it worth while to try to do what will always be "lesser" measured against what the parents can do? He refers to the joy of mastering, producing, sharing, completion, which support the child in his continuing growth.

The child can settle his own identity as a boy or a girl partly through identification with the parent of the same sex on the basis of recognized "likeness," and as he feels attractive to and loved by the parent of the opposite sex. So the base is laid for positive relationships with persons of both sexes, and an eventual primary relationship with a person of the opposite sex.

The intense struggle to achieve a sense of a separate self which is yet related to others, to establish his own identity as boy or girl, to achieve new relationships to both parents, to learn to use developing physical, intellectual, and emotional powers for production, mastery, and achievement, and still take into account the "rules of the game," in however rudimentary a fashion, abates somewhat as the child nears school age. Again he is ready, on entering school, to use new powers, new capabilities, in an environment that has expanded somewhat dramatically and offers challenges and opportunities not before encountered.

It is in school that the child has fresh opportunity to compare himself with others and to appraise himself in his difference without serious damage of self-esteem, or loss of capacity for relationship with his peers. Indeed, his opportunity is to relate to many new "others" of his age group, some more capable, some less capable than he, and in diverse areas, and to find *likeness* as a base for relating without loss of his own sense of the difference that makes him an individual in his own right. It is a sense of himself, who he is and what he is like, that is greatly stimulated by his experience with others against whom he can define himself. His capacity for using relationship to become the self he is continuously choosing to be has wider scope as he now uses relationships with peers, with groups of peers, as well as with chums and with teachers, as he had earlier used (and continues to use) relationships within the family toward this end.

Two growth opportunities afforded by the school, in addition to the central one for learning and developing skills both motor and intellectual, are the opportunity for fresh definition and affirmation of the self in its likeness to and difference from others, and the opportunity for the further development of self through expanded relationships and opportunity to learn to relate to others and to give and take, control and yield, share and assert. Also of importance is the opportunity to relate again to rules and regulations as first met in the second six months of life, and now represented in a less personal and more "fixed" way than heretofore. Law and order as a way of life are represented through the person of teacher and school personnel, and through the form and structure and procedures which characterize the school experience. They are represented as well in games with groups, which play an important part in the lives of most children. The child must ask himself, "Can I yield to the larger whole, accept outside control, and impose self-control without loss of self-esteem?"

As with his schoolmates, he finds a balance of trust and mistrust through experience with the new adult in his life. This is the period for reinforcing his sense of himself, including his identity as boy or girl, through close "chum" relationships. He decides whether he can be a "person" himself and still find a way to "fit into," and use for his own growth purpose, the experiences and relationships available to him.

To his school experience he brings not only his genetic endowment but also the attitudes and sense of himself developed through his life experiences, and what he has done with them in each successive period of his life from conception forward. Being part of a group of like age and working in concert with peers to achieve a common end are new experiences first met in any continuous and concerted way in school. Through his mastery of the skills of literacy, life unfolds, and he gains a sense of the outside —and of the world of which he is a part—to a degree not before possible for him.

Inexorably his own growth brings him to a new crisis in development—adolescence. Adolescence has been described as that longer period within which puberty occurs. The physical maturation which renders the boy or girl capable of sexual reproduction introduces strange, strong, new, and often perplexing impulses, desires, and emotions. At the same time that he is experiencing internal changes at a stepped-up rate and of a kind not always easy to assimilate into his notion of who he is, the adolescent experiences changes in his family and society's expectations of him. These expectations themselves vary from person to person and from time to time. Small wonder that his lifelong quest for a sense of his own identity is a matter of intense interest for him during this period.

Dorothy Hankins[21] refers to the task of every individual to reach and then form some balance between himself as an individual with strong needs, impulses, and drives, and himself as a member of a society which makes various and urgent demands. She writes that in adolescence the problem of achieving this balance is at its peak. The swings of mood, impulsive behavior, the going too far in defining the self against the rules of the adult world, the equally excessive conservatism as a defense against the revolutionary impulse, all characterize the adolescent boy and girl who is engaged in trying out a self in many ways new, in a new relationship to society. He may both find and lose himself anew through espousing "causes." Always he is "on the go" in sports, activity, vigorous play, or fantasy. Sex is defended as "personal and my business." But society will not let it be that way, for society has a stake in the way sex finds expression. The adolescent is ready for physical sexual expression but not ready for the commitment and responsibility which a lasting union requires.

The attempt to separate from parents, begun in relation to the mother at birth and now calling for psychological realization at a new level, may be accompanied by exaggerating flaws in parents so that they will be "bad enough" to leave or by an even more crippling clinging, with a failure to establish an own identity. Once again the boy defines himself as boy, or more properly young man, and the girl as young woman, with a need and capacity for a comfortable identification with the parent of the same sex, without loss of own identity, and with a capacity for a relationship to the parent of the opposite sex which provides a base for heterosexual peer relationships, without trapping through too close a tie to parent.

Hazardous as this phase of living may appear, it is important to appreciate that it constitutes a time of new energy, increased "life," new powers, physical, intellectual, and emotional, and widened opportunities for their use in human relationships and in productive work, as in learning. Allen's [22] reminder that the self is not merely a precipitate but has the quality of spontaneity and creativity within itself takes on fresh meaning in this age period when resources and opportunity for spontaneity and creativity are at a new height.

Erikson [23] refers to the development of fidelity, "the strength of disciplined devotion" in adolescents, with a heightening of the processes of identification both with significant persons and idealogical forces, as giving importance to the individual life through relating it to the community and so to "society."

Early maturity is characterized by still further separation from the family into which the child is born, most often through the establishing of his own family or household. He continues the development and identification of himself as an individual through educational and vocational choice and pursuit and a more responsible relationship to society, and through his identification as an adult with a new role as a "maker and shaker" of his world.

Society's changing expectations of men and women influence the younger adult's development, as do his relationships and experiences within his immediate family as he moves into maturity. Thompson [24] refers to the fact that the culture now favors the development of characteristics in women heretofore considered typical in men and takes issue with the theory of a "masculine protest" and masculinity "complex" to explain strivings and characteristics in women which today may reflect self-realization of a positive rather than a negative nature. She suggests that more basic than a reaction against being a woman, in some women's exaggerated need for freedom and independence, may be a reaction against early, too great dependency on a powerful mother which has led to damaged self-esteem. Becoming a man in today's culture poses its own problems and opportunities, as the roles of the two sexes have shifted over the last several decades with less clear-cut differentiation between functions and characteristics identified as masculine or feminine.[25]

Marriage and parenthood for both men and women constitute opportunities for further definition and further development of the self at the same time that they may constitute problems, like any new expectation and function. Work, through which a man still finds a major definition and scope for development of himself, offers such opportunity increasingly to women, particularly, but by no means exclusively to unmarried women.

Like any age period, early maturity sets its own peculiar tasks and holds its expectations. These tasks are fulfilled and expectations are realized with the resources which each individual has developed up to that point, in accordance with his genetic endowment, his own individual concept of himself, his life experiences and what he has done with them, the opportunities available to him, and the general (and far from clear or uniform) expectations of society.

Late maturity finds physical changes, sometimes the beginning of impairment of hearing and sight, perhaps loss of energy, or "vital capacity" and agility, some decline in some kinds of intellectual capacity, not uniform for all persons, with some research suggesting that the "brightest" persons tend to lose the least in intelligence in advancing years, the dullest, the most. While results of research [26] are conflicting in respect to the fact and degree of change in capacity to learn over the middle and later years, there is some consensus that the loss in learning capacity prior to any actual senile change is slight in relation to total learning, and that improvement in comprehension and judgment which may accompany advancing years sometimes offsets a loss in quick recall and rote memory.

With characteristic changes in physical and intellectual capacity which vary greatly among individuals, persons in late maturity face characteristic tasks and expectations. Responsibilities for parents, changing relationship to parents, grown old, are accompanied by changing relationships to children, engaged in achieving their own separation. Peak accomplishments in work are usually reached, responsibility to community and society is at its height. The self has achieved a kind of definition less subject to modification than when that "self" was more fluid. If embryonic life and the years of infancy constitute the periods of greatest taking in and the least giving out, the years of late maturity are likely to constitute those of greatest giving out in personal and family relationships, in work, and in community responsibility. The world is as wide as it is going to be, and one's relationship to it as a developed self as contributory and responsible as it is likely to be. Yet consistently the changing self retains the capacity for using old and new relationships, and present circumstance, for continuing differentiation and development, though at a different pace and possibly depth than is true for most in earlier years.

Old age, like the coming of dusk in the summer sky, is ordinarily gradual rather than dramatic in its onset and is characterized by difference among individuals, at the same time that it remains an identifiable and, in some ways, characteristic phase of the life cycle for all who reach it. Various theses on the nature of the aging process have been developed, with aging described as a "wearing out process" due to a decrease in the cells' capacity for self-synthesis. Three forms of aging have been identified, leading to decline of vital functions: cellular change due solely to lapse of time, senescent change resulting from hypertension, and pathological change as found in arteriosclerosis and cancer.[27]

There is common recognition, if not acceptance, that aging is a part of living and that the aging process begins at conception and ends with death. There is perhaps inadequate awareness, on the part of many, that growth, development, and maturation are as much a consequence of the aging process as are the atrophies and degenerations of senility.

The general physical slowing down, diminution of energy, slower reflexes, increased need for sleep, and the greater likelihood of certain kinds of illness and impairment are accompanied by changes in intellectual capacity. Havighurst[28] refers to the individual's "learning his way through life" but suggests that adaptive capacity to live under changing conditions may be impaired in old age. He notes an intellectual decline after the twenties and thirties in rote learning with other intellectual functions very slow to decline, usually not before the sixties, and with wisdom growing, barring organic change, and granting that the individual has been experiencing life in such a way as to produce wisdom.

Again the individual's concept of himself undergoes change, and potential development, influenced by internal factors, physical and psychological change, and by society's expectations and attitudes as communicated in a variety of ways both subtle and blatant. Again each person has the opportunity to define himself anew and to continue the creation and development of a self, in constant flux at the same time that it manifests the continuity that gives it integrity.

Pollak [29] takes note of the psychological impact upon an older person of a society which regards him as changed and limited too soon and requires him "to adjust to a social prescription of such a change before it is necessitated by his physical or mental condition." Merloo has written:

In cultures where the old are treated with veneration, old people are mentally virile, as experienced in the Orient, and hardly any coronary occlusion is known in those regions. There exists an (intimate) relation between respect for the old and their mental stability. . . .[30]

Characteristic of old age in this culture is a role ambiguity, somewhat comparable to that found in adolescence. Internal change (at a somewhat accelerated rate), plus a confused attitude on the part of society as to what it expects, leaves the old person asking freshly, "Who am I?" Frequently his position in his own family has changed. No longer head of the household, possibly dependent on children in a variety of ways, separated by retirement from the life work which helped him define himself, his task may indeed be difficult as he continues his development as an individual self and as a member of society.

It is relative disengagement which characterizes old age, just as increasing engagement characterized youth and maturity. The process becomes one of letting go. The world, which has widened throughout the growing years, shrinks toward life's end. Tasks of old age characteristically include adjusting to decreased physical strength, to illness, to degenerative bodily changes, to retirement and reduced income, to the possible death of spouse and friends. They include as well, on the more positive side, as opportunity, finding satisfactory expression for both changing and enduring interests, developing new or changing relationships with (expanding) own family and discovering ways to meet social and civic interests and obligations.

Fulfillments of old age can include a sense of satisfaction in the course run (if it has been that kind of course!), a sense of fulfillment as a person, happiness of leisure, freedom from responsibilities and a time schedule, opportunity to develop new and old interests, enjoyment of continuing family through relationship to grown children and grandchildren.

Death, as the end of life, can be viewed as a right ending, an affirmed conclusion to a process that has run its course. So can the aged person say with Stevenson: "Glad did I live and gladly die, and I laid me down with a will." [31] That it is so seldom viewed in this way may testify more to the realization of varied opportunities for living having been missed than to the fear of dying. What has been presented in what feels to the author like a "romp" through the life cycle in necessarily brief, incomplete and sketchy form is intended to convey a feeling for life as a process that has its beginning, middle, and ending.

An understanding of growth as purpose and growth as process suggests the following concepts, which have relevance as psychological base for the development of a theory for social work practice, involving as it does the professional use of a relationship between one individual, a social worker, and other individuals, in whatever configuration, toward an end both individually fulfilling and socially constructive.

   1. The individual is central in his own growth. From conception to death he is actively engaged in the development and use of himself in the direction of realization of his potential as an individual who is part of a larger whole.

2. To this end, and in every stage in his life, he makes use of his particular innate capacities and his environment, including the human relationships in his environment, both taking in what he needs and can use and putting out what he must in the interest of his growth. He both acts upon his environment and is acted upon by it.

3. The nature of this environment is continuously changing throughout every phase of the life cycle, as it moves, for the individual, from the purely physical-chemical environment of the womb to the first relationship to the mother, the immediate and then extended family, the neighborhood, the school, community, and the world at its widest as it is known in full maturity and as it narrows in old age.

4. Each individual brings continuously changing capacities (physical, intellectual, emotional, social) to bear on his continuously changing environment. Here too there is a crescendo of increasing capacity, a peak of capacity (uneven in its several aspects), and a reduction of capacity which ends in death.

5. Each age period, moving often imperceptibly to the next, has its characteristic opportunities and tasks, as posed by social expectation, which itself shifts and is not wholly consistent even at a given point in time.

6. The inner development of the individual is characterized by its own purpose to master the tasks posed, not out of compulsion from without but in response to inner readiness and capacity which has resulted in the kind of expression and activity from which the social expectations derive.

7. The environment may influence, further, retard, divert, and complicate the development of an individual, but he remains in control of his own growth, central in his own development and capable of continuing development throughout his life's course, within the limits of his particular capacities and environmental opportunity at a given point in time.

8. Cultural factors, such as social class, may affect and color social expectations of an individual and his own expectations of himself but they do not alter his continuous inner necessity to find a balance between the realization of himself as an individual

and as a member of the particular society of which he is presently a part.

Since the social worker enters into the life of individuals through human relationship, it is necessary to look at the nature of the self as capable of relationship, and of use of relationship for growth. The self has been reviewed "longitudinally," in a sense, as a differentiated growth process—What can be known of it "horizontally"—in cross-section, at any point in time?

THE NATURE OF AN INDIVIDUAL

An understanding of the process of human growth illuminates an understanding of the nature of an individual or the human self seen at any point in growth. The self is defined [32] as "having a single character or quality throughout," "the entire person," "an individual," and of particular interest for this writing, "the internal regulatory system of response and activity tendencies within the organism; the source of social adaptation and growth of the individual's personality."

The peculiar genetically determined characteristics of a given individual in interaction with its first environment, the womb, the nature of the birth experience itself, and the subsequent environmental circumstances in the changing relationships between child and mother (and others) eventuate in each person's formation of an identifiable "pattern" which tends to retain an essential identity and continuity throughout life. At the same time there is abundant evidence that each self is capable of growth within its pattern (else, how justify therapy, social work, or education?), again in response to its own push or purpose of realization of potential, and within the limits of genetic endowment and environmental opportunity. Psychological growth is achieved largely through relationships with people, social relationships. Jessie Taft wrote:

The two basic needs that form the two poles of the psychological growth process are the need for dependence upon the other, as it is first experienced in the oneness of the uterine relationship, and the opposing need for the development of self-dependence as the goal of movement toward adulthood. The two are never divorced in living, and it is on their essential conflict and interaction that we rely for the dynamic that keeps the individual moving to correct the imbalance that exists and must exist at any given moment in his use of himself.[33]

The individual pattern of any self may be understood in many ways. One way is to view it as a balance of impulse, intellect, feeling and emotion, and will. Will is used here in the sense of an organizing and controlling force. Indeed, Taft equates, or rather substitutes, it for "ego" and "self" when she writes in the article noted above, "I feel the need for the word 'will' to carry, on all the levels of growth, the controlling and creative forces that make the child hard to train and every individual hard to help."

It was Rank [34] who first developed the concept of the will as primary in understanding both the nature of the self and the nature of psychological therapy and, indeed, of all helping efforts centered in the use of relationship. The individual is first aware of himself as separate when his wanting is blocked, when desire is not immediately fulfilled. It is then that he takes in, not in any conscious intellectual sense, that he is not "all," but that there is an "other" on whom he must depend, who can give and withhold. This is what is meant by the negative origin of the will. The hungry infant who does not get the breast immediately first experiences his will, his want, in other words his self as a self, and the mother as separate from himself.

Some selves continue to define themselves negatively throughout life—sure of what they are against, less sure of what they are for. It is the will which resists help, out of fear of disorganization, change, subjection to the will of another. It is only as the will can yield to the self's own push toward more life, toward realization, that help can be accepted and used. And this is possible only through the kind of relationship which frees the self to know and claim itself. Rank sees the will as developed *through* separation, which he identifies as one of the fundamental life principles:

All organic evolution rests upon separation, but only the conscious knowledge of this life principle on the part of man who can preserve and call back the past in his memory, or can imagine the future in his fantasy, gives to the concept and the feeling of separation a fundamental psychic meaning. This explains why the first biological separation of the individual from the mother can acquire the psychic meaning that I ascribed to it in "The Trauma of Birth," likewise why all future steps on the way to self dependence, such as weaning, walking, and especially the development of the will are conceived always as continuous separations in which the individual, even as in the last separation, death, must leave behind, must resign developmental phases of his own ego.[35]

Rank refers to the guilt reaction to the will to be free, that is, that "one should have no will of his own but should be thankful and love," and identifies the problem of the neuroses as a separation problem, and as such a blocking of the human life principle, which he characterizes as the conscious ability to endure release and separation, first from the biological power represented by parents and finally from the lived-out parts of the self which this power represents and which obstruct the development of the individual personality.[36]

For Rank the aim of therapy is self-development (an opportunity for the person to develop himself into what he is in potential). This he saw as possible through the patient's capacity to discover his true self in relationship with the therapist and to bear the guilt for becoming himself through bearing the guilt of separating from the therapist. Elsewhere, Rank writes:

The psychological understanding of the creative type and its miscarriage in the neurotic teaches us therefore to value the ego, not only as a wrestling ground of (id) impulses and (super ego) repressions, but also as a conscious bearer of a striving force, that is, as the autonomous representative of the will and ethical obligation, in terms of a self-constructed ideal.[37]

Space precludes any further description of the origin and nature of the will, as an aspect of the self. Yet for any helper through relationship, it is essential to be aware of, knowledgeable about, and responsible for the way he uses his own will, and sensitive to the nature of the will in its negative-positive expression in those with whom he is working.

Individuals differ in the strength of the will, in the balance of its negative and positive expression, in the extent to which it takes into account the other, in its relation to other aspects of the self. At this writing the will is viewed neither as bad nor good but as organizing and creative force. An essential task of helping is conceived as freeing the other to claim and use his will positively toward his own self-chosen ends, within the social purpose of a particular social work relationship. Not only do individuals differ in the strength and character of their will expression, but in the strength and character of their emotional life. Feeling, the temporary and ephemeral reaction, becomes emotion as it is sustained, deepens, and is known to the person experiencing it. In her classic "Living and Feeling," Taft writes:

There is no factor of personality which is so expressive of individuality as emotion . . . the personality is impoverished as feeling is denied, and the penalty for sitting on the lid of angry feelings or feelings of fear is the inevitable blunting of capacity to feel love and desire. For to feel is to live, but to reject feeling through fear is to reject the life process itself.[38]

Just as the aim of a helping relationship is to free the other to act his will, to choose and to act on his choice, so is its aim to free the other to feel as deeply as may be in order that the true self may be experienced and known and so that its resources may become available for living. It is only as emotion is denied in the self that the individual self fears and attempts to stop it in others. As the self can know and become responsible for its own feelings, so is that self in better position to free others to own and become responsible for their feelings. Feeling develops through relationship and the relationship with a helping person is of a very special kind in which the projections of the helper are kept at a minimum, in *order* that the other may experience himself fully in his own projections, as is possible only in the absence of counter-projection.

The self of another cannot be known through intellectual assessment alone. Within a human, compassionate, and caring relationship, selves "open up," dare to become what they may be, so that the self which is known by a worker at once human, caring, and skillful is a different self from that diagnosed by one who removes himself in feeling from the relationship in an attempt to be a dispassionate observer and problem solver. As an adolescent girl once said to her new social worker, in referring to a former worker, "She knew all about me, but she didn't know me."

Impulse, the raw tendency to action in the immediacy of the moment, differs too in its strength, frequency, and nature of expression as between selves. Learning to trust one's impulse, to let oneself be enriched by the spontaneity which a healthy impulse life can bring, is part of the opportunity within a helping relationship, too. The too ready curbing of impulse, like the denial of feelings, is impoverishing and leaves one less fully human than he might be. At the same time the unbridled play of impulse can be destructive not only to the outside, but also to the self.

So each individual develops his unique pattern, his "gestalt" of feeling, impulse, will in their respective strengths and nature, and in their relative place in the self's expression. And in each self, the intellect, the thinking, comprehending, planning capacity, has its unique place and relationship to other aspects of the personality.

What makes social work possible, as a relationship process directed toward a social end, is man's capacity to establish and use human relationship toward his own inner purpose of growth. This psychological capacity has a biological base, more properly emerges from a biological base. As has been seen, the embryo from its beginning is engaged in taking from and putting out onto its environment. Without a chemical physiological capacity for utilizing the outside for its growth it could not survive.

The newborn infant has the capacity and the necessity to take from the mother physical nourishment and care and to put out, in crying, cooing, and expulsion of bodily products, what it can no longer contain without damage to its purpose of growth. The response of the mother, and consequently of others to the child, is both affected by and affects his own developing capacity for relationship. Each person develops a characteristic way of relating, in harmony with his innate nature and the fruit of his experiences, in "learning" to relate. The capacity may be great or little, blocked or fully available, but the potential and necessity for relationship are as deeply rooted in all persons as is the purpose of growth and differentiation as an individual.

In seeking to help individuals deal with some social problem or problem in social relationship, it is essential that the social worker take into account the nature of the individual who is the object of his help, as it derives from his age, his sex, his intellectual potential, so far as it can be known, his life experience and what he has done with it, his health, physical and mental, so that the helping may be realistically and appropriately directed. It is essential, as well, that he take into account the distinctive pattern or interplay of intellect, feeling, impulse, and will that characterizes his client's unique self, his way of relating and using relationship, and at the same time that he be aware of and responsible for the nature of his own self as he puts it at the disposal of the "other" for his use toward the social purpose that has brought them together. Every social worker has the obligation, and hopefully the motivation, to develop the special and detailed knowledge in depth which he needs to serve the particular age group and the kind of problem which presently constitutes the focus of his work, and to make his own, also, what he must as he moves from field to field or from process to process.

5 A PSYCHOLOGICAL BASE FOR SOCIAL WORK PRACTICE, II

SOCIAL WORKERS in the use of some processes are focused not on serving individual clients, as in the preponderance of their work as social caseworkers, but on working with groups or whole communities. An understanding of the nature of a group or community and of the nature of a specific group or community in its essence, identity, and relative stability, and through all its movement and change is essential for group and community workers. It is essential also for all social workers whose lives, like their clients, are inextricably bound to groups and communities, and whose work calls both for an understanding of the significance of that fact for the development of individuality and for a capacity to relate to groups and to communities in the very conduct of their own processes. Before some characteristics of groups and communities which require an understanding on the part of the social worker seeking to serve or work with them are defined, it seems important to emphasize again that understanding is not enough for such work, any more than it is enough for successful work with individuals as social caseworker. Unless the worker has a genuine feeling for and relationship with the group or community he serves, unless he cares about it in a human and engaged way and makes a generous gift of himself and his caring, as well as of his thinking, in his professional activity, his efforts are bound to fail of their potential. He is usable by a group or community as by an individual, only as he is a feeling,

thinking human being whose total self thus becomes available
for use.

THE NATURE OF A GROUP

No attempt will be made to give "equal time" to the group and
to the community, as phenomena served by group or community
workers, in comparison with what has been developed for the individual. This is true both because theoretical formulations are
less developed for the last two "client systems" and because the
author is less familiar with the terrain. The point being made
here is that the phenomenon served, whether individual, group,
or community, needs to be understood by the social worker giving the service as a phenomenon in its own right.

The group which is the object of the social group worker's
service is what has been defined as the "small group." It has been
the object of considerable research by social scientists, primarily
psychologists and sociologists, in both the early and the middle
parts of the twentieth century. The insights developed and the
growth of schools of thought have been helpful and useful to
group workers at the same time that they have contributed to the
quick enthusiasms and one-sided approaches that are inevitable
as a new service profession seeks to find the certainty in knowledge it needs to act effectively.

Perhaps no one on the contemporary scene has been more
helpful in evaluating current small group research and in identifying both issues which have been clarified and those which
await further clarification than Michael S. Olmsted, whose *The
Small Group* [1] is commended to all readers who wish to pursue
this subject further. Writes Olmsted:

The limited success of small group research owes something to its
common but by no means universal tendency to be concerned with individuals rather than with roles. To be sure the group is made up of
individuals, and group behavior is a compound of individual be-
haviors, but it is also a compound of social roles, of sets of expectations,
and of articulated functions which ought to be conceived of sociologi-

cally as well as psychologically. If one takes seriously the familiar sociological contention that society is a reality "sui generis," and is not simply the individual writ large, then society must be conceived as some set of institutions or some system of roles and not merely as a plurality of individuals.[2]

Olmsted defines the group as "a plurality of individuals who are in contact with one another, who take one another into account and who are aware of some significant commonality."[3] He identifies the small group as "approximately twenty [representing] the upper limit . . . with two being the lower limit."[4] Olmsted makes the further and useful distinction, found generally throughout the literature, between the primary group whose members have warm, intimate ties with one another (such as the friendship group, the gang, the family) and the secondary group, often referred to as the task-oriented group with relationships contractual and formal in the sense that members are participating in special capacities and with the group as a means to an end rather than as an end in itself. It should be noted that primary groups may have task-oriented aspects or phases, and that task-oriented groups may develop affective relationships among their members. This Olmsted notes. It is the interplay of task-oriented activity and affective relationships which needs to be understood. But at either end of a spectrum the distinction between primary and secondary groups stands and is a helpful one.

To understand any specific group being served, it is necessary to understand group behavior in general as it occurs within the small group, including such phenomena as the effect of the group on each and all the individuals who comprise it, and the role of individuals and subgroups within the group, in their interaction with each other, and as the action of each and the interaction of all constitute group activity.

The concept of leadership within the group, the way it develops, the way it is carried, whether by one or by several group members, how it shifts in relation to group interest and activity, the characteristics of the indigenous leader, all have received the attention of researchers in this field. The pioneer study conducted by Lippit and White [5] is of particular interest here. Its focus is the effect of democratic, authoritarian, and laissez faire styles of leadership on the behavior of groups.

The sociometric approach to the study of groups, developed by J. L. Moreno,[6] psychiatrist, and the psychoanalytic approach, by Fritz Redl,[7] are concerned with expressive, affective behavior within groups rather than with task-oriented or "instrumental" behavior. Despite some limitations which have been noted in the literature, they contribute their own richness to what is being evolved of small group theory. An emphasis on communication rather than affect as the crucial phenomenon of group life has been the concern of Alex Bavelas,[8] who identified and studied various patterns of communication links. Homans [9] developed a framework for study of the group which has reference to the operations people perform, with the chief conceptual elements identified as "activity, sentiment, interaction, and norms."

Of particular interest to group workers is the study of group behavior known as "group dynamics," whose founder and guiding spirit was the social psychologist Kurt Lewin. His colleagues, former students, and followers are to be found in almost all the major centers for small group research in the country.

Olmstead identifies the two problems on which group dynamics research has focused as cohesiveness and locomotion.[10] Cohesiveness refers to all the forces which act on members to remain in the group. It is seen as being furthered by an emphasis on cooperation rather than competition, a democratic rather than authoritarian or laissez faire group atmosphere, and to be affected by the status of the group. The concept of locomotion refers to the way a group proceeds toward its goal as a group as well as to the way individual members move within the group to positions of greater or less status and influence.

To understand the group as the phenomenon being served requires that it be comprehended not only as a structure but also as a process. The locomotion concept of the group dynamics school has relevance here as does the work of Robert F. Bales,[11] who developed the theory and method of small group research known as interaction process analysis.

Olmsted notes that the starting point as well as the goal of interaction process analysis is the process of problem solving:

Inspired in part by the pragmatism of John Dewey, Bales conceives of all group activity as being problem solving activity. . . . In place of the explicit spatial metaphor of Group Dynamics, an implicit image of the flow of "process" is more characteristic of Bales's thinking. Bales suggests that the process of interaction be conceived of as a continual stream of acts, of words, symbols, reactions, gestures, and so forth. . . . To complement the active pragmatist image of a natural tendency toward problem solving there is another element of Bales's thinking, one which might be referred to as the uncertainty principle. This principle states that in effect any change means the disturbance of a status quo, the upsetting of an equilibrium—an uncertainty to which the members of the group must adjust.[12]

Olmsted notes that Bales identifies "phase movement"[13] of groups and differentiates the kinds of activity which take place at different points in time, such as the initial, second, and later phases of a group meeting.

What has been so sketchily reported serves only to suggest that the structure and process of the small group are complex phenomena which have been the subject of considerable study, by no means all of which has been noted here. The small group, as focus for social work activity, requires a sophisticated understanding of the nature of a group as a sociological as well as a psychological phenomenon, having identifiable characteristics as such, and of the many differences as well which make each group and the life and process of each group distinctive, just as individuals are both like and different in their growth processes and personality patterns.

Social workers who serve small groups need to understand not only the small group as a phenomenon but also the significance of group life for individuals and for society. They need to understand as well the way their own activity can further that significance within some encompassing social work purpose. Groups served and staffed directly, or through supervisory controls, by a professional social worker provide an opportunity for their members' growth in "self-value and self-responsibility," [14] and for the development of the kind of individually fulfilling and socially responsible behavior essential for the conduct of a democratic society. Here in parvo but "for real," and not through play acting, the individual, as part of "learning his way through life," can experience being a part of a larger whole and get help with it, with resultant enrichment for both part and whole. However, the help given through group work method leading to a group *work* process rests on the group worker's understanding, first of all, of a *group* process.

Familiar group work concepts such as group interaction, bond, group goals, group structure, as characterized, for example, by the formation of subgroups and the emergence of isolates, leadership as an internal group phenomenon, group conflict and the various forms through which it is expressed and may be resolved, decision making as it occurs spontaneously and as it may be furthered and fostered have gained enormously in the subtlety and depth with which they may be comprehended through the contributions of social scientists as well as social workers to what is now a substantial literature. Running through the literature is a recognition of the power within the group for defining a purpose and moving toward it. It is to this inner power and purpose that the social worker relates, as he does in working with individuals singly. But, as has been emphasized, the task of the group worker is enormously complicated by the fact that a group is made up of a number of individuals who need to be understood as individuals, and in their interaction with each other and with the group worker, at the same time that the group as an entity is comprehended at any given point in time and as a process characterized by both continuity and change.

Only the naive and unknowing will deny the richness of the specialized knowledge which has here been only suggested in the briefest fashion but is already available and put to work in developing a social group work method, identifiable as leading to a social group work process through its use of certain principles common to all social work processes. The generic core in social work method is enriched by knowledge from this specific process methodology, but, as a methodology, it retains certain distinctive characteristics because of its purpose as method, because of the nature of the phenomenon to which it is addressed, a group, rather than an individual, having a structure and process of its own, and because of the consequent implications for a distinctive role for the worker.

THE NATURE OF A COMMUNITY

Definition of a community as one focus for social work effort poses an increasingly difficult and complex problem. Recent and contemporary writers have suggested definitions and elaborations of definitions, all with the recognition that the term "community" may be variously comprehended and used—sometimes to identify political and geographic subdivisions, sometimes in a social and psychological sense as in "community of interest," or as professional community, ethnic or sectarian community.[15] Wirth identifies as characteristics of a community "a territorial base, distribution in space of men, institutions and activities, close living together on the basis of kinship and organic interdependence and a common life based upon the mutual correspondence of interests."[16] He speaks of the growing disparity between our interdependence and our capacity to act as a unit, between our need of an organization and our defiance of this need. He sees a diminishing importance for community organization work focused on strengthening the ties and power for action of local neighborhoods, because of their loss of identity and autonomy in light of their increasing relationship to a larger community for food, services, and cultural opportunity. Wrote Werner Gettys some thirty years ago:

The Community itself is a constantly changing social entity. Not without some social stability to be sure, and to a certain degree, permanence —but with boundaries that tend to be increasingly flexible, functions that are altered in response to the demands of a super community social system and interests that have to compete with non-localized group interest for the attention of the people.[17]

In a study of 94 definitions of the term "community" it was found that 69 were "in accord that social interaction, area, and a common tie or ties are commonly found in community life."[18] It is abundantly clear from the literature of this midcentury that social scientists are making increasingly relevant and helpful contributions to social workers' understanding of the community as a phenomenon, just as they are to an understanding of the nature of the small group. Roland Warren comments on the contribution of small group research to the growing knowledge about the community in the following way: "Recent decades have seen great advances in small group research, and it is thus not entirely by coincidence that some of the most promising theoretical thinking about the community is arising today from theories about the small informal group."[19]

Warren's own contribution to a conception of community phenomena is a particularly trenchant one. After testifying to the difficulty in establishing a theoretical concept of community he writes: "We shall consider a community to be that combination of social units which perform the major functions having locality relevance," and he adds ". . . this is another way of saying that by community we mean the organization of social activities to afford people daily local access to those broad areas of activity which are necessary in day to day living."[20] He identifies five major functions having locality relevance as production-distribution-consumption, socialization, social control, social participation, and mutual support. The relation of typical community units of these major locality relevant functions to typical units of a horizontal pattern of organization and to the superior unit of a vertical pattern, presented in some detail,[21] constitutes a way of looking at the community which is useful for persons engaged in working with it. Warren's analysis of the "great change"[22] in American communities emphasizes the increasing systemic relationships of the local community to the larger society, the transfer of functions, once locally and "informally" carried, to profit enterprise and to government, the growth of bureaucratization, and impersonalization, and the constantly growing trend to urbanization and suburbanization. All of this he sees contributing to feelings of rootlessness and anomie as communities no longer contribute to a sense of "belonging" through constituting a source of daily interaction with neighbors in mutually rewarding "work and play" relationships.

He emphasizes the strengthening of the vertical ties of units of communities at the expenses of horizontal ties, as characteristic of this early century and midcentury. "Ties of units and subsystems of the community to their counterparts in the larger society are multiplying and strengthening to the extent that it is questionable whether the ties of community units to each other are sufficiently strong and meaningful for them to constitute a localized social system called the community." [23] Warren identifies the importance of any change agent (including a community organization social worker) who works with the community being clear about his purpose: whether it is *primarily* task oriented, to accomplish some "good" for the community, or primarily directed toward strengthening the horizontal pattern of the community in the sense of furthering the interest and capacity of residents of a locality for feeling, thinking, and acting "as a community" in the community's interest, with the particular task to be accomplished being secondary.

Perhaps the social worker's contribution to what is here recognized as problem and posed as dilemma can be his recognition, out of his experience, that only as these two purposes are related, only as people and units of a community are engaged in themselves identifying or concurring in a significant task to be accomplished, and in working together toward its achievement is any change for the better apt to occur and endure. This Warren himself suggests.[24]

The difficulty in understanding the community as a phenomenon to be served is summarized by Warren in the following way:

. . . a community as a client system differs from an individual or small group or an organization in ways which present difficulties to the change agent. The individual and small group are small enough to be confronted as a unit. The organization is often too large to enter into direct face-to-face relation with all of its parts, but its formal structure is highly explicit and formally at least there is little difficulty in locating the appropriate members of the structure with which to deal. The community is likewise large, typically too large to confront all the members, but it lacks the formally organized structure of an organization. This is not to say that the change agent working with the individual as a unit and the group worker do not have analogous problems of understanding the complexity of intra- and inter-personal structure and process, or that the agent working with the organization does not have a similar problem of relating himself to the appropriate people in the formal organization. But in the case of the community these problems are multiplied by the complexity of the parts combined with the absence of formal structure.[25]

Perhaps it is pertinent to suggest, in this connection, that the social worker as change agent, operating from the bases and using the principles developed in this book, is helped in knowing the boundaries of the community he is serving through his employing agency's identification of the community to be served. He is helped as well by his agency's identification of a purpose in serving the community. And he is helped by the possession of a reliable skill in a method which can be used to induce and sustain a particular kind of process, a social work process, peculiarly suited to the task of helping a community discover and act on its own power to achieve community betterment.

Social workers have profited from theoretical knowledge of the nature of the community which is being developed by the social scientists, just as they have from their own experience in serving communities, and their own knowledge, come by in the course of such service.

Harold Lewis writes ". . . whatever the dimensions used to classify communities (geographical, functional, social forces, etc.), the concern of the community social worker is with people, individually and in groups, whose relationships underpin all such classification schemes." [26] He suggests the concept of client system as developed by Ronald Lippit [27] and others to cover the understanding of "community" as it has particular relevance for the social worker who serves it. In such a view, community refers to a composite of individuals, groups, and intergroups with whom the community social worker develops direct personal relationships in offering his agency's service.

Herman Stein [28] writes of the significance of stratification theory with its objectivist and subjectivist views of social class, of organizational theory, role theory, theory of community power structure as enriching the knowledge of the nature of this phenomenon—the community, with which the social worker engaged in community organization practice, is concerned. While affirming that in community work, social workers have become more sophisticated in understanding different patterns of participation in community groups and community life, based on class position, Stein speaks to the need for both an understanding of such patterns and for alertness to the danger of stereotyping either a community or a class. Such stereotyping, as with individuals and groups, can result in failure to see and respond to differences which may be present and which carry the potential for individual fulfillment and for enrichment of a larger whole.

So it is that the community, if it is to be served by the social worker must be understood, just as an individual or group must be understood, in all its complexity as "structure." It has characteristics that it shares with all other communities, with communities in its particular "category" (e.g., rural, urban, suburban), and it has its uniqueness, too, as one particular community. It must be understood as "process" also, as being in constant flux in its internal and external relationships at the same time that it retains a relatively identifiable character.

Social problems of a community arise, in part, out of conflict between and among the various units and systems, "values" and "powers" within it. Yet the very fact of conflict, as in the individual and the group, affords opportunity for movement, for reorganization, or for development.

WAYS OF DEALING WITH
CONFLICT AND STRESS

Maintaining a dynamic equilibrium of opposing tendencies can be not only permissive of but conducive to growth and creativity. It is in this sense that Erikson has written of the "balance" of trust and mistrust, autonomy and sense of doubt, initiative and guilt as characterizing growth throughout the life cycle. Rank, in all his writings, developed the concept of conflict not as good or bad but as inevitable, and as necessary for movement. He referred to the conflict of opposing tendencies within the organism, and to the conflict between the individuals and others, and with "society."

Hans Selye, writing on the nature of stress, which he describes as the rate of wear and tear caused by life, analyzes the nature of stress, the mechanism of the organism through which the body is attacked by, and can defend itself against, stress-producing situations, diseases of adaptation both physical and mental which appear to result from failures in the stress-fighting mechanism, and concludes by suggesting some philosophic implications for the theory he has so painstakingly developed:

We instinctively feel that one final aim should somehow coordinate and give unity to all our strivings. As I see it, man's ultimate aim is to express himself as fully as possible, according to his own lights. The goal is certainly not to avoid stress. Stress is part of life. It is a natural by-product of all our activities; there is no more justification for avoiding stress than for shunning food, exercise, or love. But in order to express yourself fully, you must first find your optimum stress-level and then use your adaptation energy at a rate and in a direction adjusted to the innate structure of your mind and body. The study of stress has shown that complete rest is not good, either for the body as a whole, or even for any organ within the body. Stress, applied in modification, is necessary for life.[29]

Taft describes growth in terms of personality development as a stormy painful affair which is not to deny that we want it more than anything else in life. No love relation, however fulfilling, can outweigh the joy of a new-found self, nor can love relationship compensate entirely for the self-development it may hinder. . . . The basic need of the individual . . . is not pleasure but more life, to make more and more of the underlying energy accessible for integration, to go with the life process instead of fighting it, and to find and use one's own capacity for relationships and for creativity, however slight.[30]

An objection to the familiar concept of homeostasis is that it suggests a maintenance of the status quo as the desideratum and leaves no room for growth, development, and creativity. Insofar as it refers to a physical status, it can be conceived as the kind of equilibrium which furthers positive health. In the psychological realm the individual's thrust is not to "hold the line," but to grow, to develop, to go beyond, however blocked and distorted the attempt may be because of innate lack, crippling effects of life experience, or lacks in the immediate environment.

The effort of the social worker, then, in working with individuals, groups, or communities, is not to avoid or minimize conflict, to produce a deadly harmony, or an "as you were" condition, but to facilitate the full experiencing of conflict which presently exists. It is even to stimulate "a divine discontent" with what presently is as a base for furthering and strengthening effort to resolve the conflict in a way that "goes beyond" and constitutes growth and forward movement. Sometimes this means intervention and modification of environmental stresses that press too heavily, sometimes help toward reaching a state of physical and mental health conducive to more full and fulfilled living. Inevitably it means taking into account, as nearly as it can be known, the nature of the phenomenon being served, in its potential and limits, but always the effort is in the direction of maximizing the capacity of individual, group, or community for finding and following its own direction.

SUMMARY

This and the preceding chapter have been concerned with establishing a psychological base for social work practice, in whatever field and through whatever process. Purpose has been identified as having both biological and psychological expression in the growth of the individual, and as constituting the force, in individual, group, or community, which makes helping possible and to which the helper relates.

It is this fact of the individual as central in his own development, as capable of changing from within *through the use of inner and outer resources,* but as not susceptible to change through coercion, which has laid a psychological base for an understanding of social work processes as helping processes. Whether primary or secondary social work processes involve, essentially, putting the worker's self, as well as his knowledge and skill, at the service of the other for his use in accomplishing an own affirmed purpose. Conflict has been identified as inevitable in the life of individual, group, or community, and viewed as a condition for growth or forward movement. The social worker's task has been seen as facilitating recognition and resolution of inner conflict, valuing and development of the whole self, and use of positive will, in individual, group, or community, toward the accomplishment of a chosen social purpose.

The role of relationship in all social work processes has been identified as primary since it is through human relationship, and particularly through a relationship that exists for the other, that individuals, groups, and communities can best discover and develop their own psychological resources for courageous and creative living.

There has been some description of the nature of the phenomena with which the three primary processes of social work are respectively concerned: the individual, the group, the community. Each has been seen as having identifiable characteristics or pattern, at any one point in time, and as having a history or continuity too, as constituting a process in its own right. Sensitive and informed awareness of the nature of the phenomena with which the social worker deals can enhance his effectiveness. But a too quick stereotyping or categorizing which leaves no room for the development of what may be but is not yet can block the very development he is seeking to further.

The differences in the nature of the phenomena served, in the specific purpose inhering in the *specific* method employed, and in the consequent *specific* role of the worker result in specific characteristics for the primary (as for all) social work processes, without invalidating the concept of generic principles as characterizing all social work method, or the requirement of a common psychological base for their development.

What makes social work social, in the view here presented, is not just its concern with social relationships, the relationships of the individual to society and society to the individual, but the sanction and auspice for its practice. Social work, through tradition and in the great bulk of its present operation, consists of the administering of programs of social service, supported by society in its own interest, as well as in the interest of the immediate clientele served. The fact of its being an "institutionalized service," the service of a social agency or "department," made available through relationship processes requiring psychological knowledge and skill, has an important bearing on its nature, and can be conceived not as a limiting or inhibiting factor but as holding the promise of psychological help while assuring social responsibility.

The *social* base for social work practice inheres in the use of agency function as integral in method. It is to this consideration that the following chapter will be addressed.

6 A SOCIAL BASE FOR SOCIAL WORK PRACTICE

A SOCIAL BASE for social work practice is the fact that society's primary charge to social work as a profession is to develop and administer programs of social service. Such programs come into being when society identifies a need experienced by numbers of individuals which they are unable to meet by their own efforts; and, unmet, this need constitutes a threat both to their own welfare and opportunity for development as individuals and to society's welfare. Put positively, the social agency, through which such service programs are carried out, is "the place where the interests of society and the interests of the individual are joined."[1] In the same article, Marcus defines a social agency as "literally what its name implies, an agent to which society has delegated responsibility for carrying on a service through organized means." Every social agency, in some sense, is an expression of social policy, national, state, or local in scope. Most often it reflects an admixture of all three levels of interest and responsibility.

The way the social purpose of society, as manifest in a given agency, is interpreted and carried out becomes the responsibility of the agency. In the interpretation and the carrying out of its purpose, all parts of the agency, board, administration, and staff, have an appropriate part. Social agencies employ professional social workers (to the extent that they are available!) obviously out of a recognition that they are the personnel most surely possessing the knowledge and skill for realization of agency purpose in the particular positions for which they are engaged. Boards made up of "lay" persons (nonsocial workers) represent the wider community's stake in the program and exercise general direction and control.

The use of an agency function (or purpose in action) by the social worker gives focus, content, and direction to a specific helping process and assures its social responsibility, that is, assures that in the particular instance it is being used to accomplish the particular social purpose for which the agency was established and for which it is currently being supported. It contributes to the psychological helpfulness of the process as well, in ways later to be specified.

The development of functional social work as a form of social work practice which utilizes agency function, as an integral aspect of whatever social work process employed, has given rise to much misunderstanding and controversy, at the same time that it has enriched social work in ways readily identifiable in the literature, as well as in social work practice and social work education, generally.

One of the factors which may contribute to a difference in point of view on the significance of "function" for social work practice could be related to a difference in concept of social work purpose. If purpose is seen as therapy, as is true for those social workers who have identified strongly in purpose as well as in method (or application of method) with the psycho-analytic group, the specific purpose of the agency (that is, whatever its title or charter identifies as specific purpose or problem to be addressed) becomes secondary to the primary purpose of therapy, which is conceived as essentially an individual matter between therapist and client, or group. Indeed, as has been suggested, the agency's resources may be considered "tools in treatment," or means for accomplishing the primary purpose of therapy.

In practice generally identified as functional social work, the reverse position holds true. The primary purpose is accomplishment of the agency's social purpose whether child placement, family counseling, protective service, group experience directed toward some social end, or whatever. Developing or recovering or improving capacity for self-direction and self-control occurs through the client or group's use of a specific social service made available by a social worker who keeps a sensitive diagnostic orientation to a client's possible difficulty in making use of the service and who utilizes his skill in furthering its productive use.[2] The client may well use his experience with the agency for internal psychological change and development of great magnitude, but this occurs *as a result* of agency service skillfully offered and deeply used. It is not the primary aim of the service.

Some social workers may resist the limit introduced by identifying with the agency function largely out of the human resistance to any limit, as expressed in the familiar cowboy ballad "Don't Fence Me In!" Yet others may oppose agency controls and limits out of a feeling that employers and employed must necessarily be at cross purposes wherever found, failing to recognize the strength of common purpose which can *unite* within an organization whose goal is service and which is spending rather than making money. Still others point to the shortcomings of agencies, the "accident" of their origin in some instances, and believe this is sufficient reason to ignore their *purpose* as having any significant bearing on what the social worker does. This represents a failure to see the social worker's stake and responsibility in the continuous improvement of agencies as expressions of social policy and as context for social work practice, a responsibility equally as great as for the continuous refinement and development of skill in method. Yet others equate "being professional" with independent practice, unrelated or tenuously related to agency administration as it finds expression in supervision, policy and procedure that seek to secure a floor of service and provide for a continuously developing quality of service for which the agency is responsible *as agency*. The worker is seen as governed in what he does in the individual instance only by his own judgment "as a professional person." *

Such argument makes analogy to law and medicine without noting the distinctive character of social work as lying precisely in the fact that it is *unlike* law and medicine in that it is essentially an institutionalized form of practice, and that professional wisdom and skill can be employed to exploit, rather than to deny or minimize, that fact. Others feel the restriction in agency function as a limit on a warm human wish to help, to give "love unlimited" (however impossible and unrealistic), or whatever seems to be "needed," no strings attached—in short to "make up" to the deprived, an impulse which has been a prime motivation for social workers everywhere. It is only as the social worker discovers that he is neither as helpful as he might be nor truly responsible to the social will in establishing and sustaining a particular social agency, if he operates on an individual practitioner basis, that he can bear to discipline himself the better to do what is truly his and his alone to do, as a social worker functioning on the staff of a particular social agency.

Whatever the source of the opposition to "function" in functional social work, this book, as has been said, is written not to persuade but to expound. This chapter has been written to say how the use of agency function can contribute to a form of social work practice which is both socially responsible and psychologically helpful. Let the reader understand and use, misunderstand, oppose, or just plain differ, as he will.

In considering the use of agency function as establishing a social base for social work practice, it may be useful to examine its beginnings as a conscious aspect of professional skill, before considering how social work practice in any field and through any process can be enriched by it.

Although the concept and teaching of functional social work,

---

* Parenthetically it should be said that the worker does indeed have an individual responsibility as a professional social worker, but, as the writer sees it, that responsibility for judgment on what to do and how to do it in the individual situation includes the responsibility of functioning as a member of an agency staff with all the necessities which in that fact inhere.

that is, social work which makes use of agency function as one aspect of its helping skill, originated in the Pennsylvania School of Social Work, as it was then called, which had earlier incorporated the contribution of Otto Rank in its psychological theory, Rank, as was pointed out in Chapter 4, was in no way associated with the concept of function in social work practice. Indeed he is quoted as having replied when questioned about the nature of functional social work, "It must be very interesting, but I don't know what it is." Rank's contribution to social work theory was psychological, in such areas as the nature of human growth, and the human self, with particular emphasis on the will as a controlling and organizing force, the way help can be given and taken through relationship, the significance of the present experience for releasing growth potential and the significance of "time" and the possibilities in its conscious use in helping processes. His psychological theory was conducive to an appreciation of the psychological value in use of agency function for helping, but he himself never related his theory to this, or any, aspect of social work practice.

It was Jessie Taft who introduced the concept of "use of agency function" as basic in social work helping, an innovation which gave the Pennsylvania School its appellation as the "functional School." Although this concept had, for some time, been used in the teaching of social work practice by Taft, Robinson, Wessel, Faith, and all of the School's faculty, and in practice by the School's alumni, it was described as concept and theory for the first time in Taft's ground-breaking article, "The Relation of Function to Process in Social Casework." [3] The use of this concept, in conjunction with a psychological theory of human growth and relationship, and a theory of process as applicable to a relationship helping process gave rise to a form of social work practice for which this school prepared through a characteristic program and process of social work education.

Taft and Robinson, Marcus, Smalley, Wessel, and, later, Faatz developed functional theory in all its aspects in relation to one social work process, the process of social casework. Kenneth

Pray, and later Harold Lewis, related that theory to community organization process; Helen U. Phillips to social group work process; Virginia Robinson to the process of supervision; Pray and Robinson to a concept of administration as process; Lewis to a concept of research as process; Taft, Robinson, Wessel, Faith, Smalley, and others to the educational process. Other faculty and alumni have contributed, as well, to the continuing development, refinement, and application of functional theory as appropriate to all fields of practice and to all processes in social work.[4]

But to return to the first statement of that aspect of functional theory which refers to the use of agency function as an element in the helping skill of social work, Taft wrote [5] of the universal tendency in human development to progress by extreme swings from object to subject from the external—the social, to the internal—the psychological, and concluded that either concentration destroys or ignores the reality that lies only in the relationship between the two. She identified a movement in social casework characteristic of the period in which she wrote:

. . . the intensely psychiatric, psychological, subjective phase of interest in both clients and workers seems to be passing, along with the shift from intensive indeterminate casework by the private agency to the highly functionalized administration of public money by governmental relief and assistance boards. . . . even within the area of so-called intensive casework, interest is being diverted from hereditary factors and individual social histories, confined largely to family relationships to the larger area of economics and cultural influences.

While she identified the caseworker as "still subject to her personality handicap or emotional problems" and reaffirmed the necessity for any worker to be responsible for her use of herself in the helping relationship, she added, "She is also being held to a more objective requirement in knowledge of economic and social conditions as well as psychological understanding of the client."

She suggested a solution for social work if it intended to arrive at a technical grasp of its own process as lying in "one area and only one in which outer and inner, worker and client, agency and social need can come together effectively, one area that offers to social workers the possibility of development into a profession, and that is the area of the helping process itself."

In establishing the nature of the helping process Taft differentiated between the responsibility of the therapist and the responsibility of the caseworker, and between the nature of therapy and the nature of the casework helping process:

The Therapist is required to take an individual responsibility for what he does that the caseworker never knows and cannot know without ceasing to be a caseworker . . . the caseworker's responsibility on the other hand, real as it is, must first of all be to the agency and its function; only as agency does he meet this client professionally. There is no escape . . . from facing the necessity to establish ourselves firmly not merely on the basis of social need but on a foundation of professional skill.[6] . . . In my opinion we already have that basis if only we can relinquish the too great sense of responsibility for the client and his need in order to concentrate on a defining of what we can do and a refining of our knowledge and skill in relation to the carrying out of each specific and accepted function.[7]

Taft writes, in this same article, of the psychological as well as the social implications of this development in the following way:

To take upon oneself responsibility for complete determination of any life force in its expression is to court failure or self-destruction. This may seem a far cry from the practical problems of the social worker yet its truth, if understood with conviction, would transform much of our present practice, as science was transformed when it learned to put its effort on understanding the law of process in a particular situation, not on objects as separate entities. The approach to social work via the needs of the individual applicant is an approach that leads to inevitable failure and confusion since it focuses attention and effort on something that can never be known exactly or worked on directly. Even the client can discover what his need really is only by finding out what he does in the helping situation. If, however, we limit our study of needs to the generally recognized categories as they emerge out of the larger social problems, and leave to the individual the freedom as well as the responsibility of testing out his peculiar needs against the relatively stable function of a particular agency, there remains to us a large and rela-

tively unexplored area for future development; an area in which to
learn how to maintain our functions intelligently and skillfully, and
how to isolate whatever can be isolated from the particular situation in
terms of the law, the nature, or the general pattern of the helping process. This knowledge, however, can never be applied to the control of
the client, neither of his needs nor of his behavior, for they are always
changing, but only to ourselves, to refine and reform our professional
selves as well as to increase professional skill.[8]

Direct quotation has been used to give the reader the feel for the
origin of the concept of functional social work in the language
of its creator, but no quotation can do justice to the article, which
must be read in its entirety for its full and revolutionary impact.

To let the use of agency function become the focus of the social work helping process means to accept the fact that the social
worker's responsibility is first of all to society, that is, to administer certain social services which society has established in institutionalized form, in its own interest as well as in the interest of
individuals served. This does not mean that the particular service
or agency is the best that can be developed, is necessarily right
and good in all aspects, just by virtue of having been established
and supported, or that the pattern of services in a given community is "the best," and right and good in all particulars. It means
that social agencies *are;* they exist. They constitute the sole
avenue for social work practice for the overwhelming majority of
the profession, and to all appearances they will continue to do so
for some time to come. It is a prime responsibility of the social
worker to assess, first of all, whether the purpose of a given
agency is sufficiently right and good, and in line with the profession's own purposes and values, that he can become or can continue to be a part of it, and, second, to make available his day by
day experience so that his own agency's service, the pattern of
community services, and social policy at every level may be improved. In this sense, the practice of social work is not at all a
status quo operation, as is so frequently and erroneously charged,
but a most responsible means for administering, improving, and
developing social services and social policy. The use of function,

as an element in social work skill, means starting with the here and now, with what presently exists in the way of organized social services, the only possible starting place for the vast majority of social workers, and making a professional contribution within the "given," using the given not as dead-end but as take-off point.

The social worker whose identification is with the function or purpose of his agency is concerned that that purpose be realized not only in the *limitation* involved, in staying with what is properly his to do, but in the *fullness* inherent in his function as well. It is the professional social worker, employed by a social agency, who is in the best position to test agency policy, and the more general social policy to which it is related, for its effectiveness in realization of agency purpose, and the broader social purpose. It is also this social worker who is in the best position to participate in such change as is indicated in the direction of the democratic values which constitute this country's heritage and charge, as well as the heritage and charge to the profession of social work.

As was suggested earlier, not only does identification with agency function assure social responsibility for social work, but it is psychologically helpful as well. Secure in his identification with agency purpose, in his reason for being in the picture at all (the "client-system" picture), since it is only agency purpose that has brought worker and clientele together, he is free to relate with warm professional and human concern to the clientele, to be there *for* the clientele, in the sense of helping it realize all that it can for itself from the agency's intent and resources, and from his professional skill as social worker, in making service available. He is still concerned with need, of course, with individual client need, with group need, and the needs of individuals in the group, with community need, but, in the individual instance, with need limited and partialized as it relates to agency purpose, and so capable of being worked with, as it becomes continuously clarified and possibly modified, through the *use* of agency service.

To attempt to assess *all* of any client's, or group's, or community's needs and to decide on an individual basis which ones to meet, or in work with individuals and groups to diagnose a faulty personality development or a constellation of faulty personality developments for the purpose of putting them right, is to assume a responsibility that no social worker is prepared to carry. It is a responsibility outside his education as a social worker and outside the limits of his purpose as a social worker, as society has spelled it out through the creation of specific social agency programs and the employment of social workers to man them.

As was suggested earlier, it is only as the social worker realizes that he is being neither helpful (to the extent that he might) nor socially responsible, in the sense of discharging the particular social purpose for which he was employed, that he can willingly affirm the limit which inheres in his performance of a specific function. Only as he accepts and lives with and within the limit of his function can he discover the richness of it and experience the psychological depth at which help can be given and taken in relation to it. Both client and worker are protected by the worker's identification with his function, the worker from his impulse to give or withhold in a purely personal and individual way, or to engage in something other than social work practice, the client from asking too much or too little or something irrelevant to, and impossible of fulfillment in, the immediate situation.

All the worker's professional skill in human relationship can go into helping the client discover both what he can do with whatever service the agency is established to offer and how he can get to and make use of other community services. As Taft wrote in concluding the paper to which earlier reference has been made: "As social [case] work learns to accept its own limited area of usefulness and concentrates on the process to which it has given its purpose and determination, its capacity for growth will widen and deepen to the extent of human ability to give and to take help constructively." [9]

Criticism is sometimes directed to the client's having to move from worker to worker and from agency to agency for help with his various needs and purposes. Functional social work is applicable to practice in a multiple service as well as a single service agency, if the worker knows what service is being offered at a particular time and stays with it sufficiently long for the client to experience its helping potential in depth. One may also question whether concentrating all possible social services in one agency and in one worker can run the danger of engulfing the client, taking his life away from him, however benevolently. May the necessity to partialize his life problems, and even to take some of them to different places, agencies, or persons, serve to help him retain a responsibility for the direction of his own life, and so offset the inconvenience, and possible confusion of working with several workers at one time? The significance of interagency conferences should be noted here as one means for reaching agreement on who is doing what, and what seems to be the most critical service and social work relationship at a given point in time.

The functional social worker is constrained, as he moves from field to field, from function to function, to discover the particular psychological meaning of giving and taking help of a particular kind. It feels different to apply to adopt a child, to apply for public assistance, to be visited by a social worker because of alleged child neglect, to seek marital counseling, or group experience, or to participate in community improvement. In all the myriad of functions a worker may be called on to represent, much can be learned and much must be learned by the social worker which is specific to the particular helping situation. This includes knowledge of the "other" being served, as a phenomenon in its own right, for example, an individual, a group, a community, knowledge of a particular kind of individual, group or community, knowledge of this specific individual, group, or community; knowledge of a particular kind of problem being faced, in respect to service being given, and of general social provision, including agency resource, for meeting such problem or need. It includes, as well, knowledge of what may be involved psychologically in the carrying of a specific function, in the kind of diffi-

culty it characteristically creates for the person, group, or community served, and the problem, as well as the promise, involved
in administering it.

Only as he understands and develops skill in dealing with not
just the universal problem in taking help, particularly help
which involves internal change and reorganization, but the *specific* problem involved in giving and using a *specific* service, is
the worker capable of furthering the richness the experience can
hold for the persons he serves.

Just as functional social work requires that the worker make
his own what is necessary in specific knowledge and specific skill
(always in relation to a generic base in social work knowledge
and skill) as he moves from field to field, and function to function, so must he make his own what is necessary in specific
knowledge and specific skill as he moves from process to process
(again in relation to the use of certain generic principles which
constitute a base for all processes in social work). To be a caseworker, a group worker, a community worker, to be a supervisor, an administrator, researcher or teacher, each asks for its
own specific body of knowledge, and its own specific skill.
Above all, it asks for a psychological identification with the particular purpose which inheres in the particular functional role
being carried, just as is true for identification with agency purpose or function. To realize the richness of the role requires an
acceptance of the limits which inhere in it. If the supervisor attempts to be a "good mother," she misses the opportunity of
being fully, richly, and helpfully a supervisor. If an administrator
denies the authority and leadership elements inherent in his role
and identifies himself as just another staff member (or a "good
Joe" who disclaims his responsibility), he fails to realize for himself or his staff the richness of being an administrator, in its potential meaning for him and his own development, and in its
meaning for agency and staff. In such an instance, staff is left to
flounder about in a sea of unknowns without the direction, the
form for operation, and the leadership which is needed for effective performance, and to which staff is entitled. Once again, as

was true in carrying agency function, it is essential in carrying functional role to know, and be responsible for, the kind of psychological problem as well as promise or fulfillment a particular role creates both for the role carrier and for the person or persons on the other end.

With a clear sense of function, both of field of practice as rooted in agency, and in process role as carried by each member of the staff, it is possible for an entire staff to develop the policies, the structure, the form most promising for achieving a common, known, and affirmed purpose. A paramount psychological value in "being functional," in addition to everybody's doing what he is supposed to be doing, and consequently knowing what to count on in himself and others, is its recognition and use of the principle of partialization.

What may be felt by individual, group, or community, by student, supervised worker, staff as overwhelming need, problem, or task, with no place to take hold, is immediately broken down by a mutual recognition of purpose or function as it inheres in agency function and in functional (process) role. It is still further broken down by an adherence to what is appropriate to be worked on at each step in the process, the beginning of an undertaking, the middle, and the end, as will be developed in the next chapter. Working with a focus appropriate to, indeed necessitated by, function of agency, function of role, and particular phase of the process can release a depth of psychological engagement and movement not possible if the effort is diffuse, scattered, without focus, form, or direction.

A third psychological value in the use of function lies in its constituting a "known," a "given" for the persons served. All of life is predicated on the use of the given. Each fertilized ovum uses the "given" of its genetic endowment, the given of its particular uterine environment, to bring itself to birth as a unique infant. The human mind, as all psychologies agree, develops only in conflict, in necessity to defend the organism or fend for it, to find an answer to need outside or in. The human will likewise gets its organization and increase of power through continuous meeting of internal and external obstacles.[10] Neither the "will" nor the intellect can work on itself alone but must work on, utilize *something*, some "given" for creation.

So it is that coming to terms with the given of an agency function, or with a functional role, provides opportunity for creative use of it toward the achievement of an own purpose. A man works best when he knows what he has to work with, what he is dealing with, what the rules of the game are, what is expected of him, and what he can expect of the other. The beginning of any social work process which operates from a functional base lies, not in the worker's assessing the object in order to formulate a plan of action but in the worker's making clear the given, what the agency service is, under what conditions it is available, and with the other making clear what his hopes, wishes, needs, and intent are in relation to which he hopes to use the agency.

The feel of such a beginning is a mutual discovery of whether this particular client or clientele can use this particular service under the conditions through which it is available. It is the social worker's clear and sure hold on what he is about, what he is there to do, plus his warm and knowledgeable skill in relationship in making his service (and functional role) available, which contain the surest promise of social work help. Such helping requires, of course, *knowledge* of the other in his generality and specificity, as was earlier developed, if the held is to be offered appropriately, and effectively. But this knowledge grows out of the worker's store of knowledge about the kind of person, group, or community being served, and about the particular person, group, or community being served as it manifests itself, and *changes,* in the course of the process.

The author has noted, over the last several decades, a curious resistance on the part of a considerable number of professional social workers to acknowledging and utilizing the place of the agency in the practice of social work, expressed in a variety of ways by a variety of workers. Some possible reasons for this resistance were developed earlier. Sometimes the feeling seems almost to be that the agency is the natural enemy of professional practice, that it obstructs, interferes with, or at the very least is irrelevant to, what is truly professional. The concept of social agency is approached gingerly as the "place" where practice occurs, the "setting," the "auspice," or even as providing a "sanction." What is omitted in any of these terms is the dynamic of purpose—the purpose of the practice as determined by the *agency's* purpose.

As has been developed earlier, the purpose of the agency expresses social will that this particular service be offered to all who qualify, in their own interest and in the interest of society as a whole. It is assumed that the purpose of the agency (or social work service department as in a hospital or school) is compatible with the purpose and the values of social work as a profession, or social workers would not and should not accept employment in it. The social worker is obliged, then, by his purpose as a professional social worker to direct his energies to realizing the purpose of the agency which has employed him. He is further concerned, as a professional social worker, to seek to realize that purpose *in a way,* through the *use of a method,* through engagement *in a process* identifiable as a *social work* process, through the values, knowledge, and skill required in any social work process, and manifest in the particular social work process being employed. His "professionalism" requires of him affirmation of purpose— social work purpose, as exemplified in a specific agency purpose and in a specific functional role. It requires of him also skill in a social work relationship process for the realization of purpose. There is, then, the purpose which inheres in agency intent and program, which can be affirmed as a social work purpose, and there is the purpose which inheres in all social work methods (to make some social service usable by the clientele in its own and society's interest). This concept relates method and the nature of the specific method employed (as developed in Chapters 2 and 3) intimately and irrevocably to the purpose of the program or service which the agency, as agency, is seeking to realize. As agent of society, the social agency is constrained to offer a service society can trust, let individual workers come and go, a service designed to realize society's purpose in establishing the agency, through a method that assures a constantly improving quality in the way it is made available. It is for this reason that policy, procedures, structure, form, supervision, all aspects of "administration," are required: to produce a *service* both community and clientele can trust and from which both can profit.

SUMMARY

Identification of the social worker with the purpose of the agency of his employment, as it comes alive in agency function, assures a social base for his practice since the purpose of the employing agency expresses social will that a particular service be offered in society's interest as well as in the interest of the clientele served. The social worker has the obligation, as a professional social worker, not only to use his knowledge and skill in the administration of the service as it presently exists but also to make his experience, knowledge, and skill available in responsible ways toward society's continuous review of (1) its purpose in establishing and maintaining the agency and (2) the effectiveness of program, policy, and agency structure for its realization.

What the agency can do and the conditions under which it can be done provide something for the clientele to grapple with, to come to grips with, to find a way to use positively and constructively in its own interest as it coincides with society's interest.

This the clientele is helped to do through the social worker's relationship skill, as it is directed toward helping the other to clarify an own purpose in relation to agency purpose, and to experience, perhaps more knowingly but at any rate more deeply than has been possible for him heretofore, a way of relating to others and of working to achieve purpose . . . with the opportunity to modify that "way" constructively through experience in the social work relationship itself.

Used with understanding of its significance, both social and psychological, identification with agency function, and with functional role, becomes for the social worker not a lamentable necessity but a challenge and an opportunity for enhanced professional effectiveness.

7 A PROCESS BASE FOR SOCIAL WORK PRACTICE

AN UNDERSTANDING of the significance of process for all social work method rests, first of all, on an appreciation of process as constituting a perspective for viewing a variety of phenomena. Indeed, a "process perspective" has characterized scientific thought in the twentieth century and has resulted in the growth of what is sometimes referred to as the "new science." Man's unending quest to know his world and himself, to know his physical, psychological, social worlds, was characterized in the nineteenth century by the development of a scientific method based on concepts of continuity, order, universal laws, and predictability. The mechanistic and deterministic scientific theories formulated during this period resulted in large part from application of principles formulated by the philosopher Descartes and the physicist Isaac Newton.

Wrote Saul Hofstein in a penetrating analysis of bases for the development of process theory in social work:

The Cartesian-Newtonian generalizations as applied through developing scientific method did indeed turn out to be an enormously fruitful and productive hypothesis. Man learned to understand much that was unknown. Applied to the natural sciences these methods resulted in the insights of Darwin and the elaboration of the new understanding of biological evolution. Not only were the physical laws of nature organized, but each living organism now had its logical and consistent place in the order of nature. The biological and chemical sciences through broad application of the new methods opened channels to vast new knowledge.[1]

Marx's theory of economic determinism was in harmony with the science theory of his day. Sociologists concerned themselves with structures and functions which could be studied, analyzed, and measured. Small wonder that psychological thought had a similar character, as in the theory of conditioned response developed through the experiments of Pavlov and exploited by John Watson and others. "Methods of studying personality," wrote Lynd, "still rest on assumptions and make use of models derived from nineteenth century Newtonian science and from classical economics. This was notably true of Freud, but it is also true of some who take sharp issue with fundamentals of Freudian theory." [2]

While Lynd emphasizes that Freud's great gifts and search often took him beyond his models, she contends that he

yet modeled his theory of personality on the sciences of his youth. This meant the psychology of Bruecke and Helmholtz, both strongly influenced by nineteenth century physics. Freud's physiology and his psychology in turn were thus conceived in terms of a physics of systems of atoms moved by forces, of conservation of energy, of relatively simple lineal causation and determinism, of the belief that all phenomena are susceptible to specific quantitative treatment.[3]

Vast as were the contributions to knowledge in all fields, attributable to the use of scientific method as developed in the last century, discovery of new knowledge has resulted, as has been suggested, in a revolution in scientific thought. That revolution, which, interestingly enough, again took place in the physical sciences, may best be characterized by the emergence of an understanding of energy, movement, and so of process, with the consequent abandonment of the principles of certainty and absolute predictability on the basis of a fixed causality.

Process, as used in this book, is conceived of as "a forward movement, progressive or continuous proceeding, . . . course" . . .[4] "moving forward progressively from one point to the next

on the way to completion . . . the act of passing through continuing development from a beginning to a contemplated end"
. . . or, as appropriate to a process in which some one takes a
measure of control, through the control of what he himself puts
into it . . . "The artificial continuing operation that consists of a
series of controlled activities or movements systematically directed toward a particular result or end." [5] Hofstein writes of
process as a recurrent patterning or sequence of changes over
time and in a particular direction. [6]

New understanding of the nature of matter as energy, trig-
gered by the discovery of the characteristic behavior of the atom,
has resulted in a recognition that only change and unpredictabil-
ity can be considered universal. In the new science what generalizations can be made are based on estimates of probability rather
than predictive certitude. The data being studied are appreciated
as being in constant process of change and as depending in part
on the observer, his method of observation, and what he is trying
to explain by his observation. Physical scientists and social and
behavioral scientists, who have related their thinking to this century's discoveries, no longer seek to understand a whole by
breaking it down into its parts and studying the parts independent of their relation to each other and to the whole. There is recognition that wholeness adds a quality that transcends any of the
parts, that it is continuously modified by the parts, and that the
parts, in turn, are continuously modified by the character of the
particular whole they comprise. Assumptions are made in the
physical sciences which cannot be "proved" by facts but yet provide a base for continuing scientific activity.

F. C. S. Northrop [7] wrote that any theory of physics makes
more physical and philosophical assumptions than the facts alone
give or imply, and added that the concept of fixed causality has
been abandoned. Banesh Hoffmann contends . . . "not only does
science after all these years suddenly find 'strict causality' an un-
necessary concept, it even demonstrates that according to the
quantum theory, strict causality is fundamentally and intrin-
sically undemonstrable." [8]

In quite another field, business administration, Peter Drucker states:

All of us know and stress continually that the really important things are process characteristics, such as the "climate" of an organization, the development of people in it, or the planning of its features and purposes. But whenever we try to be "scientific" we are thrown back on mechanistic and static methods such as work measurement of individual operations, or at best organization rules and definitions. Or take the physicists. The more they discover about the various subatomic particles of matter, the more confused, complicated and inconsistent become their general theories of matter, energy and time.[9]

Drucker speaks to the necessity of knowledge becoming more general rather than specialized, of the importance of taking into account quality value and judgment without abandoning the quest for proof and measurement. He identifies today's task as being to understand patterns of biological, social, and physical order in which mind and matter become meaningful because they are reflections of a greater unity. He deplores the Cartesian split between mind and matter and contends that it ceased to be meaningful the day the first experimenter discovered that by the very act of observing phenomena he affected it, and he concludes:

We need a discipline rather than a vision, a strict discipline of qualitative and irrevocable changes such as development, growth, or decay, and methods for anticipating such changes. We need a discipline, in other words, that explains events and phenomena in terms of their direction and future state, rather than in terms of cause, a "calculus of potential" rather than one of "probability." We need a philosophy of purpose, a logic of quality, and ways of measuring qualitative change, and a methodology of potential and opportunity, of "turning points" and "critical factors," of risk and uncertainty, of constants and variations, "jump" and continuity. We need a dialectic of polarity, one in which unity and diversity are defined as simultaneous and necessary poles of the same essence.[10]

An understanding of process leaves room for the emergent, the unknown, the unpredictable, for continuous creation from a center within rather than susceptibility to or reliance on control from without for essential change. Contemporary psychologists, sociologists, psychiatrists reflect an appreciation of the central organizing, integrating selective and volitional forces in a life process, as it manifest itself in an individual life, or in the life of groups of individuals, or in whole societies.[11]

For social workers to accept the concept of process as basic in the development of a theory for practice does not at all require the abandonment of any possibility of "order" and the substitution of "chaos" in life and in social work processes. Quite the contrary. Process may be understood as involving elements which move in dynamic pattern; particular phenomena may be viewed as configurations which, through a series of changes, yet maintain an existence, an integrity and continuity. Julian Huxley wrote:

All phenomena have an historical aspect. From the condensation of nebulae to the development of the infant in the womb, from the formation of the earth as a planet, to the making of a political decision, they are all processes in time, and they are all interrelated as partial processes within the single universal process of reality. All reality in fact *is* evolution in the perfectly proper sense that it is a one way process in time unitary, continuous, irreversible, self-transforming and generating variety and novelty during its transformation.[12]

An understanding of process as it is here being developed requires an understanding of the principle of complementarity or polarity.

Two fundamental interacting tendencies exist in nature . . . the tendency toward change and transformation and the movement toward reduction of disbalance and asymmetry, toward stability and pattern of configuration. Both of these tendencies are active in any process. They may at times operate independently of each other, at times may be in opposition. They may be in balance or out of balance with each other. Changes result in fact from the movement toward the reduction of these asymmetries. . . . Lancelot Whyte has described process as consisting of "the development of form by the decrease in asymmetry." In this statement he tends to overlook the importance to process of the ever recurrent emergence of disbalance and asymmetry. "Form," in Whyte's usage, is similar to the term configuration which we have used and is defined by him as the "recognizable continuity of any process." Every process thus grows out of the successive interactions between polar tendencies, but the extent, degree, and intensity of this interaction are often unpredictable.[13]

Understanding of process as characterizing all reality requires man to abandon trying to control uncertainty and to find, instead, the courage and wisdom to live with it, and even to utilize it for his own purposes. The concepts of process and of polarity as characterizing human life, as has been seen, have been and are being developed in many quarters. Otto Rank[14] was one of the first psychologists to recognize the fundamental polarities of the life process. He spoke to man's uniqueness or particularity, to the essential integrity or unity of his being, and to his capacity for innovation, and for playing the central part in the continuous creation of himself. Such a view led inevitably to man's understanding of the relativity of any psychological system seeking to explain him. Rank's whole concept of therapy was based on a process of relationship between patient and therapist which the patient was helped to use toward becoming a more fully realized and affirmed self. It is the exact opposite of a therapy based on an attempt to know a static object in order that the therapist may know what to do in order to achieve a predictable outcome for that object.

In questioning the significance of an understanding of process as basic to an understanding of method in social work, some social workers have spoken of their wish to be "scientific" and to develop a "scientific method" for social work. Here, customarily, follows the application of the word "mystical" to a practice of social work which operates on a process rather than a deterministic base. This criticism fails to take into account two points. (1) Twentieth century science is process based. A mechanistic and deterministic base characterized science of an earlier day. In developing her concept of the helping process of social casework, Jessie Taft[15] saw it as in harmony with the transformation that physics experienced when it turned from a static analysis of substance to bodies in motion, and from the understanding of matter in general to discovery of the laws of particular moving bodies in their relativity. The papers which appeared in the first volume of *The Journal of Social Work Process,* edited by Taft, were characterized by her as reflecting two attitudes: an ignoring of the static, the analytic; and a concentration on the dynamic, on the immediate interaction between the two participants in the activity of asking and offering help. She added: "This shift from the tendency to an even deeper and more futile analysis of either side, subject or object, client or worker, to an attempt to grasp the nature of the process itself in all its relativity and immediacy is as important for the advancement of our understanding of human psychology, as it is for social work." [16] To make the first point, then, social work practice, as conceived in this writing, so far as it is science based is twentieth century, not nineteenth century, science based.

To make the second point, (2) social work is not and never can be *pure* science because of its overriding purpose, which is not to extend knowledge, let the chips fall where they may, but to give service . . . to *gain* and *use* knowledge, with social accountability, in the immediate discharge of a social purpose. Wrote Taft:

Social casework has fallen into the no man's land that lies between the scientific and the professional, between knowledge and skill. It has not succeeded yet in developing enough of either to command the complete respect of other groups or to establish its own self-confidence. That social work cannot become a science is taken for granted by virtue of its practical basis. To establish truth or to engage in scientifically valid research can never be its aim (in its service programs) since always, whatever it does is vitiated for science by its avowed purpose, which is to help. Where helping human beings comes first, interest in furthering scientific observation must be sacrificed for the one destroys the other. No one can serve two masters at the same time . . . even in the medical field we know only too well that the good research worker does not make the physician.[17]

What might be added to this forthright statement is that research, as engaged in by social workers, on the nature of the phenomena with which social work is concerned—individuals, groups, society in their interrelationships, social welfare programs, and social work processes—is essential for the continuous development and effectiveness of the profession, as is the use, by social workers, of research findings from other disciplines. Always social work is accountable for determining what research findings have relevance for practice and through what methods (and processes) they may best be integrated in the profession for use in practice. Always the social worker engaged in giving service is responsible to be thoughtful, sensitive to the more general meaning of what he is freshly discovering in the particular helping situation in order that it may enrich his own and other's understanding, and so, professional helpfulness. And always the social worker who himself engages in research is accountable for the use of generic principles of social work method in what he does in the relationship and process aspects of his task as researcher, insofar as this is appropriate and applicable in the immediate stiuation.

It was Taft who, together with Robinson and others of the faculty and alumni of the School of Social Work at the University of Pennsylvania, to which they gave leadership, worked in depth on the significance of an understanding of process, as well as of function, for the practice of social work.[18]

Some consideration of the significance of an understanding of process for comprehending both the phenomena with which the social worker is concerned and his own methods for dealing with such phenomena may be useful here. An individual, understood as a process, as one, in some respects, unique manifestation of the life process, is viewed as undergoing continuous change from conception to death. He does not stay still long enough to be analyzed and set down at some one point in time for purposes of being assessed or diagnosed as a "total person in a total situation." Such understanding is both impossible and irrelevant to the proper purpose of any social worker. Since he is constantly changing through interaction with his environment, taking in from it, putting out on it, whatever an individual is as well as his "needs" are continuously shifting in the very course of his receiving social work help. Furthermore, viewed as a process, an individual is something in his own right, and the laws which govern his growth and development are just that, laws of growth rather than laws which can account for what he presently is and predict what he will become in any final sense, given the introduction of this or that "technique of intervention." This is not to suggest that the social worker should "go it blind," without taking into account whether an individual is a child or an adult, old or young, well or sick, male or female, in one kind of environment or another, faced with this or that particular problem. Every social worker needs to use all that is available to him of understanding about the person he is seeking to help, but he gleans that understanding *only in part* from his knowledge *about* this kind of person, in this kind of situation, faced with this kind of problem.*

Rather, he is imbued with a feeling for the uniqueness of this *particular* person, at this particular time, in this particular situation, and for this person as process, in constant state of becoming something other than what he presently is, and as capable of injecting the unknown and unpredictable into the situation of which he is a part. It is this understanding of an individual as a "process" which leads the worker to engage with him in a *mutual* discovery of who he is now, what he wants, hopes or fears from *this specific* social work situation, and where he hopes to go with it. In other words, the social worker enters into the life of an individual in such a way that that "other" has the best possible chance to use him, in his own process of becoming what he wants to be, in respect to the particular problem or purpose which has brought client and worker together.

Any assumption that what the client will do with the help

* Roland Warren writes interestingly of the difference between "knowing" and "knowing about," and of the power of the poet and philosopher to understand and communicate in a way not possible for some scientists. Writes Warren: "It was the philosopher Bergson who emphasized that reason seems to proceed by means of analysis, a breaking down of that which it considers, thus missing the dynamic quality of reality, its *élan vital*, which can be experienced only through intuition, an attempt to see things whole, through "acquaintance" rather than "knowledge about." [19]

offered can be known at the point of beginning is unwarranted, since it cannot be known ahead of time. It has not yet been written.

Any seeking to know the "cause" of a client's predicament is not a one-sided discovery (on the worker's part) of a lineal cause and effect relationship for the sake of a one-sided control (by the worker), but a mutual and mutually shared discovery of various contributory factors, in order that the client may be more fully in control of a continuing life process, further developed and affirmed as his own. There is full recognition that both worker and client are living and continuously learning to live with the unpredictable and the unknown, finding the courage and increasing capacity to do it, and even to welcome the openendedness, the richness, the "life" quality of such living. "Man's only happiness is to transcend himself, his only agony is to grow," wrote poet E. E. Cummings.

Just as an individual served may be viewed as a process, and in certain respects a unique process, with resultant attitudes, purpose, and requirement for development of characteristic skill for the social worker seeking to help him, so may all phenomena served by social workers be viewed as processes, with like result and requirement. A group may be viewed as unique, as having the integrity of a characteristic pattern, and at the same time as being in constant process of development and change. It may be viewed as comprised of interacting individuals, each one a "life process" in his own right, yet having its own life and process as a group. So can it be understood as utilizing the worker and its present opportunity of agency purpose and resources to achieve its own ends for itself as they are congruent with the social work ends which brought worker and group together. So viewed, the whole effort of the social group worker is on developing skill in his own part in a process—the process of social group work—so that the group and the individuals who comprise it have the best possible chance of realizing their own developing purposes for themselves through a maximizing of their own capacity to do so.

A community may be viewed as a living process of great complexity, involving interacting processes both individual and group, yet possessing a wholeness, an integrity, a character of its own at the same time it is in constant flux. Such a view, on the part of a social worker, sees the community, as it sees an individual or group, as having both the responsibility and the potential for formulating and achieving its own ends, with social work help, as those particular ends are appropriate to the purpose which brings community and community worker together.

The social worker who operates from a process base sees any "assessment," any understanding, of the phenomena being served as: (1) being characterized by a high degree of particularity . . . a phenomenon unique within its own category (individual, group, or community); (2) tentative, since the "phenomenon served" is in a constant state of becoming something other than what it presently is, within the integrity of its own character; and (3) mutually arrived at in the course of a service being given, which service continually affects the "assessment" and is affected by it.

Working from a process base the social worker uses the dynamics in his polar identification with society and clientele to help the clientele find self-development and self-actualization that is in society's interest as well as its own—in other words a balance in its own individual-social polarity.

Working from a process base, the worker recognizes and makes use of form and movement, of pattern and process, with recognition that it is possible for phenomena to have an individual character, an individual integrity, a uniqueness, and at the same time to undergo change, development, growth within the pattern. Such a view appreciates that phenomena change from their own bases, within their own patterns, as living processes making use of their own inner resources as well as outside resources toward their own growth.

Understanding that any human process of psychological growth is furthered by the introduction of difference which another can use in his own process of becoming what he may be, the social worker introduces the "difference" which is real and appropriate to the particular social work situation, the difference which inheres in his function or reason for being in the picture at all, as it lies in the function of the agency he represents, and his role within it.

Understanding the relation of form or pattern to process, the social worker facilitates the development of whatever form, pattern, structure is particularly appropriate for the giving of a particular service in a way that most surely conduces to its productive use by those for whom it is designed. Such understanding leads to the formulation and continuous modification of policy and of procedure, as, for example, through the construction and use of application forms in intake, reporting, and other schedules, the establishment of patterns of interviews or meetings, the form or "agenda" for the conducting of meetings.

Just as the processes of individual, group, and community life have certain characteristics in common, as processes, so is it immediately obvious that they are differentiated as processes by the nature of their own particular configurations—the individual as interaction of biological, psychological, social, and cultural factors; the group as interaction of individual life processes yet with a character of its own; the community as interaction of individuals and groups yet with its own integrity and wholeness, as community. The differences in the particular process (individual, group, or community), as well as the likenesses, need to be appreciated and understood. Inevitably the particular social work process used to affect the particular phenomena, viewed as process, while based in principles generic for any process in social work, will have its uniqueness too, appropriate to the particular configuration of interacting forces which constitutes the process affected, and to its own purpose as a specific process in social work.

In short, working from a process base the social worker conceives all phenomena as unique within classes or categories, as characterized by continuous change and direction toward an end, as embodying potential for such change which itself shifts in the course of time. He uses a process, a professional social work process, to affect processes, that is, the life process of an individual, group, or community, in order that the processes affected may have the best possible chance for self-realization in relation to a purpose which has brought worker and clientele together.

SUMMARY

Twentieth century science, in turning from the mechanistic and deterministic science of an earlier day and in developing the concepts of relativity, energy, particularity, emergence, and potential, has laid the base for the development of a theory of process. Applied to the practice of social work such theory leads to revolutionary changes in social work method.

The essence of the method here presented is its recognition of all phenomena served as processes, marked by a high degree of particularity, possessing integrity and wholeness, yet characterized by continuous change, and embodying a potential for realization or actualization which can be furthered by the social work process itself.

Such a theory leaves room for the emergence of the unknown, the unpredictable, for "becoming" through the utilization of the immediacy of a continuously shifting life situation.

It calls for the development of a method which requires the social worker's engagement of the other in a relationship process through which that other may both discover and modify his own wanting, and develop new power for satisfying his own wants.

Social work method (in process-based practice) is not a method of study of a relatively static object, whether individual, group, or community, in order that the worker may apply specific techniques to achieve the workers' own preconceived ends for client, group, or community. It is rather a method for entering into a process of relationship with another or others, with mutual and continuous discovery of the nature of the phenomena being served, what it is seeking from the present situation and social work relationship, as both change in the course of the service being given, and with the intent of providing the best possible opportunity for the other to achieve its own continuously shifting capacity for achieving its own goals, as those goals are appropriate to the purpose which has brought social worker and clientele together.

Social work practice which is process-based requires that the worker control not the phenomena being served, but his own part in the social work process, through application in the specific instance of certain generic principles, principles which characterize any process in social work, and others congruent with the generic principles but specific to the specific social work process engaged in.

It is the generic principles which will be developed in Chapter 8.

8 *FIVE PRINCIPLES GENERIC FOR SOCIAL WORK PRACTICE*

THE FIVE principles for practice which will be developed in this chapter derive from the psychological, social, and process bases which have been presented in the preceding chapters. In other words they rest on an understanding of the nature of human growth which affirms the central role of the individual in growing and changing and identifies the way he uses his inner resources as well as his environment (physical, psychological, and social) for his own growth purpose. Such an understanding of the nature of growth and the power for growth in the individual identifies, also, the power in the group, a plurality of individuals yet an entity in itself and the power in the community, a plurality of individuals, groups, and institutions yet an entity in itself for growth and change and for using inner and outer resources (including the "resource" of a social worker) for that change.

The five principles rest as well on an understanding of the significance of social agency purpose for giving direction and form to social work practice, and so for conducing to both its psychological helpfulness and its social accountability. Finally they rest on an understanding of the nature of process which makes it possible to appreciate both the phenomena served as processes and the social work skill itself as a process. It is this process skill which calls for the use of a method designed to initiate, sustain, and bring to an end processes of human interaction, directed toward an identified social purpose, through which mutually affirmed goals may be discovered, chosen and rechosen, and realized.

The use of the five principles constitutes the core of the method which leads to the particular social work process in which the social worker is engaged. Their use is appropriate for the practice of social work in all its processes, both primary and secondary, and in any field within the general purview for social work, established earlier.

It is not contended that the mastery of these principles provides an exhaustive and foolproof armamenta for the practice of the profession. It *is* suggested, however, that their understanding, use, and further development can form a unifying theoretical framework for method in social work, within which elaboration, additions, and refinements of generic principles as well as the development of principles specific to the several social work methods may take place.

Without any order of importance, the principles may be stated in the following way.

PRINCIPLE I

That diagnosis, or understanding of the phenomenon served, is most effective for all the social work processes which is related to the use of the service; which is developed, in part, in the course of giving the service, with the engagement and participation of the clientele served; which is recognized as being subject to continuous modification as the phenomenon changes; and which is put out by the worker for the clientele to use, as appropriate, in the course of the service.

This principle has to do with the nature of "diagnosis" and the use of diagnosis by the social worker. Elaboration of successive parts of the principle stated may clarify its meaning. For effective social work service to be given, the phenomenon served must be "understood." But *what* must be understood? *How* is that understanding arrived at? How is it *used* in the giving of service?

Those who hold the view of social work practice presented in this book do not see, in the use of the method of social casework, for example, any need to understand "the total person in his total situation." This is both impossible and irrelevant to the particular purpose being discharged. Similarly, less than exhaustive and exhausting study of a group or a community can serve as basis for offering a service, with fuller understanding developing as the phenomenon (individual, group, or community) changes in the course of using, or not using, the service offered.

To the beginning of the process the worker brings his own understanding, developed, organized, and available, most surely, through a process of professional education, of the nature of the particular phenomenon with which he is immediately engaged, whether an individual, a group, or a community. Within these broad categories of phenomena he brings understanding of particular *kinds* of individuals, groups, or communities. Important here in his understanding of an individual, by way of illustration, is his knowledge of the growth process, the characteristics and needs of any and all individuals at various points in the life process, the varied ways of dealing with stress both external and internal, the nature of the more common illnesses, physical, psychological, and psychosocial, and their more usual meanings to the individual affected and to others in his environment.

Similarly, the social worker is aware of different kinds of groups: for example, the formed group, the interest group, the natural group, the large group, and the small group. He understands, as well, various kinds of communities, such as geographical communities, ethnic communities, small neighborhood communities, urban communities, rural communities.

The worker brings, or should bring, to his work a rich understanding of the particular phenomenon he seeks to serve. Some of this he will derive from records and reports of various kinds, available or "securable" within his own and other agencies and institutions. But he brings, also, a capacity to let this particular and unique individual, this particular and unique group, this particular and unique community discover, reveal, and modify itself in the course of using or failing to use the service offered.

So it is that the worker's understanding develops *in part* from what the other brings to and does with the service offered. And one aspect of his skill is his engagement of the "other" in making itself known, both to the worker and to itself, in the immediacy of the moment.

Such a view of diagnosis recognizes that people, groups, and communities do not stay put in categories and that any attempt to place and keep them there and to plan service or help on the basis of a "firm diagnosis" made denies potential for growth and change, and can actually be stultifying and inhibiting of growth through too arbitrary an expectation of what can be expected from "this kind" of individual, group, or community.

However, the point has been made and is here reinforced that the worker brings an understanding of the phenomenon served, the kind of phenomenon served, and the particular phenomenon which helps him to be realistic at the same time that he is open-minded. For example, the worker does not approach a mentally retarded person with a communicated (or uncommunicated!) expectation that he may want to think about going to college or a particular group or community with a similarly inappropriate possibility in mind.

What has been developed is the *way* understanding is achieved in the course of giving service, through engagement of the clientele in development of the understanding and *through observing what is done in using the service,* with recognition of the tentative nature of diagnosis at any one point in time, within a solid knowledge base of what is realistically possible.

A further understanding of the principle stated has to do with the nature of the understanding itself. As was earlier suggested, no attempt is made to know and set down on paper a "total individual in a total situation," nor is there a like attempt for a group or a community. Rather the focus from the beginning of the relationship is on an understanding of the phenomena *as related to the service being offered.* For example, a couple applies to an adoption agency or service for the purpose of adopting a child. The effort of the worker is to understand husband and wife *not* as separate individuals, or even as a married couple with various "assets and liabilities" as individual persons and as a couple, with the intent of then making a decision as to whether this kind of man and this kind of woman and this kind of couple are suitable as adoptive parents as measured against some concept of an "ideal family." Rather the effort is to help the couple as well as the agency discover in the course of the application process whether they want to be and can be adoptive parents through this agency at this time. There is opportunity to discover this as the worker presents what the agency requires of couples seeking to adopt a child, and what adoption itself requires of adoptive parents. Into the interchange with the worker will go much about the past life of the prospective parents and their present relationships with each other, with extended families, and within the community. But the purpose of the understanding or "diagnosis" being developed is kept sharply in mind by the worker, with the result that the investigation becomes less intrusive and "for the worker and agency's sake" and more acceptable and reasonable as part of a mutual effort toward a mutual discovery of whether the client's request for a child can be granted by this particular agency at this particular time. The final judgment, must, of course, be made by the agency, with respect and consideration for the meaning of the decision to the applying couple.

Imagination will suggest the way an understanding of any client, and the *development* of an understanding of any client, comes to a focus in an assessment of this person's capacity to use this service toward an end that is or can become his own, as it relates to the purpose of the particular service being given. The mother who is neglecting and abusing her child discovers, no less than the agency discovers, whether she is or can become the kind of mother who can meet the minimal requirements of the community *as a mother*. The boy on probation discovers, no less than the probation officer, whether he is or can become the kind of boy who can realize his own potential in a way that does not

violate society's laws. The married couple seeking marital counseling discover, no less than the worker, whether they can or
cannot make a "go" of their marriage.

Similarly, the group discovers what kind of group it is, idiosyncratically, and what it can do or become as a group in relation to some project or program appropriate to the sponsoring
agency's purpose, just as each group member discovers freshly
who he is and what he can become through participation in the
life of the group. The community discovers itself, its tensions, its
conflicts, its wants, its power for realizing its wants in the course
of using a service, related in the immediate moment to some particular aspect of its life which is in harmony with an agency's
concern in making service available. So in establishing a diagnosis, individual, group, or community, each in a sense "writes
its own ticket," makes its own diagnosis of itself, and revises that
diagnosis as it, in fact, becomes different. However, it must be repeated here that the worker brings to this process of diagnosis his
understanding of the phenomenon served, and the particular
kind of phenomenon served, as well as his own developing understanding of *this specific* phenomenon. The understanding out
of which the worker continually acts is enriched and accompanied by the phenomenon's understanding of itself, in all of its
particularity, and as it grows and changes. And this brings us to
the final implication of the First Principle, which has been concerned with the nature and use of diagnosis in social work practice.

Instead of making his judgment on what this individual or
this group or this community is "like," noting it in the record, or
sharing it with his supervisor, or even using it as a base for his
own planned action, the worker puts out frankly and freely,
with professional caring and relatedness, for the "other" to use
for the achievement of his own purpose, his (the worker's)
present understanding. This, of course, is not done indiscrimi-
nately but with a sense of timing and of the readiness of the
other to use what is being shared, constructively. However, the
free sharing of understanding, within the limits indicated, itself

conveys an appreciation of the other as a unique individual, group, or community, a belief in the capacity of the other to use what is being expressed, in his own behalf, and it furthers engagement in the relationship process, as well.

A caseworker may say to a client: "You tell me you are a mousy person who can't stand up for her own rights, and yet the way you are with me today, coming late to your appointment and wanting everything pretty much on your own terms, suggests a lot of strength to control." Or discrepancies in what the client is putting out can be pointed up, not for the purpose of catching him in a trap but for the purpose of helping him experience more deeply his own ambivalence as he discovers and develops that part of himself most true to what the self as a whole desires.

A group can be helped to know itself as a group through the worker's sharing his understanding of it at a particular point in time, and it can use that understanding toward accomplishing a purpose of its own which is in harmony with the agency's reason for being. A community, through the individuals and groups who comprise it, can profit from the worker's pointing up the way the community appears to him as he works with it. He works for the purpose of helping the community experience its own conflicts and wants more deeply and more knowingly, as a base for moving on whatever concerted and constructive want it can discover and maximize in respect to the particular service being offered.

It should be clear that all that has been said about the nature of diagnosis, the way it is arrived at and the way it can be used in the primary processes of social work, is equally true for the secondary processes. The supervisor, the administrator, the teacher, the researcher must make a "diagnosis" of the person or group he is serving in his particular functional role and within the function of the agency he represents or serves. This diagnosis is *not* of the total person or group as person or group, but as relevant for his relationship to them, his *purpose* in relationship to them. The supervisor must judge what is facilitating or interfering with a worker's giving service that reflects both his own developing professional skill and the requirements of the agency for effective helpful service to all clients. The administrator makes continuing diagnosis of his staff as a whole as well as of individual staff members in relation to their part in the production of that service with which the agency is charged. He diagnoses, as well, the continuing role of the board in facilitating or impeding the agency's achievement of its purpose, as well as the agency's relationship to the community for what it portends of the role the agency should and could play in the community. The teacher in a school of social work must diagnose or evaluate a class as a whole, as it moves through the semester or year, in respect to its mastery and use of a particular content. He must evaluate, also, the learning problems and promise of individual students. The adviser has a very special responsibility for arriving at and acting on an educational diagnosis of each of her advisees. The researcher, gathering data as a member of a social agency staff or as consultant on the staff of a social agency, must understand factors interfering with as well as furthering staff's furnishing of data and engaging in the research process in such a way that research findings will stand the best possible chance of being used in the interest of worker, agency, and profession.

In all these instances the social worker is constrained to make a diagnosis or diagnoses. In all, the participation of "the other" in arriving at a diagnosis is essential. In all, the diagnosis shifts in the course of time. In all, the diagnosis is related to the purpose of the worker and clientele in coming together. In all, there is appropriate and potentially fruitful opportunity for sharing with the "other" the understanding or diagnosis arrived at by the worker, for the other's use in the achievement of own purpose, as it coincides with or is appropriate to the purpose of a particular undertaking. Such a concept and such a use of diagnosis reflect a belief in the individual (the group, the community) as being its own center for change, capable of continuous growth and development and of using the "outside" (including a relationship with a worker) to achieve that growth. They reflect an understanding of the significance of the agency function at every step of a social work helping process, including its beginning. They reflect, as well, an understanding of all of life as process, of the phenomenon served as a process, and of skill in the use of a social work method as constituting a "process skill," or skill in the use of a process to affect a process.

Diagnosis is used here within the context of an understanding of method in social work not as involving a "way of study of an object," formulation of a plan and carrying out of a plan through enlisting the cooperation of the other, but rather as involving a way of engaging in a human relationship process which frees the other to define his own goals for himself as they fall within or coincide with the goals of the specific program being administered, and to work toward their achievement with the worker's help. In other words, method in social work as implied here is viewed essentially as method not for studying or diagnosing phenomena served but as method for affecting phenomena served. The method for studying and diagnosing in order to affect has its own characteristics as a particular kind of study and diagnosis. It finds its place *as part of* social work method whose essential quality is that it seeks to affect, to induce change, to help. Social work method which, in use, leads to social work process involves an interaction of study *and* affecting or helping with each being continuously altered by the other. How is the study, the development of understanding, modified by what has happened in the process of helping? How can the other participate in the study of himself with more accurate understanding resulting and with the process of helping furthered? How can what is freshly and newly known and discovered be immediately utilized in the helping? An understanding of social work method as requiring the social worker's utilization of self in a relationship process with the clientele served, according to defined principles of action and toward a defined social purpose, eschews diagnosis by fixed catagories and leaves room instead for the emergence and utilization of the unknown, the unexpected, the newly possible in the course of the helping process.

PRINCIPLE II

*The effectiveness of any social work process, primary or second-
ary, is furthered by the worker's conscious, knowing use of time
phases in the process (beginnings, middles, and endings) in
order that the particular potential in each time phase may be
fully exploited for the other's use.*

An understanding of process as characterizing all of life can
conduce to the development of a capacity to go *with* life, to *be* in
effect a process, in relation to other processes, with affirmation
and with exploitation of each present moment for its full and
unique value. It is this capacity, developed in himself, which the
social worker seeks to use in furthering like capacity in those he
serves. A heightened understanding of time phases as characterizing process makes possible their use in the interest of the clientele served and furthers the clientele's going with, and utilization
of, each present and passing moment.

Beginning any venture in which there are bound to be elements of the unknown, particularly a venture involving human
relationship and within which the one served by the worker is
expected to do something or become something, leads inevitably
to feelings of hope, excitement, and the mobilization of energy.
At the same time it evokes fear, uncertainty, and even a "setting
of the self against," perhaps to protect a hardly won inner balance and sense of integrity. The particular gestalt of feeling
about a beginning for an individual client, group, or community
depends on the character of individual, group, or community, a
characteristic way of beginning, as it has evolved through experience, and on the nature and significance of the particular undertaking which is being begun. For the individual the beginning of
life *as* an individual is birth. Subsequent beginnings reflect and
carry some of the "feel" of that experience, in a generic sense and
idiosyncratically, for each individual as well.[1]

It is the worker's sensitivity to what is involved *in this particular beginning,* within the context of his understanding of what is

true for beginnings in general, which makes it possible for him to lessen the fear and resistance and exploit the marshaling of energy and use of new life which attend beginnings. This he does by such "techniques" as making the unknown known through, for example, being clear about his agency's service, the conditions under which it is available, what can be expected of it and of him as worker, and what the requirements and expectation of the "other" are. The known is less feared and more manageable than the unknown. At the same time the worker encourages immediate engagement of the other in expressing hopes, intentions, fears in respect to what is being offered in the way of service. The more quickly the other gets into action and makes clear to the worker as well as to himself his part and stake in the situation that brings them together, the more readily his life force and energy can be directed toward, and utilized in, dealing with a situation rather than in protecting himself against its impact, and against the impact of the one who may represent the threat of change. As the "other" experiences through entering on a relationship with the worker both what he wants, and what he is like, and what the agency in the person of the worker is like and expects and requires (stripped of some of his projections on it of what he wants it to be or fears it is), a working relationship develops which the other is free to use in his own behalf, yet within the known purpose and intent of the agency or service with respect to him.

Additional ways of furthering fruitful beginnings include the partialization or breaking up and breaking down of what can be felt as total problem or global purpose into something that is small enough to be encompassed, and get started on, as one piece of that problem or purpose. The worker's responsibility is to help the other find a place to take hold, to *begin* with some aspect or part of his problem, need, or intent. Experience in staying with and using the partialized, focused service leads to the development of confidence and competence to cope with other and related problems and needs. Nothing is so conducive to frustration and scatter as trying to do everything at once.

Perhaps most essential of all are the worker's sensitivity to what the other is experiencing in beginning and his response to that feeling, *in a way appropriate to the situation,* so that the other is freed to move through and beyond feelings which may be impeding his getting started. It cannot be overstressed that it is the worker's appreciation of the promise and problems in beginnings in general and his capacity fully to exploit this particular beginning for this particular client or clientele, *to stay with the beginning and let it be a beginning* in all its inevitable awkwardness and tentativeness, rather than to rush to try to solve all the problems in the first interview, group meeting, or conference, that embodies skill in this aspect of social work process. The warm human connection which the worker is ready to extend to the client or group can be felt and responded to and so facilitate entering on the new experience. But love is not enough, and it can be overwhelming if put out too totally or in a way that leaves the other carrying all the "bad" feelings of fear, suspicion, and ingratitude for help extended.

The goal in any beginning is to facilitate finding a common base for worker and clientele to work together toward a common purpose, with the rules of the game known and its elements broken down into what can be encompassed for immediate engagement. Beginning social workers in *their* beginnings, with clients or with groups, are sometimes reminiscent of the "poor young poets . . . who have so much to say, and try to say it all in one sonnet." To let a beginning be a beginning, furthermore, to *further* a beginning's being a good beginning in all the fumbling and discomfort that so frequently attends it, in all the trying out and experimenting involved in finding a base for continuing work, ask for knowledge and disciplined skill in a process that is truly professional.

It will be immediately clear that beginnings in the broad field of social work are of many kinds. A client begins with an agency through a relationship with a worker. Each interview that follows the first one will have its own beginning, middle, and ending until the service is terminated. It is possible to feel and utilize the rhythm of these time phases and to do what is appropriate in respect to beginnings, big and little, major and "sub," within a process which is already underway.

The same is true for meetings of groups. The first meeting of any group is alive with the feel of beginning. Members are filled with hope of what this can mean for them, and with fear and uncertainty too. The group as a whole, if it is being newly formed, is not yet a group but is already started on the fascinating discovery of whether it can become one. A community roused to a point of action in respect to some community problem or aspiration, either on its own initiative or through the initiative of another, is just beginning to feel its identity as a community in a new way, as it discovers whether it can act in any whole or concerted fashion *as a community* for all the diversity and conflict within it, in its own interest and toward its own welfare as well as the general social welfare. Beginnings are no less real in the secondary processes. A supervisee, starting with a supervisor and in an agency, is entering on a long process within which there will be many beginnings. A staff beginning to work with a new administrator has its way to find; and the administrator, in making his own beginning, has the responsibility for furthering staff and board's beginning with him, as parties to an agency's producing service, ever more effectively and responsibly. The life of any administrator is full of beginnings, beginnings of a new year following vacations, of a new "budget year," beginning of series of meetings and of individual meetings with board and with staff. As administrator he must find the rhythm and must identify and exploit beginnings big and little as they occur in order that they may be fruitful toward the accomplishment of common purposes.

The researcher knows well what is involved in beginning a project which is going to involve others in supplying data, in looking at their work, in having their work looked at. Not only does the social work researcher who, in addition to possessing research skills, takes responsibility for the use of the generic social work principle of recognizing and utilizing time phases for their full value stand a good chance of being more helpful as a researcher to those he serves, but his research itself stands a better chance of being valid as others are freed to participate wholeheartedly and frankly in the undertaking.

Nowhere are the potentials in using beginnings more keenly felt than in a school of social work. Here the rhythm of the school year highlights the hope and fear which attend beginnings —the reaching forward, the fearing, fleeing from, or fighting, so characteristic in varying pattern in all beginnings. The administrator of a school of social work has much to do to recognize and utilize those beginnings in which he has a responsible role to play, the beginning of the undertaking as a whole, in getting each school year underway, as he works with individuals and groups, students, faculty, staff, board, university administration, community. Certainly all teachers and all advisers know that "this is a beginning" with their students and respond in a way appropriate to their functional roles as teacher or adviser within a school of social work.

"Middles" are generally conceived as more difficult to understand and utilize. Indeed Taft[2] once disposed of them by saying, in respect to therapy, that there are no middles. Once a patient is thoroughly "in" he is seeking and finding the way to get "out," to leave, to end. There is application of this truth for social work processes. Yet middles do exist, and they have their own character. Social workers in all functional roles have felt the dead level quality of middles, the slump that follows the exhilaration of truly beginning and precedes the getting ready to end and continue on one's own. However, they are characterized, or can be characterized, also by the other's taking over increased responsibility for his part in the situation and by a deepening of the relationships involved. How can we keep middles from being flat, stale, and unprofitable, unproductive of movement? Social work method is directed toward helping the other feel and take increased responsibility for his part in the project. The very act of working together and what the worker puts in of professional concern, respect for the integrity of the other, and skillful help conduce to a deepening of worker-clientele relationship which is then available for the other's use. There is always opportunity for the *new* project, venture, focus, or experience within the ongoing experience. Intuitively, workers, whatever their functional role, make use of introduction of the "new" to capture the new life potential of beginnings, to deepen the engagement and relationship, and to make it possible for the other to gain a new sense of accomplishment and new power through bringing something to conclusion. In any event, middles need to be understood as time phases in their own right, as the worker takes the responsibility for knowing how their particular potential can be fully utilized for deepening of engagement and movement toward capacity for more independent functioning.

Endings have their own feeling and quality. Just as beginnings are psychologically imbued with the feeling of birth, so endings are imbued in varying proportion and degree with the feeling of death . . . of separation. As such they may be resisted and feared.[3] When one has had an experience of significance, it is hard to end. There is always the question of whether the self can survive the ending. So students nearing graduation sometimes wonder aloud: "What will I do without the 'School'? I feel lost." Clients and groups may resist and postpone endings even after the relationship has lost its meaning or is necessarily to be terminated under the conditions of agency service as, for example, when a client is no longer elegible for public assistance, or a mother (client of a protective agency) is giving her child care above the "floor" required by the community. Or endings may be rushed toward prematurely by clients or groups, students, or supervisees, to *prove* that "I can get along without you very well," when the self doubts it.

Yet endings are welcomed, too, and even invited. In truth, we "thank whatever Gods may be, that no life lives forever, that dead men rise up never, that even the weariest river winds somewhere safe to sea."[4] For every ending carries within it the potential for a feeling of accomplishment, a sense of something lived through and taken into the self, and there is the wish to be free, to try it on ones' own, to use the new power and the new self in new situations.

"Patterns of ending" will be as diverse as patterns of beginnings for individuals and groups . . . and for the same reasons, derived from past ending experiences and evolved ways for dealing with them, and as affected by the nature of the particular ending situation presently faced. What is the significance of what is being left behind? of the new beginning which is to follow? Social workers, both intuitively and knowingly, have done more with beginnings than with endings. The literature speaks to "intake procedures" and "getting started" in various professional situations, with varying degrees of skill consciously identified and utilized.

Endings on the other hand, are usually allowed to happen when the client is worn out, "wearied out," and the relationship has lost its meaning. The same may be said for the life of a group. There is room for the use of as much skill in exploiting the significance of endings in social work processes, as in exploiting the significance in beginnings, though much less attention has been given to it. Sometimes the ending is fixed by the situation. For example, as was earlier suggested, the public assistance client may no longer be eligible for financial assistance. Exploitation of any ending involves recognizing either that it is going to occur or *should* occur in the interest of effective service, and helping the other to recognize it, look at it, and capture his own accomplishment within it. This he may be helped to do through recapitulating the meaning the experience has had for him, assessing his own learning in it, expressing whatever of regret, sadness, or fear of going on alone he may feel, as well as the wish and readiness he feels for what now looms as a new beginning of other ventures with their promise and hope and opportunity for using what has been learned. To "end" is to experience the new self, with its fresh courage and power and, perhaps, capacity for relationship, through what has been done, in relationship with the worker, and others involved in the undertaking being completed.

The "use of ending" as one aspect of skill in social work process has been much misunderstood. There should never be a practice of setting a rigid and arbitrary time limit at the point of entering on the giving of service as a "technique" unrelated to the needs and requirements of a particular situation or service. When the ending is *in the stiuation,* it can be used with sensitivity and skill, which involves not only technical capacity for dealing helpfully with what is involved in ending for the other but also the worker's own capacity to let go. Where there is no ending inherent in the situation, it can be psychologically helpful to establish one at the point of beginning. The ending time established will be based on the time usually required for something productive to be done in a particular kind of situation. Setting an ending can alleviate a client's feeling of being trapped in something that may go on forever, with his own will and self lost to the control of an outside force. It can serve as an incentive to him to use productively the present moment, out of the recognition that the relationship and service are not going to last indefinitely. In developing capacity and courage to enter on something, use it, and let it go, he develops capacity and confidence in living with all things temporal, and in small degree with the fact of life itself, with its inevitable physical ending.

When an ending is set, on the basis of collective agency experience, it is in some such way as "Let's work on this for three months (or six months or six weeks, or twelve sessions, or three, or six) and see where we are. It may be that by that time you will have found what you wanted to or can find here. If more time is needed we can talk about it then." Such a method is particularly helpful in family and marriage counseling services which lack the external form and structure of services that carry their own endings in their function or nature, for example, probation, parole, protective services, public assistance, convalescent leave from a mental hospital, and the like.

In certain situations "natural" time periods can be used, such as in school counseling, the school year, or "until Christmas vacation." Sometimes a short time period is indicated by the nature of the problem and is consequently established. And time structures may be used to break up a long process as through the establishment of a time structure for an application process to be followed by a period of continuing service, with a still different time structure for ending the service.

Imagination is needed to develop an appropriate and skillful use of endings—major and minor, within whole processes of service, and within individual interviews or sessions for all the processes both primary and secondary. The essential thing, again, is that endings be understood as a psychological experience having the potential for another's more sure possession of a more fully developed self which can be "owned" or affirmed through the very act of ending. As is true for beginnings and middles, both the promise of ending and its problems can be consciously exploited for the value the ending can have for the other's use of service.

In writing of this principle of social work helping as briefly as must be within the confines of this book there is a risk of being superficial. A volume could be devoted to the nature of beginnings, middles, and endings, as characteristics of any process and particularly of the life process, and as significant for the social work processes, primary and secondary. And another volume could be written on the nature of the fine-grained professional skill which can go into their exploitation in each of the several social work processes. What has been identified is a principle as part of a frame of reference within which skill in social work processes may be considered, leaving it to the reader to pursue elsewhere, on his own, through study, experience, or both, the value that can derive from the use of the principle. Neither is the writer unaware that social workers have "always done that" in the sense of developing "intake procedures" (one form of utilizing beginnings as a time phase) or helping groups and communities summarize what has been taken from or learned through an experience for future use (one form of utilizing endings as a time phase). What *is* claimed is that when those activities are viewed not as disparate "techniques" but as ways of relating to and making appropriate professional social work use of "time," a comprehension of their significance as related to a general principle results. It can lead to the affirmation and full and imaginative exploitation of the activities as one essential of professional social work skill. Such full exploitation, it is here suggested, increases the helpfulness of the process for the clientele served.

PRINCIPLE III

The use of agency function and function in professional role gives focus, content, and direction to social work processes, assures accountability to society and to agency, and provides the partialization, the concreteness, the "difference," the "given" which further productive engagement.

Use of agency function in the social work processes, both primary and secondary, asks that what the social worker does, his *part* in the social work process in which he is engaged, be not only *related to* but also embody and constitute an implementation of, the purpose of the social agency or institution within which he is functioning. The "content" of what goes on between the worker and those he serves is determined both by the purpose of the agency of his employment and the purpose of his role within it. His goal is always to realize those purposes, to make them come true to the fullest possible extent in the interest of the supporting society and agency and of the clientele served. Indeed the first task in the use of agency function is to determine, through initiating the process for which the social worker is responsible, whether the purpose or purposes of the persons he seeks to serve and the purpose of the agency service or institution he represents can come together in fruitful engagement toward a common end.

So a social caseworker, in an agency whose purpose is child placement, in all that he does seeks to carry out that purpose, if it develops in the course of making the service available that this is indeed a service needed or wanted by the clientele served, and in their own interest as well as the general social interst. This will involve him in work with own parents, not just at the point of their application or referral for the service but throughout the period of placement, as their participation is required to help the placement work both for their child and for themselves as parents. It involves continuous determination with them of whether placement of the child is the right solution, for how long, whether changing circumstances or attitudes or capacities on their part or the child's make a different solution possible, whether and to what degree their continuing participation in the life of their child, as parents of a placed child, is indicated, what form that participation can best take. Into the relationship with the worker may come much of the parent's own past and present as he tries to learn how he can best be parent to his child at this particular time, whether through placement or otherwise. But the focus of what is done inheres in the purpose of the service which has brought worker and own parent together.

The very concreteness, definiteness, and sharpness of the focus facilitate psychological engagement, since the own parent has something to struggle with, to work with, a purpose which animates and gives form to his relationship with the worker. As a result of his own searching inquiry into what he wants to be and can be to his child at this time, and his relationship with a skillful and compassionate worker who is joining him and helping him in that inquiry, he may achieve substantial growth, development, and integration as a whole person. But such development is a by-product of a social service skillfully made available, not its primary aim.

Similarly the placed child, through a sustained relationship with the worker, has the steady, dependable support of the "agency" as society's instrument for assuring him that he will have a home, physical care, and family life, which his own parents are not able, for a long or short period, to provide. To the worker the child brings his accomplishments and problems in the "way of life" that is his as a placed child. By her, he is helped to utilize that way of life to the full for his own growth and development.

The foster parents, in applying to the agency to become foster parents, discover with the worker whether they can be foster parents for this agency, at this time, to their own satisfaction, and to the satisfaction of the agency. For it is the agency which must keep the responsibility for determining whether this home and these parents are right, and right for this particular child at this particular time. Again, both foster child and foster parents may bring to the relationship with the worker, past and present, interests, concerns, problems that cover the range of human living, but always the worker is kept on course by agency purpose. It is this purpose which acts as compass and assures a focus and direction in what is being done that is not only appropriate but essential if agency purpose is to be realized. The partialization of total problem of own parent, or child, or foster parents, which is introduced by agency function, serves as a safeguard against their whole lives being taken over by a worker who then tries to set them right. It assures that some *part* of what is currently being experienced in the placement situation, a part which can be grasped and taken hold of, can be used by them to find a solution to a social problem or responsibility which is right and satisfying to them, and acceptable to the agency (agent of society) making the service available. As was earlier suggested in the case of own parent, either foster child or foster parents may use the experience with worker and agency for growth, the development of new capacity for productive, individually fulfilled, social living, but this accrues as a by-product of a social service skillfully made available through a psychological relationship process.

Use of agency function as an integral part of social work skill offers a "difference" to the client or group who may come to an agency full of own problem or need or intent, and full of projection that the agency will or will not be well disposed and helpful to them. The introduction by the worker of who he, as agency, really is and what he can and cannot be or do in relation to them and their problem or purpose helps them to take account in a fresh and more responsible way of themselves as separate from the outside. It also gives them something to struggle with and against, to try to control and to yield to, and so to develop new and more effective ways of dealing with the outside, of relating to others, of becoming responsible for their own selves, and their own will, and, through their experience of ending with worker and agency, of managing on their own.

Agency function requires the worker's use of all the resources of the agency and all the resources of the community, medical, psychiatric, educational, recreational, economic, religious. These resources are not only made available by the worker but it is a part of his skill that they will be made available, as appropriate to any need expressed for which there is community resource, at a time and in a way that gives them the best possible chance of being used.

In relation to the kind of situation just described (child placement) the individual judgment of the worker and the resources and structure of the agency will determine whether the placed child having severe problems in growth (and this is increasingly true for most placed children) shall be offered a sustained period of psychological help by his caseworker. This help necessitates something over and beyond skilled social casework help of a placement worker. It may require therapy made available by his caseworker, a group therapy experience made available by the agency, the help of a psychiatrist on the agency staff, or referral to a community clinic, toward freeing him to get on with his growth and to use the months or years of his being a placed child to do it.

No agency is limited to a single primary method for the accomplishment of its purpose. Increasingly, social agencies whose primary method has been social casework are seeing and making use of the possibilities in group process, in working with families, and in multiple client interviews. It is within this context that work with groups is being instituted on an ever-increasing scale as a part of a child-placement agency's service and as one of its established methods for accomplishing its purpose. So work with groups of foster parents, long used by child-placement agencies, is becoming increasingly effective for achieving agency purpose as the dynamics in use of group process is increasingly well understood and provided for by the agency, and used as skill in group work method, or, more properly in this instance, adaptation of group work method.

Not only does use of agency function introduce a focus, a partialization, a difference which serve as a dynamic in the worker-client relationship and which the client may and often does use for psychological growth of great depth and pervasiveness, but it assures social accountability as well. For whatever reasons it came into existence, so long as an agency continues to exist and to receive public support through tax monies, voluntary contributions or, both, it can be assumed that it is fulfilling a needed social purpose for which the public is willing to pay. Obviously the public wants the service for which it is paying carried out with the greatest possible skill and efficiency. Use of agency function or purpose to provide content and give direction to worker activity assures that society is getting what it is asking for and paying for in the way of a particular social service.

Certainly it is true that agencies outlive their usefulness, that community conditions and social needs change, and that patterns of social agencies and social resources change, and should change. It is also true that boards and staffs of agencies may develop vested interests and, sometimes without conscious intent, struggle to keep an agency alive because of their personal investment in it rather than because it is a vital and currently needed social resource. The responsibility of social work in these instances is to assess continuously the needs for change within a community's total pattern of social services and within a single agency. Here social work makes its contribution through constituting staff of planning agencies under both public and voluntary auspices, and staff of licensing and certifying groups. And here each social worker has an obligation to assess continuously his own service agency from his own vantage point, as worker within it, and to share his findings through appropriate channels toward his agency's change, expansion, or decease in line with the public interest—the interest of *all* the public. What is spoken for here is evolutionary change achieved through the use of social work method, in respect to the forms, the institutional forms, through which social work is practiced, rather than revolutionary change achieved through revolutionary methods which seek to "smash this sorry scheme of things entire and then rebuild it nearer to the heart's desire."

There is no intent to minimize the problem in such evolutionary change or to deny the existence of the conflict of interest, the struggle for power, the overlapping and duplication of presently existing social services, and the uncovered, the insufficiently covered, the poorly covered areas for service, the lag between identification of social need and provision of social resource to meet it. However, change that comes from within as a result of starting where an agency is or where the community is, and working with disciplined social work skill to accomplish a deeply felt social work purpose of adequate and adequately administered social service for all the people, is here set forth as the most sure way for achieving a change that can be lasting and that is the "peoples' own," through their own choice and responsible action.

So long as agencies continue to exist as the primary media for social work practice, it is not only possible but also essential to use that fact as opportunity for increasing the accountability and effectiveness of the service offered. To deplore or ignore or minimize the significance of the social agency as the medium for social work practice is to distort social work's purpose and lessen its helpfulness.

The use of agency function as a generic principle of social work practice is as true for group-serving agencies, within which group work method is the primary method for making the service available, as it is for those agencies within which casework is the primary method. Just as work with groups is becoming increasingly a part of agency service once carried primarily through social casework, so work with individuals, a part of group-serving agency programs since their beginnings in the early settlement house movement, is becoming an increasingly effective part of the service of such agencies. It becomes effective, in large part, as "work with individuals" is established, seen, and practiced in relation to the agency function being discharged, and in appropriate relation to the primary method of the agency.

Use of agency function then is an integral aspect of skill in the primary processes of social casework, social group work, and community organization. Whatever the primary social work process being employed, it is necessary to ask "To what end? To what *agency* end or purpose is this method being used?" The answer to that question gives focus, content, direction to what is being done, and, in the ways described for the process of social casework, assures social accountabliity and furthers the psychological effectiveness and usableness of the service being made available.

Use of agency function is effective as well for the secondary processes. Supervision and administration, for example, are inevitably used to accomplish a purpose, and that purpose is some agency's production of service. The social work educator, whether teacher or administrator, is gearing his whole effort to the accomplishment of an educational purpose, the purpose of a school of social work. The researcher who serves a particular social agency or field of practice is making his research available to the end that that agency or that field of practice may use the findings to improve service or, put another way, may more effectively realize its function.

Utilization of agency function as a principle of all social work processes may be thought of and implemented in its richness, its potential of breadth and depth, rather than viewed and offered as a lamentable constriction of help. Lack of imagination and range in any worker can result in a rigid wooden "hewing to the line" that fails truly to realize agency purpose in its potential fullness through failure to see the connection and relevance of the range and depth of content and experiencing possible in any social work relationship whatever its focus. But failure to use this principle consciously and skillfully as an element of helping for which the worker takes responsibility can result in dispersion of effort, want of purpose and direction for the worker, vagueness and lack of forward movement for the clientele, and no assurance to the community that what it supports as purpose is truly being realized.

The multiple-service agency can make as full use of this principle as the single-function agency so long as it is responsible for the several services it is making available and establishes a structure for their administration which makes them most usable. For a worker to work on all fronts or problems at once can be confusing to both worker and client and wasteful of time and energy. It has been suggested that partialization, focus, the introduction of difference, and the "given" of agency purpose and terms of service or requirement are dynamics in the forward movement of social work processes, and that one responsible way of achieving such dynamic is through the use of function as it inheres in a particular service. A client can be both comforted and helped when confronted with a sea of troubles, if he is asked where he would like to start, and is held to some continuity of focus until some resolution of problem is achieved. A total life problem can best be worked on as it manifests itself in a specific life problem; as the specific life problem is met, the gain in capacity to cope with social problem is pervasive for the total self.

While use of agency function is a generic principle in all social work processes and in every field of practice, one of its aspects is that each function, field of practice, or service is recognized as having its own body of knowledge and its own "psychology" which the worker must make his own and integrate in his helping skill as he moves from field of practice to field of practice.

No school of social work can prepare any student with all he needs to know and all he needs to have as skill to practice with equal effectiveness in any and all fields. But it *can* hope to graduate him in possession of a general body of knowledge, possessed of a skill characterized by the use of certain general principles of action which he has developed within some specific field, and with a commitment which includes a commitment to make his own what he must of new knowledge and skill as he moves from one function to another. What is essential is his recognition that there is something new to be learned and, in a sense, to become for every field which can improve his effectiveness in the use of those principles which are generic to all fields and processes.

As was suggested in Chapter 6, applying to a public assistance agency *feels* different from applying to adopt a child, and both feel different from going to a group serving agency for leisure time activity or from being on probation, or seeking marital counseling, or working with professional staff to achieve some community objective. Just as there is a certain "psychology," a constellation of feelings and attitudes within which each individual client develops those unique for himself in respect to every field of practice, so is there a certain *worker* psychology or constellation of feelings and attitudes within which each *worker* develops his own psychology for every service.

It is the responsibility of the worker to understand what these two psychologies are, for the other and for himself, in general for a given field of practice, and specifically in a given situation, and to be responsible for his own "psychology" and responsive to the "psychology" of the other. It is the responsibility of the worker as well to make his own the very substantial specialized body of knowledge he will need to master as he moves from field to field—knowledge in all the traditional social work areas: social policy and services, human behavior and the social environment, and appropriate adaptation of social work method.

Use of function in professional role is as significant for effective social work practice as use of agency function, and for the same reasons of psychological effectiveness and accountability, in this case accountability to agency as well as to community. An assumption is being made here that a professional social worker is accountable as a professional person to society, which the profession purports to serve, and to his own professional group. That accountability includes his subscription to his profession's code of ethics, for example as established by his professional membership organization, which is binding on him as an individual. It includes, as well, a responsibility for the continuing development and use of professional knowledge and skill and a specific accountability to whatever agency constitutes the institutional medium or form for his practice. Through his accountability to agency, he is accountable, again, to society, which supports the profession through supporting the institutionalized forms for its practice.

It is imperative for every social worker, whatever his role, whether caseworker, group worker, or community organizer, supervisor, administrator, researcher, or teacher, to possess what he must in knowledge and skill to carry that role in all its *specificity* of purpose and method, as well as through the use of principles which are generic to all process roles, as they are here being developed. The richness and helping potential of every role is most fully realized as the worker stays with what his role is in the particular situation. Here again, not only is accountability assured, with the employing agency knowing that a supervisor is supervising, a caseworker is practicing casework, a group worker is practicing group work, a teacher is teaching, but the person or persons served meet something stable and steady in role to which they can relate, against which they can struggle, from which they can take, as they find their own way toward the accomplishment of their own purposes within the purpose of the agency.

An administrator who fails to grasp the essential meaning of being an administrator in that role's responsibility for embodying the whole of a service, and for furthering the continuous contribution of the several parts of an agency in relation to each other and in relation to the purpose of the whole, will fail to realize his full potential as an administrator, no matter how effective he may be in his use of isolated "techniques" of administration. And, as is true for the use of agency function, not only must he possess the knowledge and skill (in distinction from *skills*) of the administrator, but he must also understand the psychology of "being an administrator" and the psychology of "being administered" and be responsible for the one and responsive to the other. Many an administrator, as has been earlier suggested, has foundered on the rocks of having to be liked, of being psychologically unable to carry the difference and separation his role necessarily imposes. The resultant attempt to be "one of the boys," in feeling and nature of responsibility carried, inevitably lessens his effectiveness as administrator.

Whatever the method or process role carried by a given worker at a given time, he can learn to use it knowingly, skillfully, with relatedness to those he serves, and through taking responsibility, as part of his professional skill, for any problem his particular functional role may create for the other. It is possible in carrying agency function, and the professional role function to *be* that function, be *only* that function, and be *fully* that function. Only so may the richness in use of functional role and in use of agency function be truly realized.

Attention was give in Chapter 2 to the nature of the several processes, both primary and secondary. The specifics in the process roles carried are determined by the particular purpose of the role (for example, for the primary processes, the purpose of a caseworker, a group worker, a community organizer, as it inheres in the process itself and not in any specific field of practice or agency function) and by the particular configuration of relationships involved. The same principle holds true for the secondary processes. The specific purpose of the process role, and the configuration of relationships involved, both affect and determine the worker's role, for example, for the supervisor, administrator, researcher, teacher.

One of the aspects of the generic principle related to the use of functional role is that each role must be appreciated and understood and utilized in all its complexity and specificity if its full potential is to be realized. Every social worker has the responsibility for learning and becoming what he must as he moves from process role to process role. To think of social work method as "the same" for all of the processes, both primary and secondary, is as fallacious and impoverishing for practice as to think of practice in all fields as "the same." However, the more fully and deeply generic principles of social work method (including the use of distinctive functional roles) are grasped, the more readily the social worker can move from method to method, making his own what he must to carry the new role responsibility.

PRINCIPLE IV

A conscious, knowing use of structure as it evolves from and is related to function and process introduces "form," which furthers the effectiveness of all the social work processes, both primary and secondary.

Dictionary definitions [5] of *form* may be helpful in clarifying what is intended here:

the peculiar configuration by which (an object) is recognized (by sight or touch); the outward or visible shape; established or prescribed method; hence an established or conventional rule of observance, procedure or practice, orderly arrangement, symmetry, shape; style or manner of expression as opposed to inherent qualities. . . .

Definitions of structure include "a combination of related parts; the arrangement and organized union of parts in a body or object; specific mode or way in which anything is made or put together"; and (in reference to rhetoric) ". . . in such a way as to bind all the members into some compact whole." Definitions of structureless may be equally helpful, for example, "devoid of arrangement or correlation, amorphous."

Structure or form in each of the social work processes should arise from the process itself, and serve to channel, contain, and make that process effective toward the realization of some agency function or purpose.

Time itself may be used to give form or rather calls for the development of form and structure in order that its potential may be realized (see Principle II). If the importance of *beginning* is appreciated, appropriate structure for beginning will be devised and utilized. Not only will the content of a first interview or a first group meeting or a first class session or a "first" in any of the processes be structured, in part by the fact that it is a "first" with due attention given to that fact in the content of what is done, but also the very *form* for beginning will be given attention. Is it preferable to begin with a group by seeing the leader of the group, the president, before a group meeting? Why? What about? What will it do to the process? Is this structure for beginning the same for all group work beginnings, for certain kinds of group beginnings? Different in each instance? Is it better in working with a marital problem to see husband and wife together for the first interview, or separately, and what is the desirable pattern for the succeeding interviews which constitute, taken together, the beginning phase of the process? Can *anything* be established as a most effective form for starting in this kind of situation? or is "every situation different," calling for something different in the form required for meeting it? What is the pattern for beginning a school year in a school of social work? What groups of faculty, students, board, committees need to be called together? When, in what relation to each other, in order to make getting the school year under way most effective? What is the content of those meetings as it is related to their being "first meetings?"

A myriad of forms conduce to beginnings: application forms, intake forms, registration forms for each of the processes. What "pieces of paper" are necessary to starting, and what should be their content and use? For every process it is necessary to establish a pattern, to continue, to sustain the process through a form, a series of meetings or conferences or interviews or sessions in such configuration, frequency, and overall duration as seem most likely to conduce to the realization of a particular purpose through a particular process.

Sometimes "time structure" inheres in the situation. A class term is so many weeks long, by university definition. Then how can this *fact* of duration be utilized as a pattern, as form, with a sense of and response to the shifting movement to which the known fact of duration conduces? If a teacher misses a class session, if a client or a worker misses a scheduled interview, if some circumstance interferes with the regular scheduled meeting of a group, the skilled worker knows that that break in the process, the disruption of the form, must be taken into account and dealt with in subsequent interviews, meetings, or sessions. Every experienced teacher knows how hard it is to "get back in the swing" after a break occasioned by vacation or other interrupting factor has interfered with the rhythm of the whole. The time form contains, holds, keeps something going by its very "fixity," by its regularity. Where there is no time form inherent in the situation, it must be introduced—for example, by suggesting a series of interviews, sessions, or meetings leading to an appropriate ending or to a time for stocktaking as a help for continuing.

As endings near, again it is necessary to develop the form appropriate to maximize their meaning. Structures for ending include setting the ending or identifying an ending which is imminent. The actual *content* of the ending, what is talked about, response to, and even, as appropriate, elicitation of feeling about the ending—all are instances of form introduced by the time factor of ending. Structures for ending include as well development and use of such forms for ending as evaluation forms of various kinds, as appropriate for various processes and agency purposes, ending letters, and ending interviews or sessions or meetings. Perhaps enough has been said to suggest that the conscious use of form or structure to facilitate process includes awareness of time as one factor giving rise to and occasioning the development and use of appropriate form.

Place constitutes a kind of form and *gives* form to the several processes as well. Although a caseworker knows that an interview can be held "anywhere"—in a car, on a street corner, in the client's home, as well as in an office—and that circumstances will suggest the most effective place in the individual instance, he knows too that holding a series of interviews in the same office can itself conduce to a stability, a form, a structure, which makes the interviews more usable by the client. Indeed when the place of an interview (which is one in a series of interviews) is changed, backward movement in the casework process may result. Certainly, as a part of helping skill, the fact of the change needs to be noted in the interview as an aid to the client in taking in and encompassing the shift. Similarly a group finds value in having the same meeting room and may evidence confusion and loss of forward movement as a group if the meeting room is changed from session to session. It is not only administratively necessary for classes in a school of social work (or any school) to meet in the same room week after week or day after day, it is psychologically and educationally helpful as well. Old classrooms may be recalled with a variety of feelings as the *place* where so much happened, and the very fact of its being the *same* place for the entire process has often helped it to happen. So an agency conducts its business in a certain building, and if a move to a new building is contemplated, not only must account be taken of the suitability of the new structure (form) to the undertaking but a process also established for moving into and adjusting to the strange place.

Place, as structure, needs not only to hold steady but also to be suited to the undertaking, the function to be discharged. For the student entering on field work in the agency or for the worker coming newly to an agency, the place, the office, where he will work has importance. The desk and the other pieces of physical structure need to be planned and valued for their appropriateness to the process being engaged in, and as constituting an element of form which makes the operation possible. Writers often return to the same place to do their writing, sit in the same chair, use the same typewriter or pen. These various elements of structure, including the structure of place, through remaining constant, can further the flow of the process.

Policy itself serves as structure and gives form to an undertaking. Once policy is established through an orderly process, and with the intent of making more effective the carrying out of some agency purpose, it gives form to the particular undertaking and avoids the inequity and chaos which could result from lack of policy. Policy is designed to assure an operation that always works the same in like situations and that carries the intent of the program in its design. It embodies the comfort and accountability of a form, a structure, on which the community, the worker, and the client can rely. It constitutes a given, a known, a something concrete and real which the client or group can grapple with, something which will hold steady and hold still and so facilitate the client or group's own movement in relation to it, in doing something with it.

From the establishment of policy flows the development of procedures, or specific methods, ways of implementing policy. Policies require constant scrutiny and evaluation, testing in the crucible of actual operation. As agency purposes are modified, policies must be modified to carry the changed purpose. Similarly, procedures need constant evaluation. They may be too many, too few, inoperable for one reason or another, overelaborate. They may actually impede the process they were designed to further.

Agency function influences form and gives rise to the development of structure for making a particular kind of service available, as suggested in Principle III. The configuration of relationships implicit in each of the social work processes itself constitutes a form which can be utilized well or poorly.

Structure or form of any kind, *time, place, policy, agency function, relationship configuration,* may be used rigidly, woodenly, without imagination, without a sense or appreciation of its potential significance for the conduct of the process it is designed to further, or of its relationship to the purpose of the particular undertaking, comprehended as a whole. Skill in the development and use of form or structure requires that it be employed in quite another way, with full comprehension of its necessity, with wisdom in its employment, and with constant testing and modification in the interest of its effectiveness for making a service available in a helpful way. Too much form can stifle creativity and result in working from the book, with the own self and opportunity for the new and emergent left out or minimized. But too little form or absence of form can be wasteful of effort, lead to purposelessness, disorganization, confusion, amorphousness, or outright chaos.

What is suggested here is that acceptance of the use of form and structure as a principle of practice for all the social work processes can lead to its imaginative development and productive employment as a required element in social work skill.

PRINCIPLE V

All social work processes, to be effective as processes in social work, require the use of relationship to engage the other in making and acting on choices or decisions as the core of working toward the accomplishment of a purpose identified as own purpose, within the purpose of the service being offered.

The common phrase used to describe this generally accepted principle is "helping people help themselves." All the principles described in this chapter come to focus in this central and final one. All are designed to further what is here established as the essential generic core of social work practice in all its processes, both primary and secondary—the engagement of the other through the use of a relationship process in working toward an own social purpose.

This principle is operative only if the psychological base established in Chapters 4 and 5 is accepted. This base sees the individual as chief actor in his own life, creator as well as creature, actuated by inner purpose, biological and psychological, to "become," *able* to become, and able to use a relationship to become, to make, and to act on choices or decisions throughout all his days.

It is operative as well only as the process base for practice, as established in Chapter 7, is accepted. It is this understanding which makes possible the development of skill in engaging the other in a continuing human interaction, which has duration, which has direction at the same time that it is "open-ended," and through which the other discovers in the very course of the process what he wants to do and can do in his own behalf. And it is operative only as the social base as vested in agency function and as developed in Chapter 6 is affirmed. It is agency function which defines and focuses the particular social purpose toward the realization of which the other is engaged.

The nature of "engagement" requires some elaboration here. It characterizes all the processes in social work from beginning to end. It is as true in beginning, in establishing diagnosis, as it is in ending. This is not to imply, for the process of social casework, for example, that everything the social caseworker does is in immediate relationship with the person or persons served. The worker may bring about change in the environment, may enlist and utilize community resources in addition to the resources of his own agency, but everything he does has its focus in releasing the client to use himself and his situation as it is, as he makes it different, as the worker makes it different toward the fullest possible realization of own individual and socal potential, in respect to the problem of immediate concern.

Similarly, in social group work, the central focus is to engage the group in accomplishing some social purpose as a group, and to engage individual members of the group in using the group experience for their own development as individuals who are social, in respect to whatever content or program is appropriate to the organization within which the group service is being made available. When the group process is used in an agency which does not have as its central purpose "service to groups," when, in other words, the agency is not a group-serving agency, the engagement is not of the group as a group, but of the individual group members, in using the group experience toward whatever purpose led to its formation. For example, social work service in hospitals for the mentally ill may include work with groups of patients as a way of helping individual patients use a group to work toward their discharge from the hospital, get ready to leave the hospital.

In community organization process, the principle of engagement is applicable in all programs including programs of community development. The Economic Opportunity Act requires the "maximum feasible participation of residents and areas and of persons served." [6] In community organization processes, personnel other than social workers, such as physical planners, city planners, and others, may be employed to assist in "planning social change." The social worker's unique contribution as community organization worker is vested in his skill in enlisting the participation, "engaging," the individuals and groups who comprise the community in finding their own connection with what is being planned; in contributing to the planning; and in implementing the plan. Here the focus is *more* on the community welfare goal or task to be accomplished and *less* on their personal development as individuals who are social, or their increased ability to function as part of a group whether as leader or member, or on helping groups achieve desirable purposes as groups for the meaning the experience can have for the members, although these may be and often are by-products of the process. But it is the community organizer's understanding of what is involved in helping individuals and groups mobilize and use inner and outer resources for a constructive social purpose which is at the heart of his skill.[7] A social plan for a community, developed without its participation and superimposed on it for its "good," ignores the human factors involved in social change and is less likely to accomplish its social purpose fully and with lasting results than one which takes into account and utilizes the *human* resources for social change which inhere in the members of the community themselves. Community organization which is focused on the coordination of social resources and the development of new resources again requires the participation, the engagement of individuals, groups and organizations in effecting the change through their own efforts, with the assistance of the community organization worker.

The principle of engagement is operative in the process of supervision as the supervisee is helped to identify his own stake in "being supervised" and to enter into and use the relationship with his supervisor (and with a group of supervisees if that is the process being used) to achieve ends important for him as a professional person, for example, the continuous refinement of his professional skill, the capacity to function productively, contributively, responsibly as a member of an agency staff. The agency purpose in providing supervision is steadily maintained, that is, to assure a base of service for which the agency as agency can be accountable in coverage and quality, and to foster the continuous improvement of the skill through which the agency's services are made available, and of the agency form, structure, policy for administering them. But the essence of supervisory skill lies in its engagement of the supervisee in moving, functioning, developing, learning out of an *own* motivation, and through the use of *own* feeling, thinking, willing resources. In other words, the essence of supervision as a process is its engagement of the supervisee in affirming and acting on his own stake in the process of being supervised, as it connects with the agency's stake in requiring it.

The administrator's whole intent is to engage the many others whose total work comprises the agency undertaking, in finding and acting on their own stake in their job, in their performance as individuals and as members of groups such as staff, professional and clerical, board, board and staff committees, and others. The well-known word *Posdcorb* [8] in listing the responsibilities of an administrator fails to grasp engagement of others toward realization of common purpose as the unifying focus and core of an administrative process. The word *enabling,* as suggested in Chapter 3, leaves out the concept of the administrator, the executive, as head-end leader, in a way that the concept of engagement need not. The term *intervention* fails to embody the concept of another being involved in an enterprise that is characterized by both mutuality and direction. It is the administrator's skill in the *engagement* of others in a common undertaking which is focal in the success of the undertaking. Every part and party to the operation is "engaged" by the administrator, through appropriate channels, in making creative contribution to the total effort, out of an own affirmed stake in it, because of the opportunity within it for his own personal-professional development and for the achievement of an agency purpose with which he is identified. Administrative skill characterized by this kind of engagement not only elicits everyone's best effort for the common undertaking but also tends to assure stability of staff. Personnel are slow to leave an operation whose purpose they have affirmed as significant and identified as their own, and where their own fulfillment and professional development are consistently furthered.

The necessity for engagement is no less real for the researcher who serves a social agency. In helping an agency develop and conduct a research program, the social work researcher cannot limit himself to drawing up a design for getting the facts, and summarizing findings, if he is concerned about the social usefulness of what he is doing. As a *social work* researcher he makes use of the generic principle of engagement to help the staff connect with the research project, identify their own stake in it, find a way to participate in it and to use the findings. This calls for the researcher's use of himself in a relationship process marked by engagement of others in a social work (research) process.

The teacher in a school of social work who has knowledge to impart and skill to develop is responsible for testifying to learning, its quality, and whether in the particular instance it is enough, but central in his own process skill as teacher in class or in field is his capacity for engagement of the student in learning, for furthering the student's capacity to act on his own interest and will-to-become, for his own sake, rather than purely or primarily to satisfy the school's requirements.

Teaching method is characterized by skill in engaging as well as in imparting. And the adviser in a school of social work directs his whole energies to freeing the individual student to take hold positively of his own will to learn and to become a professional social worker, through working with him on what is standing in the way of what he needs to know or experience for a fuller engagement of himself in learning.

Engagement of the other in using his own powers to work on his own problem or intent, through making and acting on choices or decisions, can be identified as central in all the processes of social work. But what specifically makes it possible?

How does it take place? What *in method* accomplishes it? Identifying a purpose, as it inheres in agency purpose, discovering with the other whether it is or can become his own purpose for himself, whether he can *choose* it as purpose, facilitating the expression of the other's own purpose for himself, clarifying both what the other is saying and asking and what is available in agency and community recourse to meet expressed need or intent, questioning to develop further mutual understanding of problems and choices for solution, identifying conflict or ambivalence for the other to resolve, introducing facts or information which may be useful, eliciting and responding to thinking and feeling as appropriate to the situation and the particular phase of the helping process—a whole array of "techniques" is useful to further true engagement of the other in working on his problem or intent in relation to a mutually affirmed purpose. Indeed, the use of all the principles previously developed is necessary for furthering productive engagement of the clientele served toward the accomplishment of own purpose, through the use of own effort and power, with the worker's help, made available through a relationship process.

The significance of *choosing,* of making and acting on decisions for affirmation of, and development of, capacity for responsible action, is developed with penetration by Faatz in *The Nature of Choice in Social Casework,* to which reference has been made.

The role of feeling and response to feeling in furthering productive engagement is generally accepted as primary in the practice of social casework and perhaps to a somewhat lesser degree in social group work. Always, in both processes, such expression is in relation to client or group feeling, thinking, understanding, planning, decision making, and acting on decision, with respect to some social purpose. Feeling and thinking occur and are utilized in changing balance in the individual instance and, as between situations, in all the processes. It is through the relationship with the caseworker, to illustrate through reference to one of the processes, that the client discovers his own self, his own feeling, his own willing, as he takes back some of his projection on the worker and on others in his life situation, with the worker's help, and as he identifies with the worker and so makes some of *The Worker's* quality as a person, *The Worker's* strength for coping, his own. His discovery entails not just (and sometimes very little) intellectual assessment of what he is like in theoretical terms, but it always involves an *experiencing* of what he is like in the situation with the worker, for a surer possession of a more developed and a more affirmed self. This knowing, experiencing, possessing the self occur in relation to what he and the worker are working on together, in his own life situation as well as in relation to the worker. As he leaves the casework situation it is a "new self," a more courageous and able self, within its own pattern, which he takes, as it has emerged through work as a whole self on a limited situation or problem. It is this new and whole self which is available for subsequent living in the variety of relationships and situations he will encounter.

In processes other than social casework and social group work, that is, in community organization and in the secondary processes, response to feeling and eliciting of feeling may play a secondary, even a minor, part in relation to eliciting of thinking, response to thinking, and putting in what can move thinking and decision-making forward. But it is never absent from the process if engagement of the other in a relationship process toward some social purpose is accepted as central in identifying the process as a process in social work. For unless the engagement is more than purely intellectual, the whole man, or the whole group, is not in full possession of itself for choosing, acting, learning. Thinking can be distorted and forward movement checked in any of the processes by failure to appreciate and engage with feeling. For example, if a new housing development is coming into an area, residents need help not just in thinking what the new development will mean to the community and to them as part of the community, and what they choose to do about it, but in feeling and expressing the feelings that are aroused as a base for clearer thinking and more appropriate action, lest there result what Bertha Reynolds [9] once referred to as "ill-timed explosions, inappropriately directed."

A research project may not get off the ground until the projected participants have a chance to express what they feel about having their work studied, with a sense of having those feelings understood. In every process in social work, marked as it is by engagement of the other in a process of human relationship, feeling as well as thinking interchange is involved. Skill in the worker's use of himself in any of the processes asks for self-awareness and self-discipline of a very high order, for the worker is part of the relationship and responsible for his part in it. It asks also for capacity to lend the self to the other, to be there for the other, to make a "gift of the self for the other" [10] with professional concern and human compassion as well as with knowledge and skill in the technical aspects of making a service available through some social work process. What the worker puts in, how he puts it in, and when he puts it in to advance the process call for judgment in the individual instance.

Use of the five principles of social work process, taken together and in their inter-relationship, constitutes for each of the processes a helping skill whose character is determined partly by the configuration of relationships involved, and by the purpose of the specific process, partly by the purpose of the service (agency) and the use of the structure and social resources it entails, and partly by the phase of the process in which the worker and the other are engaged.

Each social work process is distinctive and is unique both in the way it makes use of the generic principles which have been described and in its requirement of use of additional principles specific to and appropriate for the particular process. As was earlier suggested, it is immediately apparent that description and analysis of any one of the processes would require its own volume. For each a whole array of "techniques" or "skills" are involved, but in this writing those "skills" are viewed not as discrete entities, a "repertoire of interventive acts," but as integral parts of a process that has unity and wholeness and is directed toward a central purpose which inheres in the process, and in the purpose of the agency within which it is being used. Each process, for all its difference and uniqueness, is identifiable as a process in social work through its use of generic principles of practice common to them all.

SUMMARY

Five principles for the practice of social work in all its processes have been developed. They are:

Principle I. That diagnosis, or understanding of the phenomenon served, is most effective for all the social work processes which is related to the use of the service; which is developed, in part, in the course of giving the service, with the engagement and participation of the clientele served; which is recognized as being subject to continuous modification as the phenomenon changes; and which is put out by the worker for the clientele to use, as appropriate, in the course of the service.

Principle II. The effectiveness of any social work process, primary or secondary, is furthered by the worker's conscious, knowing use of time phases in the process (beginnings, middles, and endings) in order that the particular potential in each time phase may be fully exploited for the other's use.

Principle III. The use of agency function and function in professional role gives focus, content, and direction to social work processes, assures accountability to society and to agency, and provides the partialization, the concreteness, the "difference," the "given" which further productive engagement.

Principle IV. A conscious, knowing use of structure as it evolves from and is related to function and process introduces "form," which furthers the effectiveness of all the social work processes, both primary and secondary.

Principle V. All social work processes, to be effective as processes in social work, require the use of relationship to engage the other in making and acting on choices or decisions as the core of working toward the accomplishment of a purpose identified as own purpose, within the purpose of the service being offered.

While these principles characterize all social work processes, and, used in concert, identify them as processes in social work, there are specifics involved, too, for each of the primary processes and for each of the secondary processes. The worker who moves from process to process must make his own what the specific process requires in knowledge and skill if he is to be truly effective, just as he must make his own what is necessary in specific knowledge and skill as he moves from field of practice to field of practice, from function to function.

The whole emphasis of this book is on the development of principles which are generic in social work method, characterize all social work methods, and establish a commonness for method in social work just as truly as a commonness in social work purpose can be established. But it has been emphasized that to try to develop a social work method in the large, which can be taught, learned, and practiced as such, obscures the differences which a specific purpose as it inheres in a specific method and in a specific configuration of relationships introduces, and so impoverishes what is done. However, the more fully and deeply the generic principles of social work process are grasped, the more readily the social worker can move from process to process and make his own what he must to be effective.

9 GENERIC PRINCIPLES OF SOCIAL WORK METHOD IN SOCIAL CASEWORK

BECAUSE social casework as method is practiced in agencies differing widely in specific purpose, with clients of all ages and all degrees of physical and emotional health and of intellectual capacity, of diverse nationality backgrounds, races, creeds, economic and social statuses or conditions, faced by a great variety of problems, it is impossible to select a single case record which could be considered typical of the practice of social casework, if "typical" refers to a "kind of client" or to a kind of problem or to the nature of a specific service. However, it is possible to select a piece of material typical of the *method* used. The judgment of the social worker is always required to adapt the method appropriate to the particular service being offered to a particular client, faced by a particular problem.

The record material used in this chapter and in Chapters 10 and 11 was chosen to illustrate the way the generic principles of social work method, as developed in Chapter 8, manifest themselves in actual practice. It is not possible to show work in process detail and at the same time of any considerable duration, for any of the three primary processes within the purpose of this writing. Nor did it seem desirable to attempt illustration of the way generic principles of social work method manifest themselves in the secondary processes through specific case illustration. What has been presented represents not a blue-print but, as has been said, a frame of reference within which social work method may be examined and developed in depth for all of the social work processes, primary and secondary, in their common characteristics and in the ways in which they are distinctive.

An illustration of social casework method, which in use becomes an illustration of social casework process, follows in this chapter. Approximately three months of after-care service to a former patient in a hospital for the mentally ill is presented in "Miss Amy Devlin Lives Outside." The record, as excerpted by the worker, is here reproduced in its entirety for the period covered. The discussion which follows suggests how each of the generic principles previously developed is manifest in the service given.

This is not a "completed case" but covers a sufficient length of time (2½ months, 7 interviews) to serve the purpose for which it is being used.

MISS AMY DEVLIN LIVES "OUTSIDE"

Miss Amy Devlin, now 29 years old, was admitted to the State Hospital in 1950, at age 16, from another state hospital, where she had been a patient since she was 8 years old. The diagnosis upon admission was: Primary Behavior Disorder.

Her family had consisted of her parents and seven brothers and sisters. A twin sister and one of the other children were said to be mentally defective. Her twin had been committed to an institution for mental retardates when Miss Devlin was first sent to a state hospital. The home was described as being in poor condition and all the children as neglected, physically as well as emotionally. Fourteen different agencies in the community, including the court and child protective agencies, had worked with this family. Miss Devlin, prior to her first hospitalization, had attempted to burn down her family home on two occasions.

During the patient's first hospitalization in 1943–50 her parents wrote that they would visit or take her home, but they rarely fulfilled any promises and visited infrequently.

On admission to State Hospital, Miss Devlin was fearful, anxious, tearful, appeared younger than her stated age. During the early part of her hospitalization, she showed evidence of a preoccupation with sex, by exhibitionism, and by writing frequent erotic letters to a brother who had re-established contact with her suddenly. Psychological testing revealed that Miss Delvin had an IQ of 74 (borderline mentally defective).

Efforts at reaching the patient's family during her hospitalization in the hope that they could be helpful to her were not successful. The family resisted all contact from the hospital. When the patient became pregnant as a result of her promiscuity with patients on the hospital grounds in 1953, again no replies were received to our letters to her family. With the patient's consent, the baby was committed to the care of a child-placing agency.

In 1955 a brother of the patient expressed interest in her, and she was granted restricted home visits in his care, until her inability to control her sexual acting-out impulses resulted in loss of these privileges and she had to be detained on the hospital grounds.

For several years, until 1960, the patient's sexual behavior, which included soliciting when she was on her work assignment in the hospital, was the focus of medical attention, until she appeared to have this behavior reasonably under control.

From 1960 through 1962 Miss Devlin was allowed city privileges to go on day visits unattended. She used these privileges often and responsibly. She secured a job at a local nursing home, working there during the day and staying at the hospital at night. After 30 days of a satisfactory beginning adjustment she was presented at the medical staff and released on Trial Visit on 12–11–62, with referral to social service.

1-4-63

The patient arrived at my office as we had arranged by telephone at her place of business on 12–31. Miss Devlin, although 29 years old, presented a very youthful appearance, chiefly because of her hair styling, head scarf, and bobby socks. She was visibly quite tense, and gave me a bright smile. I introduced myself to her as her social worker and remarked that from her chart I understood that her last contact with Social Service was in 1953, quite a long time ago. She answered yes, in a little girl voice. I asked her how she had felt about coming to the hospital today to see me, and she burst out with "I don't need a social worker. I've had enough of people trying to control my life." I said I could appreciate that having a social worker could have this kind of meaning for her. I knew that she had felt "pushed" out of the hospital, which had exerted some control over her for the last 12½ years since her admission. She responded quickly to this, telling me how she was always pushed around. I remarked that she really had no reason to think that I might represent something different for her. "I don't want you to run my life, too. I'm out now, and other people are running my life where I work. I'm an individual. I don't like that," she said.

I told Miss Devlin that I would be offering her a new kind of service if she wanted it. My purpose was certainly not to run her life. I wondered if we could discuss the kind of help that the hospital could now offer her. Miss Devlin said, "I don't want to come back. I've had enough of this place. I did not want to leave, but now that I'm out, I don't want to ever come back." I remarked that she could well feel this way, but things sometimes were not as one-sided as that. She replied that her job was located very close to the hospital. I picked this up and suggested that it could feel comforting to know that she was close to the support of the hospital should she need help. She agreed, and said that many times in the last month she had been out, and she had felt like coming back. Living outside was so new to her and got "pretty scary" at times. "But," I put in, "you have been able to stay out this long. Apparently you have found a way to be happier out in the community." She agreed that she had, and smiled, looking quite proud of herself. We agreed that she had reason to feel proud. It was quite a hard thing to do in the face of so much newness.

I said that as she had learned from me in our phone conversation, we would be discussing the Out-Patient Clinic today, and how she might use it. We talked in detail about how and where the Clinic functioned and what it could offer her now that she was out and feeling well. Part of Clinic Service would be my help as her individual social worker, to assist her with any problems she might have in connection with Clinic, and also to help her in any way she needed in regard to her living situation now.

Miss Devlin said she did not feel that she needed medicine, but, since

Clinic was voluntary, she might try it out. Could she have her former doctor? Her former physician was not on the Clinic service, and the chances were that she would be meeting someone entirely new to her, with whom she would have to make a beginning, as she had with me this morning. How did she feel about my introducing her to someone new? She said she would not like it, and it came out that she was feeling some guilt about having behaved badly toward some of the doctors during her hospitalization, and hoped it would not be one of those. I asked her how much responsibility she could take for her behavior when she was ill, and how she was different in the kind of responsibility she needed to have now. Miss Devlin said she was able to put up with a "lot of stuff" from the people she worked with at the nursing home. She just might be able to put up with a Clinic doctor too. "And with me?" I asked. She said she could if she had to. I remarked that she did not have to at all. If she felt I could help her, she might want a social worker. Her doctor had recommended that she attend Clinic as the best way the hospital knew to help her to remain well. If she needed time to think more about it, I could plan another appointment with her. If not, I was prepared to offer her a Clinic card with her first appointment written on it. Miss Devlin sat in silence for a while, and looked at me and at the Clinic card in front of her. She took the card, and said she thought she might attend Clinic.

We arranged to meet again on 1–25, the date of the first Clinic appointment, and she knew from me that she could telephone me in the meantime, or my supervisor in my absence.

Prior to the interview that followed on 1–25, there had been several telephone calls from the patient and her employers, since Miss Devlin was feeling persecuted in her work situation. My work with them centered around helping them to become more able to talk together about mutual problems, and Miss Devlin decided to discuss this further with me on 1–25. On that date, however, the patient canceled her Clinic appointment because she did not wish to "associate" with the other patients who were also coming to Clinic that day, sharing a taxi because of the transportation strike, and she could not afford to get there by herself. Recognizing that part of this might be her fear of meeting that first appointment with the doctor, I arranged for her to receive her medicine later, but I told her that she would still need to be responsible about keeping the alternative appointment I set up.

1-25-63

Later that morning Miss Devlin arrived unexpectedly after her Clinic appointment had been canceled and her Clinic physician had left. She said that she had been forced to come to Clinic by her employer, who had not understood that we had made alternative arrangements. I said that I could not accept her having been forced to come, wondering where she was in this. Where was the self-assertion that she had shown with me and her employer prior to this? Miss Devlin was able to have a beginning awareness of how she was a willing victim of being "pushed around." She said, "I am twenty-nine years old and everyone treats me like a baby." I valued her being able to say this to me, but she had been responsible for her actions so far in working with me. What did she think about how others see her? She answered that she kept to herself, minded her own business, and wanted no one to bother her. People would not let her alone. I said that this might be all right if she were living by herself and did not need to earn money, but she did have a job, and there were things expected of her. We discussed her feelings about herself, and she was able to agree that she did not give people a chance to understand her with this kind of attitude.

Was she happy in her job? "No. I want to leave that place. I can't stand it." What did she want to do if she left? "I'll just come back to the hospital." I questioned her about this. She had told me in our first interview that she did not want ever to return here. Did she just want to prove to the hospital that she should not have been pushed out? She did not want to return. She wanted to find another job, but she did not know where to look, and did not want to discuss how she might do something about keeping her present job. It was much too late. I helped her to understand that she might at least end responsibly with her employers so that she could use them as future references if necessary. We arranged to meet at my office on 2-8-63 to discuss her use of the job leads I had given her, and how she might make better use of herself on her next job.

1-28-63

I received a telephone call from the patient's employers, who said they were discontinuing her employment as of that day. Miss Devlin had accidentally dropped a bed patient and had become belligerent and defensive, causing quite a turmoil. After confirming with them that they had already let her know she was discharged, I spoke with Miss Devlin on the telephone. She was filled with hostility and had no insight into her part in the situation. She said she would return to the hospital. As we went into her feelings about returning more in detail, Miss Devlin was still able to affirm the gains she had made in her two months of living outside the hospital, and she was not feeling she was in need of care. She responded with interest to my suggestion that she could find another place to live temporarily. She telephoned the manager of a women's residence with whom the agency had good experience, and then she told me she was scared but willing to try it. Because of the transportation strike and her limited amount of money, we arranged that I would transport her there.

During the trip she was frightened, and I said that there was little I could say to minimize her fright. Moving into a new home with all of her belongings, even though she had never seen the place, made her choice very limited, but still she had a choice as to whether she could make use of it at all.

When we arrived, Mrs. Baker, the manager, greeted us warmly, and instinctively put her arm around the patient. I began to prepare to leave shortly after the rent agreements were signed. We arranged that she could telephone me if she needed my help prior to my visit to her one week later, on 2-5, and Mrs. Baker agreed to help the patient to get to the local public assistance office within the next few days to apply for an emergency grant. Miss Devlin seemed to become more comfortable, especially since her moving in was witnessed by other hospital patients whom she knew and who responded to her warmly.

As I was leaving, Miss Devlin ran over to me and said, "Miss F., don't leave me here. I don't like it." As tears rolled down her cheeks, I said I could understand what she was feeling, and it was taking a great deal of courage. However, the only alternative seemed to be a return to the hospital. What did she want? As she firmly held to her desire not to come back to the hospital, Miss Devlin turned from me and said, "I can make it," waving goodbye.

In the next interview with Miss Devlin at her residence on 2-5-63 I found that she had in one week's time made quite a positive impact on others around her. Her little girl appearance and manner of helplessness had quickly won over most of the women around her, and she was enjoying her role. She attempted to manipulate me by asking me to do something about her having to have a different worker at the office of public assistance. Although I appreciated her feeling of confusion and her long standing fear of control, I stood firm on the necessity for her to comply with the conditions of another agency, as she was doing with the hospital, if she wanted help.

2-25-63

The patient arrived at my office as we had arranged, dressed in slacks, jacket, and scarf. I commented that from the way she was perched on the edge of her chair it seemed that she was planning not to stay very long. She answered that she "might not." She had told me in a telephone conversation earlier that the women's residence where she lived had been without a manager for over a week, and she now told me more freely how bad she felt, since the former manager had made her feel so accepted, a rare occurrence for the patient. She did not now like "that place," and there was nothing but trouble for her there. She knew she could move out, but she still preferred to stay.

Miss Devlin talked more in detail about the things she did not like, and one of her concerns was that the men in the neighborhood seemed to know her name. They had been coming into the residence and asking for her, and shouting up to her fourth floor room from the street. As she talked she was able to tell me that she had "innocently" encouraged friendliness of strangers on the street, saying "I have to be civil to people," defensively. I pointed out to her that she was complaining about being bothered on the one hand, and yet was encouraging this on the other. Perhaps she had not realized it, but was this the case? She quickly responded that I was like that "bossy woman" tenant at the residence who was now "running the show." The woman kept accusing her of being a "chippie." She went on to say that the same thing had happened to her on her job at the nursing home. People were always getting the wrong idea about her, blaming her for everything. Whenever there was trouble, an accusing finger was always pointed at her. She had no use for people. Why couldn't they leave her alone? She began to cry silently, but she quickly wiped away the tears.

I said it looked to me as if she was feeling very deeply about this, but the only way I could help her was to point out her own part in these instances and to help her to see what she was doing. She said, "I try to live with other people, but I just can't. I think the only thing left for me to do is to drop dead!" After a few moments of silence I said gently, "Is that all there is left for you?" Miss Devlin answered that it was, and then became very loud, swearing at me and saying "D—— you all you do is nag at me, to get me to say things are my fault! I hate you and this —— hospital. I don't know why I came all the way up here today. What for. You're supposed to be a psychologist or social worker or something, but you don't understand me." She did a very good imitation of my voice, mimicking my concern, in soft tones. Then she looked around her, at the tiled walls of the office, and shouted at the top of her lungs, "Why am I here in this office, in this hospital that I hate so much? I can never escape you. I feel like pressure is pulling me back!" When she was through, I said quietly, "If you feel I can't help you, why don't you just get up and walk out?" She looked at me squarely and broke into a torrent of sobbing which lasted for several minutes.

Afterward I waited for her to speak, and she said, "I think I really do need to come back to the hospital," in a very self-defeated tone. I asked why. Miss Devlin said she just felt it was so hopeless. Still she was able to affirm her own strength in staying out this long, and said explosively she would not return to the hospital. She would make it. She only needed a job. That would make everything all right. I said that she had told me this before. As soon as she could leave her last job everything would be all right, but was it? She answered, "To make it in this world it seems that you need other people, even though you don't want them." I answered that it did seem this way. She said, "I'll let them know how I feel, just like I did with you." I said she had yelled and screamed and called me names today, and maybe she had to, to get anywhere. I could still accept and value her feelings even more for her having been able to do it, but I was still sitting here with her. She had not destroyed me with her anger, but that is what I was there for. Did she think that employers and fellow employees would be able to accept this? She guessed not.

I suggested that perhaps I could be of help to her if she wanted to try to change. Miss Devlin started talking rapidly about what kind of jobs she wanted, but I held her to the fact that she had decided she must do something with herself first. She did not understand. I said that if she would rush into a new job at this point, she would risk losing it. She thought for a moment about this, and said she couldn't take that again so soon.

3-8-63

Miss Devlin arrived for her Clinic appointment, and seemed in good spirits, but quite nervous. Since there were five other patients before her, we asked to be interrupted when the doctor was ready for her, and went to my office. She was going to let her doctor know that she wanted her medicine decreased or discontinued altogether, whichever the physician would agree to. I commented that she seemed to have gained some courage since the last time we had talked about her first Clinic visit. She affirmed this and pulled out an envelope quickly, telling me all she had accomplished since she had last seen me.

Miss Devlin had gone to the Social Security office and received her card, and was able to realize that she had not followed through correctly on her last application. She giggled and looked down, saying it was really her fault all the time. Next she showed me her income tax statement and we discussed how she could obtain a Form 1040 and fill it out. Also Miss Devlin told me that she had no intention of paying her rent this month unless the real estate company corrected the heat and electricity problems she was having. Her requests for help to the current managers, whom she forced herself to communicate with, had been ignored repeatedly. As we discussed this, Miss Devlin said that people out in the community were supposed to help patients like her. She supposed that the owner of the property could be made to be very sorry he had "crossed" her. I explained to her that the owner of the property really had no obligation to help her. If she did not feel satisfied with her living arrangement and he did not make needed adjustments, he probably would give her the choice of remaining or moving, and her threat of not paying the rent might not be as effective as she would like. We discussed how she might try to deal with the managers a little less belligerently, since she did not want to move.

She had followed up an advertisement in the newspaper for a mother's helper and was going to wait another week before telephoning the woman to get a definite answer about being hired. The job was located near the hospital, and she intended to commute from her residence in Center City, even though it was some distance away.

Before we could discuss this further, Miss Devlin said she was going "to college for four years." I was quite surprised at this, and it took some time before she could help me to understand what she meant. She had a habit of making up words as she went along, making it difficult to understand her. She showed me a contract she had signed with a correspondence school for a four-year high school education, having agreed to pay $295.00 for the course, in $10.00 monthly installments. She said that she realized that she could get much further if she could learn to communicate better. I had just prior to this asked her if others had difficulty understanding her, as I did at times, when she seemed to make up new words on the spot. She knew this to be true. The representatives of the school had come to see her and had carefully gone over the agreement with her so that she knew what she was signing. She wanted to do this because she was afraid to go out at night to evening courses at a high school, which I had suggested as a possibility. I asked her how she could afford $10.00 per month, and she told me in detail about how she budgeted her $69.00 public assistance grant so that she had this money left over anyhow. I pointed out that her public assistance grant was supposed to be for living essentials, as far as I knew, and she angrily retorted that what she did with that money was her business, not that of public assistance.

Besides this, she was receiving money from her friends (all male). After some questioning she understood that I was asking her in effect what she was giving these men in return. She promptly denied any involvement with them and said she just asked them out of friendship. "Could this go on until the whole $295.00 was paid up?" I asked. She answered that she would be getting a job soon anyway. When I told her that receiving unreported money from outside sources was also a violation of her grant, she became angry and said they would never know about it unless I, her "social work girl" blabbed to them." I replied that I would not violate her confidence by informing on her, but angry as she was, I still needed to point out to her what her responsibility was so that she could decide more effectively.

In answer to her question as to what was the worst thing that could happen to her if they found out, I said she might wind up in jail and have to find some way of paying back the money to public assistance. She said, "So I'll go to jail. I'll stay there thirty days or whatever, and then come home. I'd rather be in jail than in the hospital." I asked, "Is that how much regard you have for yourself?" She said it was her life! I agreed that it certainly was, and felt that now she understood the consequences fully. She would not be taking this up with her public assistance worker. I said this was up to her.

Aside from all of these new things that were happening to her, I wondered if her living situation had become any more comfortable for her in regard to her interpersonal relations there. She said it had, and said she had reported the men who were bothering her to the police, and then had no more trouble. We talked about how this situation was troubling to her, and she said, "You bring up my friendships with men because you know from my record that I got messed up here in the hospital when I was very young and did not know any better. I can take care of myself now. I'm a girl who likes fun and is pretty, and who likes to give men love. Besides, I'm learning jujitsu from the girls at the residence." I commented that her behavior in relation to men was certainly her own affair if she was feeling no problem with it, but she was very attractive and was dressing seductively. Could she not expect to attract men all the time this way, even the kind she had needed to complain to the police about? She agreed to this, and we were interrupted since the doctor was now ready for her.

When we again got settled in the office, Miss Devlin told me that her next Clinic appointment was for May 31st. The doctor had taken her completely off medicine, as she had requested. They had spent the whole interview, she said, talking about her dealings with men. The doctor had shown her the information in her chart which dealt with her pregnancy during her hospitalization, and this was very painful for her to recall.

Miss Devlin became very angry again, and poured out her feeling about everyone's bringing up her past. She threatened to find a way of destroying her chart, as she had "set fire to [her] parents home when they had crossed [her]."

In trying further to establish in what area she might need my help now, she said, "I don't need help. I'll go out and get a job now, and tell public assitance to ———." Getting a job was not going to be easy for her, I said, to which she took offense. Most of our patients whom I helped were finding it very difficult to get a job. Well, she would show me. "I can get a job right now, before you could; you with your fancy desk and soft words. You're not supposed to upset me. You make me angry and nervous. I'm a patient. You did the same thing to me last time; I don't know why I have to see you again." She told me that Dr. Smith had recommended that she keep seeing me, although she would not be seeing him for about two and a half months, and she did not like this. I said that although this was the doctor's recommendation, she already knew from me that attending Clinic and having a social worker were both voluntary. Did she need help from me now? She thought she might want to discuss getting jobs with me. Rather than have a definite appointment, she asked that we set up a date for her to telephone me and make an appointment, depending on what was happening to her. I agreed to this and set up a time she agreed on, for 3-22.

Since Miss Devlin did not telephone me on 3-22, as we had arranged in our last interview, I telephoned her at her residence on 3-25. She had not called me because she "had no use for me," and asked why I had to bother her now, since all I did was upset her. I let her know that if she no longer wanted my help she could end with me right now, but she might do it more responsibly with me in person. She finally told me she was feeling very upset and was staying in her room, to the exclusion even of meals. She responded to my concern about this, and accepted an appointment at her residence for 3-29.

3-29-63
On 3-29-63 I visited Miss Devlin, and her manner was bright and friendly. I remarked that this was very different from how she was feeling in our telephone conversation, and she told me that she had been very distraught during that week, and had moved out of her residence for two days. Finding loneliness unbearable in a furnished room, she came back. She attributed all this to her being disgusted with herself. Our last interview had "shook her up" so much that she felt she could not go on the way she had before. She had attempted to phone me for help prior to my calling her, but had been unable to reach me or my supervisor.

Lately a number of things had happened to make her situation more favorable. Her brother had telephoned her after a year and a half, and had taken her to meet her twin sister, from whom she had been separated since she was two years old, when the family home had broken up. She had reacted to this meeting with shock, and its impact had been powerful, but she was now looking forward to becoming reunited with some semblance of a family again. She took her sister's institutionalization much for granted and did not care to question why she had been committed to a mental hospital and her sister to a training school. Her brother had offered her money, but she let him know that it was "illegal" for her to accept outside resources while receiving public assistance. She had stopped accepting money from her male friends, letting them know that her "body was not for sale." She had been through enough with her former pregnancy and was not now going to risk disease, pregnancy, or jail. I said I was surprised a little, because her feelings regarding male relationships had changed so much since our last interview. She told me that had been the hardest hour of her life, but she wanted now to be able to "look into the mirror and say to herself, 'Amy, you're all right.'" I said I could respect and value all this was demanding of her, but what of her own needs? She picked this up quickly and said that she had a boy friend who really cared for her, and she could have her needs met in this relationship. In talking about this, she let me know that she all along was protecting herself by buying contraceptives for use with her casual acquaintances, but now she was feeling different. This was not the way to get love. She could derive far more satisfaction with someone whom she really cared for.

Miss Devlin had also telephoned her public assistance worker to reveal that she was using $10.00 per month from her grant for her correspondence course, which she said was now the most important thing in her life. I could appreciate the risk that this involved. But I had misinformed her, and in the light of new information I now had I clarified for her the fact that she could use her assistance grant to meet this expense. The violation of her grant was in the area of accepting money from outside resources. Perhaps she would need to discuss this aspect of it more fully with her worker. She told me that even though she had told her brother of her trust in my not "blabbing to public assistance" what she had told me in confidence, she felt the responsibility herself.

Now that she was no longer accepting money from men, she found it barely possible to get along on her grant, and wanted very much to find employment. She asked if I could help her by telling her where to go in search of a job. I said I could, but questioned whether she was ready for this step. She was able to recall with me how she had refused my help with this before. What was the difference now? She had been hearing from the other residents how jobs were hard to find. I agreed that they were, and put in that finding a job might not be as difficult for her as to hold one. She had been fired from her last job. We discussed her former employment in detail, and I noticed that her defensiveness about this subject had diminished greatly. We looked together for reasons her employers had not accepted her attitude, the reason for her dismissal. As Miss Devlin related each instance of interpersonal friction to me, I ended her sentence with "and then you blew up," to which she agreed. She said she had always been like this, unable to control her temper.

I commented that in our recent telephone conversation it had taken all my self-control to meet her hostility and still want to be of help to her. We had apparently touched on something that was a real problem for her. At that moment someone opened the door to the room and came in, and Miss Devlin took command of the situation by politely asking the woman to wait until we were through. I picked this up with her, asking how she felt about how she had used herself just then. She agreed that she had felt angry but had controlled it. "Why?", I asked. "I owe people some respect," she answered. I asked then if it did seem possible that she was able to have self-control at times? She sat back abruptly and smiled and swore, agreeing with me. I asked her what most frequently made her angry about people and she answered, "When they boss me." I responded to this by asking who was the first person she thought of in a job situation. She quickly said, "The boss." She thought about this for a while and then said, "I thought I hated you, but I don't. You really understand. I need something greater than myself alone, and maybe you can help me." I certainly wanted very much to help her. But she already knew what taking help from me was like. Here I was offering her help with becoming employed, but expecting a lot of work from her, a lot of looking at herself, a lot of headache. Was it worth the effort?

Miss Devlin said, "I want your help. You're my caseworker until I tell you I don't need you anymore, and I need you now. I don't want to sit around here. I'll go crazy and I need a job badly." I said I could help her, but I could make no promises as to how quickly she would find herself ready for an actual job interview. She said she did not care how long it would take and we tentatively reached the time limit of about one month, when we would evaluate our progress. I said I should just let her know that I had only visited her at home this time because she had sounded upset enough for me to do this as an emergency. I knew she disliked coming to the hospital, but after all, I was a hospital worker, and offering her a hospital service. She moved on this to accept an appointment at my office on 4–5, in one week.

As we ended the interview I helped her to review what we had discussed, and she was able to accept responsibility for this swift surge of forward movement with the realization that it was probably still going to be a hard battle for her to work on a pattern that had been her way of coping with life for almost twenty-nine years.

PRINCIPLE I: *That diagnosis, or understanding of the phenomenon served, is most effective for all the social work processes which is related to the use of the service; which is developed, in part, in the course of giving the service, with the engagement and participation of the clientele served; which is recognized as being subject to continuous modification as the phenomenon changes; and which is put out by the worker for the clientele to use, as appropriate, in the course of the service.*

The worker knew a good deal "about" Miss Devlin before she met her. She understood her in quite a different way, and Miss Devlin became a somewhat different person, in the course of service given. The record reveals a young woman, limited intellectually according to recorded psychological test results, with a psychiatric diagnosis of primary behavior disorder, who had lived the last twenty-one of her twenty-nine years in hospitals for the mentally ill, estranged from her family, unable to control her impulsive acting out behavior even within the hospital. A relatively recent (two-year) period of gradually increased opportunity to try herself out in being on her own, including her management of a day job outside the hospital for one month just prior to this referral resulted in her being presented to medical staff and released from the hospital on trial visit, with opportunity to use the clinic for psychiatric help.

It is at this point that the social worker, whose social casework method is being examined, entered the situation. Her purpose, as a hospital clinic worker, implicit in the record, was to see whether social casework (the method used to carry the trial visit service for the hospital in this instance) could help this young woman stay out of the hospital, using the psychiatric service of the hospital clinic, as indicated, and live responsibly, with some measure of personal fulfillment, in the community.

The worker's understanding of the client, or "diagnosis," is at all times related to this purpose, both as she makes her own what is available in the record and as that understanding develops and changes in the course of giving the service. "Diagnostically" she consistently addresses herself to the question, "Can this young woman as she is now, as revealed in what she is doing with me, with the clinic, on the job, in her living situation, in the community, maintain herself outside the hospital with profit to herself and without gross 'danger' to the community?" The worker relates to the further question, what does my present social work diagnosis of her, as she is now, call for in the way of social casework help to facilitate her discovering, with me, whether she wants to and can maintain herself outside?

It should be clear that the worker is not offering treatment for a primary behavior disorder. She is offering a social work service, the service of trial visit, through the method of social casework, toward the achievement of a limited purpose—the purpose of trial visit. The worker is not defeated by what the record has to say about this patient's present capacity, psychiatric diagnosis, and past experience in the hospitals and earlier, although any worker might well have felt defeated by such a "history." She sets no arbitrary limits on what can be expected from "this kind of patient" with respect to capacity for life outside. However, she does take into account, and uses in what she does with Miss Devlin and in how she does it, all that is available of hospital diagnoses, psychiatric and psychological, past history of behavior, family relationships, and present resources in family connections and community services and opportunities. What she knows of the patient helps the worker to be realistic about the kind of living-outside opportunities most promising for this particular client, but the final answer to the question of whether Miss Devlin can "do it" remains with Miss Devlin. It is a question to be answered only in the course of time as she and the worker discover together what it is possible for her to do with the worker's help.

As Miss Devlin, even within the short time covered by the record's span, becomes able to use trial visit service fruitfully, as made available through her relationship with the worker, there is some evidence that a shift in her "total personality" may be taking place, that she is different as a whole person, with changed goals for herself and changed capacity to reach them. This change occurs as a result of the skillful offering of the specific service of trial visit. The worker's social work diagnosis at the end of the three-month period would be different in certain respects from what it was at the beginning of the service, for the client has made it different through what she has done with the worker's help.

There are several points in the record to indicate that the worker's understanding of her is being shared with the client, that Miss Devlin is being helped to understand and evaluate herself—to "catch herself in the act of being human" in relationship with others, on the job, in the residence, with the worker— as the "way she is" shifts and changes.

When Miss Devlin suggests that living outside is new to her and is pretty scary at times, the worker interjects: "You have been able to stay out this long. Apparently you have found a way to be happier in the community." She agrees that she has and smiles, looking quite pleased with herself. This diagnosis of her as a person able to live in the community, this sharing with her of the worker's diagnosis, helps Miss Devlin to possess her own gains and to see herself a little differently, without minimizing the problem, and the remaining question of what is possible for her.

The worker's challenge of her statement (Interview 1–25) that she had been "forced to come to the Clinic by her employer" leads to Miss Devlin's diagnosis of herself and her situation as "I am twenty-nine years old and everyone treats me like a baby." The worker accepts this, and the courage required to say it, but again interjects her seeing another side of Miss Devlin: "She has been responsible for her actions so far in working with me." This helps Miss Devlin to see herself, to understand herself more "wholly" and accurately, and to possess her responsible as well as her immature self.

In the residence to which Miss Devlin goes after her "blow up" on the job, in the nursing home, the worker describes her in the following way: "Her little girl appearance and manner of helplessness had quickly won over most of the women around her and she was enjoying her role." However, the worker does not let herself be drawn into Miss Devlin's pattern of control and manipulation of others through helplessness, but stands firm on the necessity for Miss Devlin to comply with the conditions of another agency (Public Assistance) as she was doing in complying with the hospital's conditions, if she wanted Public Assistance help. In other words, the worker acts on her diagnosis that Miss Devlin is manipulating others and offers her a living and present situation with her (the worker) where that kind of behavior does not work, with the result that Miss Devlin finds she can manage this particular situation (her relation to the Public Assistance agency) in a more responsible way. This kind of help to effect change in Miss Devlin's use of herself derives from the worker's purpose as a social worker, and as a hospital clinic trial visit worker, and from Miss Devlin's own purpose for herself—to become the kind of person who can live outside.

When Miss Devlin complains about being bothered by men, the worker points out to her that she is complaining about being bothered, on the one hand, and encouraging it on the other. This sharing of the worker's understanding of the client for the client to use in understanding herself, as a base for being different (if she wants to be different), leads to an outburst and tirade, and real rechoosing on Miss Devlin's part of whether she wants to live outside the hospital in view of what it asks of her. When the worker points out that she took Miss Devlin's outburst and was not destroyed, that that was what she was there for, but asks whether employers and fellow employees will take it, Miss Devlin guesses not. She gains a new understanding of herself, her part in what happens to her, and what is required of her in responsible behavior.

After the considerable change in her way of life, which Miss Devlin initiates on the basis of wanting to look into the mirror and say "Amy, you're all right," she begins to plan again for employment. She is helped to an understanding of herself as related to her chance of getting and holding a job in the following way (Interview 3-29):

As Miss Devlin related each instance of interpersonal functioning to me (in past employment) I ended her sentence with "and then you blew up," to which she agreed. She said she had always been this way, unable to control her temper—at that moment someone opened the door to the room to come in. Miss Devlin took command of the situation by politely asking the woman to wait until we were through. I picked this up with her, asking how she felt about what she had done just then. She agreed that she had felt angry but had controlled it. "Why?" I asked. "I owe people some respect." I asked then if it did seem possible that she was able to have self-control at times. She sat back abruptly, smiled and swore, agreeing with me.

Here Miss Devlin has a new picture, a new understanding of a new self—a self that is only at the beginning of being new—with recognition that it "is going to be a hard battle for her to work on a pattern that has been her way of coping with life for almost twenty-nine years." What is significant here is that Miss Devlin's experience in being different reinforces her own choice to be different, to be different in a way that means living on the outside, and using the worker's help to do it. "I want your help." She accepts an appointment in the worker's office for the following week.

There are many instances, of which those noted are only a few, of the worker's consistent relating of her understanding of Miss Devlin to the purpose of the service, for example, to help Miss Devlin use trial visit to live outside in the community; of her changing understanding of what Miss Devlin is like as a person as Miss Devlin becomes different in the course of using the service; of her sharing her understanding with Miss Devlin herself, not in technical terms but humanly and simply with warmth and strength, so that Miss Devlin can have that understanding of herself to use toward becoming the kind of person she now wants to be. "My body is not for sale." "Amy, you're all right." What is understood, in other words, is put to immediate use to help.

PRINCIPLE II: *The effectiveness of any social work process, primary or secondary, is furthered by the worker's conscious, knowing use of time phases in the process (beginnings, middles, and endings) in order that the particular potential in each time phase may be fully exploited for the other's use.*

The worker's use of this principle is evident in the way she begins with Miss Devlin and helps Miss Devlin begin with her; in the way she helps her begin in the new living situation; in the way she helps Miss Devlin take increased responsibility for herself and what she is doing in the "middle," in the use of appointments to sustain continuity; in what she puts into the ending of each interview that helps Miss Devlin pull together the gain from the interview and make it her own as a base for going forward.

There might have been a firmer and more defined use of time as structure for the entire process had the worker clarified with Miss Devlin at the outset the duration of the trial visit period, and the frequency of interviews with the caseworker available within it, together with planned periods for review of what had been accomplished. The worker emphasizes the voluntary aspects of the client's use of the clinic service, including the interviews with the worker (good in itself to help her find her own motivation and wanting) but perhaps a little "looser" and with less support in structure than there needed to be.

In beginning with Miss Devlin the worker makes the connection with the earlier experience with social service, ten years before, as a way of helping Miss Devlin find what is new and can be different in this present experience, through asking how she feels about coming to the hospital today. She elicits and accepts the feelings which beginning again with social service stirs up, identifies this as a new kind of service, clarifies what the outpatient clinic service has to offer Miss Devlin, and what her own purpose as a social caseworker is within the overall hospital purpose of extension of its care, "to assist her in any problems she might have in connection with the Clinic and also to help her in any way she needed in regard to her living situation now."

Miss Devlin is helped to begin through the worker's recognition of her ambivalence about wanting to start again with the hospital in a new relationship to it and with the worker, the fear and the wanting, through being specific and concrete about what is being offered, what is voluntary in it, when and where the next interview will be held. Anticipating an ending to the relationship at the time of the beginning with the worker, as it would inhere in the ending of Trial Visit, or at least projecting a time for review along the way, might have helped this client feel less trapped and "permanently connected" with the hospital she was trying to leave. In the interview on 3-29, a time period is used, "about one month," following which there is to be an evaluation of progress in relation to Miss Devlin's readiness to apply for a job.

Continuity is sustained not only by setting a next appointment at the end of each one but also by suggesting a focus or purpose for succeeding appointments. "We arranged to meet at my office to discuss the use of the job leads I had given her and how she might make better use of herself on the next job."

At the time of the move to the new residence (another beginning for the client) the worker helps through not minimizing the fear involved or trying to smooth it over. "I said there was little I could say to minimize this for her. Moving into a new home with all her belongings made her choice very limited, but still she had a choice as to whether she could make use of it at all." What the client is helped to possess here is a sense of herself, as not a helpless pawn of circumstance but as having some power in the new situation, a way of easing her fear of an "outside" she does not know.

The ending of this particular interview calls for skill related to the use of time phases. The fear of the new is stirred up again by the worker's departure. To her tears and pleas not to be left the worker replies with understanding of her feeling and the courage it is taking to meet it, but with a pointing up of the alternative of hospitalization, with the requirement that Miss Devlin choose. In this ending of the interview and in staying in the residence, the client experiences her power—what she can control in the situation (whether to stay or return to the hospital) and what she cannot control.

The worker makes appropriate response at the beginning of each interview by noting how it seems to be for Miss Devlin. At each interview's end there is some summary of what had been accomplished, in order that Miss Devlin may possess her gains more fully, some choice about continuing, the setting of the time, and frequently the focus, for the next interview.

At the end of the interview on 3-8, a date for Miss Devlin to telephone to set an appointment is given, rather than an appointment, "depending on what is happening to her." When the telephone call is not made, the worker calls the residence and goes to see the patient at the residence. This reaching out and flexibility in the time and place of the interview are indicated by the patient's upset and confusion, but the regularity of spaced interviews is again established, once the crisis has passed, as a way of sustaining the process.

At the end of the series of interviews recorded here, as a way of helping her face and meet backslidings inevitable in the weeks and months ahead, there is an attempt to help the patient claim and possess her movement, "the swift surge of forward movement," and at the same time to look at how much she is trying to do. She is trying to "work on a pattern that has been her way of coping with life for almost twenty-nine years."

Within each interview, and particularly marked in 2-25, there is a rhythm, a tentativeness and ambivalence in beginning, a deepening of engagement and intensification of feeling in the middle, and a quieting, a letting up, a moving out, a disengagement, as well as a looking ahead to what comes next, at the end. Characteristically, a total case shows this same rhythm for the case as a whole. In this particular series of interviews the clear climax and turning point occur in the interview of 2-25.

Throughout the recorded interviews runs the worker's recognition of the life process that is Miss Devlin, having continuity, yet permissive of change, of growth within its own pattern, a process into which the worker enters through the use of a method which leads to a helping process having its own character and continuity, and in which Miss Devlin is helped to engage, to use, toward changing her own way of living, in respect to a focus appropriate to the service being offered.

PRINCIPLE III: *The use of agency function and function in professional role gives focus, content, and direction to social work processes, assures accountability to society and to agency, and provides the partialization, the concreteness, the "difference," the "given" which further productive engagement.*

Throughout this series of interviews the worker's own clarity about her function or purpose as a hospital social worker offering service to a patient who is attempting to live in the community gives form, content, and direction to what she does. From the first interview this purpose is shared with the client so that the reason for worker and client being together is clear to the client and provides a basis for her own choice of using or not using what is being offered.

"I told Miss Devlin that I would be offering her a new kind of service if she wanted it. My purpose was certainly not to run her life. I wondered if we could discuss the kind of help that the hospital could now offer her." The "function" of the trial visit worker is expressed simply in order that this particular client may be able to grasp it. There is engagement of the patient in finding whether she has a purpose of her own (to try to make a go of it outside the hospital) which unites her with the purpose of the worker in making this particular hospital service available to her. It is the patient's own purpose which provides the basis, the motivation, for her to continue to use the worker's help.

Throughout the stormy sessions which follow, the aim of the worker is clearly not to improve this client's adjustment "in the large" but to work step by step on the problem and the success she is having in living outside, and to help her to take what responsibility she can for her own part in both problem and success. As a result of this focused help, the patient begins to feel and take quite a different kind of responsibility for herself as a total person. One can speculate that intrapsychic change may follow (is occurring) as a result of what she is doing with the worker's help in certain areas of her life, getting and holding a job, finding and staying in some home or place of residence, getting along with people in the community—all clearly related to the purpose of the worker's seeing her.

Helping the patient discover whether she can, at this time, live outside the hospital is of course the immediate focus within the larger function of helping the patient make use of the hospital's service in a way appropriate for her "now." This includes helping her use the outpatient clinic and the psychiatric service available within it to the extent that her psychiatrist finds indicated, and helping her return to the hospital should *that* be indicated. The function which inheres in the professional role "social caseworker" leads to engagement on an individual-to-individual basis with the purpose of helping the patient use this relationship to achieve the maximum fulfillment of herself possible as an individual who is social. This broad purpose finds realization in the specific service being made available by the social caseworker. It involves the worker in relationship not only with the client but with her employers also, the heads of residences where she lives, the Public Assistance agency, the psychiatrist in the hospital, and others not specified in this brief excerpt. But all the worker's activity as a caseworker comes to focus in the specific purpose which brings worker and client together. It is this purpose which provides continuity and the specificity which makes the engagement fruitful both for the worker and the hospital offering the service, and the client seeking to use it.

The worker's warmth and human compassion and her willingness to modify the "structure" within which help is given (for example, to go out to see the patient in the home instead of holding to an office interview) suggest that the worker is using function to help and not "for function's sake."

Time and again, when the client is angry or discouraged, the worker helps her to find her own wanting of what is being offered, her own strength and forward movement, and to choose again whether she will continue.

In the interview on 2-25, the worker does not accept the impulsive decision to return to the hospital as total but helps her look at the other side ["Miss Devlin was still able to affirm the gains she had made in her two months of living outside and was not feeling in need of care"] and to make a more responsible choice that represents the most responsible self she can be at this time. Conversely, the worker had not accepted the first impulsive "I don't want ever to come back," but had helped Miss Devlin look at the security the hospital could mean for her, to know that it is there for her if she needs it.

The worker's clarity about her own role as distinguished from the role of the Public Assistance worker is marked when she presents Miss Devlin's obligation to report income. She takes responsibility for her error in interpreting "wrongly" that the Public Assistance grant could not be used for the correspondence course. Consistently the worker's effort is directed toward helping this client use the community resources available to her—and to know and take responsibility for the way she uses them, as a help to her in becoming what she wants to be—all in respect to her expressed wish to stay outside the hospital, and the worker's interest to help her stay outside, if she can.

The function of the worker in offering the hospital's help, as appropriate at this time, provides the concrete, the substance, with which the client can engage. But the essence of what she is doing is finding her own strength, capacity, and will to engage with life, and developing that capacity through what she does with the worker. It is the human connection with the worker which makes it possible for her to identify with the worker and her strength, and to use the help offered to find and increase her own strength through actually trying herself out in the many relationships on the job, in the homes, with the agencies, with the psychiatrist, and discovering what she can do with them. "I thought I hated you, but I don't. You really understand. I need something greater than myself alone. And maybe you can help me." There follows Miss Devlin's commitment to use the help and the real moving in, the note on which these excerpts end.

PRINCIPLE IV: *A conscious, knowing use of structure as it*

evolves from and is related to function and process introduces "form," which furthers the effectiveness of all the social work processes, both primary and secondary.

In the preceding paragraphs reference has been made to the use of structure in this material. The purpose or function of the worker itself constitutes a structure and gives content or form to what is discussed in the interviews and to the activity of the worker in the client's behalf, in relation to employers, careholders, psychiatrist, and others. The professional role of social caseworker establishes the structure of a series of interviews through which the relationship develops essentially on a one-to-one basis. Holding the interviews in the worker's office on the hospital grounds constitutes the use of place as structure. This can be thought to constitute a hazard and to serve to tie the patient back into the hospital at the very time she is seeking to leave it behind. However, another way of looking at it is that it concretizes or identifies for the patient that she is discovering a new way to use the hospital, and she is using a hospital service to do it. In the interview of 2-25-63, which, as has been said, constitutes the turning point in this series of interviews, she "looked around at the tiled walls of the office and shouted at the top of her lungs, 'Why am I here in this office, in this hospital that I hate so much? I can never escape you. I feel like pressure is pulling me back!'" The worker uses the patient's actually being in the hospital for this interview to help her to test out whether she wants to come all the way in or trust the gains she had made in staying out, truly to leave it behind a little bit more. There is never any denial of the fact that Miss Devlin has been a patient and may need to return to the hospital. But there is a consistent generous offering of what is as much this hospital's concept of its function, that is, trial visit service to leave the hospital, as the offer of bed care.

When the patient's upset suggests the wisdom of a different place structure for an interview, a visit to her in her residence, this is done, but the reason for the shift is made clear to Miss Devlin and the place of subsequent interviews re-established as the worker's office on the hospital grounds. "I said . . . I had visited her at home this time because she had sounded upset enough for me to do this as an emergency. I knew she disliked coming to the hospital, but after all I was a hospital worker and offering her a hospital service." She moved on this to accept an appointment at my office on 4-5 in one week.

The place remains constant as a help to the client, as providing something fixed, known, the same, embodying in a sense the purpose of the relationship, with which she can struggle, and within which she can find, and make her own, forward movement, including the eventual leaving of the relationship. The "place" becomes, in the excerpt quoted above, the focus of her struggle. "You are the hospital. I want to leave you." "Can you?"—and the decision to keep on trying, with affirmation that the very help being struggled against is needed in order, eventually, to be able to get along without it.

Time is used as structure in the setting up of regular interviews and in the way beginnings, middles, and endings are consciously used, as discussed earlier in this chapter. As was suggested, there might have been use of a firmer overall time structure related to the length of Trial Visit service, broken up into periods for review of progress. Such use is furthered by the establishment of the structure of social service department policy, which can set up a time structure within which such service is given, with whatever departure may be indicated, in a specific instance, permissible under overall hospital policy. In the last of the interviews, in this sequence, as earlier noted, a time structure to help Miss Devlin get ready to apply for a job is used. "We tentatively reached the time limit of about one month, and then we would evaluate our progress." The setting of the month for this particular focus for work conduces to the patient's purposeful use of the interviews with an end in sight, in contrast to their use for Miss Devlin to recount "how things are going" in an unfocused and purposeless way.

The use of the appointment card in the first interview is an instance of use of structure, which again serves to concretize the service and to engage the client in a responsible choice. The way this structure is used reflects this worker's understanding of its significance as part of a helping skill in engaging the client in making a decision. "Her doctor had recommended that she attend Clinic as the best way the hospital knew to help her remain well. If she needed more time to think about it, I could plan another appointment with her. If not, I was prepared to offer her a Clinic card with her first appointment written on it. Miss Devlin sat in silence for a while and looked at me and at the Clinic card in front of her. She took the card and said she thought she might attend the Clinic."

PRINCIPLE V: *All social work processes, to be effective as processes in social work, require the use of relationship to engage the other in making and acting on choices or decisions as the core of working toward the accomplishment of a purpose identified as own purpose within the purpose of the service being offered.*

At first diagnostic glance, we might question Miss Devlin's capacity to use a relationship process within which she might, progressively, be able to make and act on responsible decisions toward the accomplishment of a purpose which is her own, within the hospital purpose in offering her its service. It is in the course of the service that she not only reveals but also develops that capacity. From the beginning, the worker's effort to engage the patient in a process of relationship is apparent. Her first question, after her introduction of herself and her identifying of herself with the hospital's social work service, is to elicit from the patient her feeling about coming to the hospital that day and specifically about seeing a social worker, in the light of her earlier experiences with both hospital and social service. Without the resultant explosive "I don't need a social worker, I've had enough of people trying to control my life" there would have been no basis for a true engagement which could establish this relationship as a new one, with a purpose different from the one Miss Devlin was ascribing to it.

The first engagement is around function, the purpose of the social work relationship. Because it is a voluntary service, it is so presented, and this gives Miss Devlin her first chance to choose whether she will have it at all. In social services which are not voluntary, the patient's freedom to use or not use what he must have still offers him choice, limited though it is, and it is this choice that he is consistently helped to know and act on.

In presenting what will be involved in using the service, for example, seeing a psychiatrist in the Clinic, seeing the worker, the client is engaged each step of the way: Does she want to? Can she do it? She is not hurried into a decision; she is helped to separate herself "then" from her self "now," since engagement is possible only in the present. "I questioned her about how much responsibility she could take for her behavior when she was ill (when she had fought with the doctor) and how she was different in the kind of responsibility she needed to have now."

In the second interview, when Miss Devlin arrives unexpectedly, having earlier called to cancel the appointment, the worker challenges her statement of having been forced to come by her employer, as a way of helping her feel and possess her own strength and choice in situations. "I said I could not accept her having been forced to come, wondering where she was in this. Where was the strength, the self-assertion that she had shown with me and her employer previously?" This kind of engagement with her on what she says and does in relationship with the worker is consistent throughout all the interviews and reaches a crisis in the interview which has been identified as the turning point for this series (2-25-63). The worker receives Miss Devlin's rage, but questions her conclusion: "I think I really do need to come back to the hospital," pointing up, for her to claim, her strength in remaining out as long as she has. Yet, when once more Miss Devlin chooses the outside and speaks of finding a job, and the way she plans to be with others, "I'll let them know how I feel just like I did with you today," the worker skillfully and warmly points out the difference in what Miss Devlin can do with her, and what will "work" with others. "Did she think her employers and fellow employees could accept this? She guessed not. I suggested that perhaps I could be of help to her if she wanted to try to change." This experience, this engagement with the worker, is used as a basis for a rechoice by Miss Devlin. She wants the worker's help, and she has a deepened sense of her own purpose in using it—to change.

The worker not only furthers engagement with herself in the helping relationship, but she also furthers Miss Devlin's engagement with the outside. There is a minimum of doing for and a maximum of fostering Miss Devlin's own doing, as when she makes her own phone call to arrange for new living quarters, after being given the "name to call" by the worker. She makes her own contacts with Public Assistance. Individual judgment is used throughout as the worker sometimes "does for and in behalf of," as when she accompanies Miss Devlin to her new home, and sometimes helps Miss Devlin do it herself and by herself. But the direction is always toward Miss Devlin's assuming increased responsibility for herself.

The warmth, compassion, and human concern are evident by implication in what the worker does. When Miss Devlin fails to phone on 3-22 the worker telephones, receives the "I have no use for you," and responds with concern for Miss Devlin's upset state, with the result that the client agrees to the worker's coming to see her at her residence. It is in this interview (3-29) that Miss Devlin's surprising accomplishments in what she did with the Public Assistance agency, with her brother and family, in deciding about her relationships with men, come tumbling out. This activity illustrates so graphically the way functionally limited help to a whole person spills over and can result in pervasive personality change that results in changed capacities and motivation for coping with all life situations. And it is here that Miss Devlin so touchingly chooses again to use the worker's help. "I need someone greater than myself." Here the worker's engagement of her asks her to look at what taking help is like. "Here I was offering her help with becoming employed but expecting a lot of work from her, a lot of looking at herself, a lot of headache. Was it worth the effort?" Miss Devlin's choosing to continue is on the basis of her experiencing what "use of casework help involves" and on the basis of her wanting to work toward a purpose that is her own. "I want your help. You're my caseworker until I tell you I don't need you anymore and I need you now. I don't want to sit around here. I'll go crazy, and I need a job badly."

Part of the skill of engagement involves controlling the tempo, slowing the patient down when she tries to rush ahead too fast, as in setting up a time within which work will be directed toward getting ready to apply for a job instead of encouraging an impulsive seeking that may well end in failure. Part of the skill involves helping the patient see a different side from the one she is presenting—her accomplishments when she is feeling discouraged, and yet her power to alienate when she is affirming a "way of acting" that is bound to defeat her. "I commented that in our recent telephone conversation it had taken all of my self control to meet her hostility and still want to be of help to her."

In summary, the engagement appropriate for social casework, as is so evident in this excerpted material, consists of giving the client an opportunity to experience the way she is in relationship through what she does with the worker and with others, as she works on what is involved in achieving the purpose which has brought her and the worker together. It is this experience in living, with its opportunity for identification with a caring person making the service available, and for such self-awareness as is appropriate and useful and timely, which makes it possible for the client to make and act on decisions in real life situations. This use of social casework help can eventuate in Miss Devlin's increased capacity for responsible living—for living with increased fulfillment of the self's potential as an individual who is social.

SUMMARY

Discussion of the way each of the generic principles of social work practice is evident in one short series of interviews with one client may leave the reader with some wish to put Humpty Dumpty together again and to grasp the essence of "what helped." It has been abundantly clear that is is not possible to consider the application of one principle without considering how it is related to or also expresses the application of others. It has not been possible to avoid overlappings in describing the use of principles which have been isolated as separate principles for purpose of analysis. It is obvious that all the principles are effective only as they are used in concert, in relationship with each other, and as appropriate not only to this particular social work process (social casework) but also to this particular client, receiving this particular service. What is here presented is not "techniques" or "skills" or "rules of thumb" but *principles,* whose use requires individual judgment in every instance. The integration of the principles occurs or should occur within the worker so that what is made available is skillful help based on (1) a diagnosis related to the service given, shifting in the course of the service and put out for the client to use and conducing to (2) an engagement of the client in a process of human relationship, which (3) moves in time, makes conscious use of time and time phases, and constitutes the medium for (4) offering a service determined by the agency's purpose and the client's own purpose in using it (5) within a form or structure appropriate for the service being offered, toward the client's full use of the service for his own and the community's welfare.

10 GENERIC PRINCIPLES OF SOCIAL WORK METHOD IN SOCIAL GROUP WORK

AS WAS TRUE for social casework method, it is impossible to find any record of the practice of social group work which could be considered "typical," in the sense, for example, of kind of group served (formed, voluntary, specific size of group) or characteristics of individuals who comprise it (age, sex, health, social condition) or purpose of agency making the group work service available. A further problem is introduced since social group work, long used as a method by agencies making available leisure time programs for persons seeking group association, is being increasingly used as method by social agencies with social purposes defined by social problems which the agencies have been established to meet. The earlier basic method for realization of purpose by these agencies has been social casework. The traditional purpose of social group work—to help individuals find individual and social development, self-value, and self-affirmation through group association, and to help groups as groups accomplish social purposes—is somewhat modified in the nontraditional group-serving agency. In the first place, the social purpose of the agency is more defined and specific than is the traditional group-serving agency's. This defined purpose gives both form and content to what is done in the group.

In the second place, the achievement of the group *as a group* has little or no importance in the agency established to meet a "problem." It is what each individual can achieve *through* the group which is primary. Although many caseworkers, often without benefit of further study, supervision, or help from social workers trained and experienced in social group work method, have begun to work with groups as ways of accomplishing their social work purposes in the nontraditional group-serving agencies, evidence is already available to suggest that the social group worker, well prepared through group work process concentration in his social work education and through his subsequent experience, has both knowledge and skill of considerable range and depth to bring to this new development. He has also much to contribute to social caseworkers who work with groups as part of their functioning as social caseworkers as in interviews with several members of a family in the "joint interview," or in their participation in committees and other groups.

Difficult, and indeed impossible as it is, then, to select a typical group work record, it *is* possible to identify what is typical in group work method within the frame of reference of what is generic or common to all social work method as earlier established, and to suggest (as well) some of the knowledge and skill which remain specific to the method of social group work, whatever the group composition or purpose.

Two pieces of material will be presented here: (1) a single meeting of a leisure-time group of adult women (fifty-five to seventy years) being served by a Jewish community center; (2) a series of sessions with a group of chronically ill, mentally ill men patients as part of a hospital social work department's pre-parole service.

These very different forms for the use of group work method will be discussed from the point of view of their reflection and use of the generic principles of social work method previously developed within the scope and purpose of this writing. It will not be possible to analyze in detail the refinements of social group work skill which are, or might have been, present in each. But it is hoped that the discussion will make clear both the value in the use of a general frame of reference for analysis of social group work (or any social work) method and the necessity for the recognition and development of what remains specific to the specific method being employed.

The two group work work records will be presented in sequence. Discussion of both will follow.

RECORD I. A GROUP WORK SERVICE
FOR OLDER ADULTS

The meeting recorded below is of a group of women fifty-five to seventy years of age. Thirteen of them are Jewish, four are Christian. With one exception, all are widows, and all belong to the middle economic class. Originally, the group was organized and sponsored by a volunteer organization of Jewish women, but for three years it has been affiliated with a Jewish community center, which provides the worker for this leisure-time group.

Meetings are held in the *clubhouse of a large suburban apartment,* where many of the members live. Although their major interest is in playing cards together, they have gradually, with the help of the group worker, extended their program to include occasional speakers, cultural events, and discussions.

The worker's focus has been on helping the members to value themselves and their group increasingly as they take more responsibility for their group life. Tensions have been evident, related to their nonacceptance of each other's many differences—political, cultural, religious, and personal.

Mrs. Mary Stone is the president; Mrs. Ruth Dubin, the program chairman; Mrs. Etta Fox, secretary.

March 5, 1962. There were a few women already setting up tables when I came into the clubhouse. They greeted me warmly. Some of them came over to shake hands with me, and all of them said how glad they were to see me. I was openly pleased at their interest and responded by saying to the women standing around me that I was glad to be back and had thought of them. The "tone" was set, and the ladies were very cheery, calling back and forth one to the other, making jokes, giggling. As each member came in, she was greeted with a loud hello, and most of them fell in with the spirit that was created.

As usual, I circulated, saying something to each woman. I spoke to several women about having a Purim party. Ruth Dubin reacted strongly by saying that this was impossible since we couldn't bring religion to the group. I said that it seemed to me that Purim has more than a religious meaning, and this was what we could bring to the group, that it was all in the way that we did it, all in the kind of attitude that we brought to the group. She said that we have to be careful not to discriminate. I wondered against whom we were discriminating, against the Christians or against ourselves. She wanted to know what I meant by this. I said that this is a Jewish-Christian group sponsored by a Jewish agency, and I wondered if it might be possible to celebrate naturally each other's holidays, instead of doing the unnatural thing of avoiding or ignoring them. Ruth then said: "I'll tell you. I don't really know. You may be able to do it. Bring it up to the group and have the women vote." I said that I thought this was a good idea. I felt that some progress had been made if Ruth Dubin at least thought that this could be discussed in the group. I also spoke to Lisa about having a Purim party. She responded in a most positive fashion, saying: "Yes, let's have something." I wondered if the Christians might feel uncomfortable in this kind of situation. Lisa answered: "We have to acknowledge differences, don't we?"

The conversation was general. There was lots of joking and "kidding" back and forth. When it came time for the business meeting, some of the women began putting all the tables together so that all the women were sitting in a "round table" style. Mary Stone called the meeting to attention, asking the secretary and treasurer to report, and then she called on me. (I had spoken to her before the meeting and told her I had some items to bring before the group.) I said that I wanted very seriously and openly to discuss the program for the month of March, that again I had been "told" that too much time was being taken away from the card playing for planned programs. I went on to say that I wanted to put this issue before them frankly and bluntly. The immediate and spontaneous response was that the club should continue having programs. Sylvia Weber said: "Having something besides card playing adds something to the group." Mary Stone said that the club could have business and card playing. Ruth reacted by saying that the group wouldn't be a group if they didn't do all kinds of things and she thought that when parties were held, they should have some music.

Lisa said that she thought that the group should sing more. "No one can sing and be sad," she commented. There was a small silence, and I wondered if the others would like to comment on this; I was sure everyone wanted to hear what they were thinking. Etta then said she would like to speak, and with great emotion she spoke in this vein. She said that the group should face it, that the ladies come to play cards and aren't interested in anything else. Some of the women nodded their heads at this; others murmured that this was not so. At this point Ruth interrupted and said impatiently that "we are what we are." She went on to say that the group was small and that its purpose was social. Etta said that this was the trouble, that the group was "stupidly social." The ladies looked in my direction. I immediately reacted by saying that I thought that Ruth Dubin had described the group nicely, that a group could be small, social, and do all kinds of interesting things as we had been doing and surely could continue to do so in the future.

Etta wanted to continue, and all of us said to go ahead. She said that "you ladies" don't even pay attention when someone is ill or has a birthday and that she always makes it her business to find out. Gladys interjected that she had always understood this to be the responsibility of the secretary (Etta is the secretary). Annie Miller (treasurer) said that she always sends out birthday cards. Etta ignored the two comments and went on to say that she had sent a card to Debby Silver, who had been taken to the hospital again, and had paid for it out of her own money. "But I don't care. I did it to make her feel that the club was thinking about her." Gladys spoke up again and said that this was the job of the secretary, and she thought that no one would be against her getting the fifteen cents back. Etta was rather disconcerted by the reaction, but stuck to her guns. At this point I said that making sure that every sick person got a card and every birthday person got a card was certainly a good idea, and I saw that the ladies felt this way too. I wondered if the ladies wanted to appoint someone to be responsible for this. Ruth Dubin then said: "Yes, let the secretary be responsible. And that means Etta." The ladies said, "Yes, let Etta be responsible." Etta reacted by saying that if the group thought the secretary should be responsible for things of this nature, she would be very glad to do so.

She said that she had some other things to say and she hoped she wasn't talking too much. Murmurs of no, go ahead, everyone has the right to express themselves. She wondered what Ruth Dubin was doing as program chairman. Ruth was really disconcerted and said, stumbling a little, that she had cooperated with me and done what she could. I supported Ruth by saying that this was certainly so and that I wanted to point out to Etta and the group that we had, at least once a month, brought program ideas to the floor of the meeting and had been interested in the group's suggestions and reactions. Ruth then said rather defensively that it was true that [the worker] did most of the work but that she had tried to help. Ruth and the group were very annoyed with Etta and made comments to the effect that the meetings were nice, they didn't understand what was going on, etc. Etta then said that she had one more comment to make, and she spoke strongly about "that nice Ella" who couldn't come to the meetings because of the weather and that *she* called her up and that Ella was so grateful. She wanted to know why the other members weren't concerned. At this there really was a storm of protest, and the women related how they had called her, visited her. I interjected that I personally had called her once a week during the entire winter. ("You did?" Etta asked, apparently in great surprise.) I then suggested to the group that since Ella was a shut-in these days it would be nice and a welcome gesture if the few who hadn't contacted Ella do so.

Ruth Dubin said that she would like to say that the group had been "accused" and that she thought the women came to meet other people, to talk, to be social. Mary Stone said: "Look, Etta, perhaps there are some things wrong with this group but it must be satisfactory. The ladies like it. They keep coming every week." Etta, who was sitting next to me, murmured in my ear that these ladies just don't understand.

It was clear that the women felt attacked and rose up to defend themselves and the group. However, all this was done in a rather good atmosphere and with a lot of amiability, despite some slight attitudes of impatience.

I then went on to say that since so much had been said we could now continue to talk about the program. Since this is a group and obviously an alert group, I wondered if some of the ladies could see themselves giving some of the book reviews or leading the discussion. I wondered if they felt that more of the programs could come from the group. There were many protests from the group. Lisa verbalized it by saying that she disagreed with this. "That's what you are here for." She then murmured something about my being an "employee" of the group. I reacted by saying that I didn't understand this, that it seemed to me that I was here to help the group help itself. Several of the women said that they looked forward to hearing the talks and the book reviews but didn't think they could give them. Sadie said that when Ben worked with the group, he actually read excerpts from books and that they had thought that this is what I would be doing. Lisa said that Miriam always "entertained" her group. I looked at Lisa with a half smile, shook my head, and said to her that I didn't really think that "entertainment" was what she wanted from me. At that she smiled and shook her head. The ladies also shook their heads. Gladys said: "Rose, we're just too old to start doing different kinds of things." I answered this by saying: "Too old? Are you sure?" Sylvia then chimed in with: "We're satisfied with you!" I then said (deciding to end this part of the discussion) that I really felt pleased they felt that way but I did want them to think about all the talent in this very group.

I then picked up once more the program "thread" and said that I was hoping they had some program "likes." Sadie said she would like to say something about some of the suggestions the speaker had made two weeks ago. She went on to say that she thinks she speaks for the group when she says that they don't want to come around to sew, or play checkers, or put out newspapers. Lisa interrupted and said with really great emotion, in trembling voice: "Ladies, Rose. Don't you see? This is it. This is why we come. Just sitting around like this and talking." She spread her arms outwards to include the entire group, looked around and said: "I love it."

There was a moment of silence—a nice silence with everyone beaming at everyone else. I said that it seemed to me by the faces that everyone loved it. I went on to say that the discussion had given me lots of ideas which I would like to present to the group. I proposed that we have a Purim party by saying that I wondered if everyone remembered that Purim was coming up and, since we had talked several times about knowing more about each other's holidays, the group might like to know more about Purim. There was a murmur of laughter in the group. I went on to say that Purim had in it the idea of giving, but instead of giving gifts to each other I wondered if the members liked the idea of bringing in a small, inexpensive toy that we could give to the kindergarten here or an orphanage in the name of the group. The women received this enthusiastically. I said I would get an idea of some of the children's institutions in the city and let them know about this.

Ruth Dubin said she would very frankly like to ask the Christians if they objected to the celebration of Purim. They (of course) said they didn't object, while Connie added that she, for one, was interested. A general discussion ensued, and the ladies began to have ideas for the party. The enthusiasm grew, and the ladies volunteered to bring in tablecloths, flowers. Sylvia agreed to buy Hamantaschen. Ruth Dubin thought that the Christians might not like this. I commented that I had an idea that people like to taste new kinds of cakes. Mary and Connie immediately said that there was no question about this. Fay volunteered to bake some Hamantaschen. Annie then said that she also would bake Hamantaschen. I mentioned that the tradition was that one was to be very gay on Purim. Sylvia then said she would bring a bottle of wine. The ladies giggled and looked in my direction. I smiled, and said I thought it would be good to put in the punch. Some of the women murmured: "Who needs punch?"

Connie then commented that she thought I should tell the story of Purim. The ladies nodded "yes," and I said that I thought this was a very good idea and that I would find something suitable. At this point Etta whispered in my ear that the story of Purim might offend the Christians. I again reiterated that I would find something suitable, something that everyone in the group would be interested in and enjoy.

I said that I had another idea that I would like to present to the group. (One of the ladies exclaimed: "Boy, she's hopping today!") I said that I would like to pick up on something that Connie had said previously and suggest that we have a dinner-theatre party. The group took this very well. Connie immediately elaborated on this by describing how nice it would be, how much fun, etc. There was some discussion about when it would be, and it was decided to have it in April.

Mary then read a poem "Never-Old" with a lot of feeling, and it was received with a lot of feeling (the group by this time was in a "feeling mood"). Lisa then read two poems, which were also received with a lot of emotion. Actually, the meeting program was now at an end, but the ladies somehow couldn't leave. Fay said that she would like to tell a story. This started the ball rolling, and the jokes and stories came thick and fast. The ladies were animated and literally rolled with laughter at some of the jokes. At one point I turned to some of the quieter ones and said "Let's hear from this side," but they smiled and said very little.

The atmosphere was most congenial; the ladies seemed reluctant to move and only when I saw that a lull was in the offing, did I suggest that they might start the cards, if they felt like it.

RECORD II. PRE-PAROLE SERVICE FOR A GROUP OF MENTALLY ILL MEN

The following excerpts are drawn from a record of group work practice in a hospital for the mentally ill. They represent the use of the group work method by the social service department of the hospital to discharge the function of pre-parole through offering assistance in planning to patients, thought by the hospital to be ready to consider the possibility of leaving the hospital. The function of pre-parole is discharged in this hospital by the social casework method as well. While one of the reasons social group work method was employed to carry this function was the need for additional social work staff to serve the "backlog" of patients awaiting pre-parole social service, experience revealed that for some patients social group work was the method of choice. An attempt was made, subsequently, to make selective assignment of patients to social casework or social group work service in accordance with their particular needs. Pre-parole service is conceived by the hospital as an opportunity for the patient to "test out his own will, direction and the strength of his impulse toward new life." * When the patient is considered ready, and after his use of this service, he comes before the Social Planning Staff to present his request to leave the hospital to the psychiatrists, social workers, and other hospital personnel who comprise that group, for a hospital decision on his leaving.

At the first meeting of the group whose record follows, nine patients attended—all men—all long-time patients of the hospital. The group worker opened the meeting by identifying the

---

* Manual, Social Service Department, State Hospital, as quoted in the Project from which this material is drawn.

purpose of the meeting as being to help the patients work in a group, for a maximum of eight meetings, on whether, as individuals, they wanted to try life on the outside. They were informed that the hospital (including their psychiatrists) considered them ready to examine this question, but that they would be free to decide against it as well as for it. Indeed, their first choice would be whether they wanted to use this service at all. Several of the patients immediately mentioned their relatives in connection with their plans. An excerpt from the record follows:

November 9. First Meeting

I said they all seemed to be thinking of involving their relatives, which was good. Before we went any further I wanted them to know that if they decided to use the service I would be getting in touch with their relatives, as this was one requirement for using the service. They didn't have to decide if they would use it this morning, but later I would give them a choice of times when we could meet again and explore further whether they wanted to or not. I continued that some of them might find it a little hard to take if their relatives were unwilling or unable to be part of their planning for the future. This led to a real expression of disappointment on the part of the group as well as some anger at relatives who had refused or might refuse to be part of the planning. Mr. Kaye, with much feeling, told how his brother in Washington, D.C. would have nothing to do with him and how hard this was to take, but he had to. I voiced sympathetic understanding of the pain involved in facing this, and the group came out with the fact that, if relatives wouldn't help they still wanted to leave the hospital and asked if I would tell them the ways they might do this.

After this session, several patients dropped out of the group, and others joined it. When I visited on the ward the men who had dropped out, I found that though they had decided against using the service, their one contact with the group had started something stirring within them, in each case, and had often contributed to a better ward adjustment and group living.

December 16. Second Meeting

Mr. Kaye began speaking of how this was the Christmas season, and how he tries to help his fellow men always, not only during this season. He went on to describe what he does in the hospital and how much satisfaction he had got from helping "those old men in the Building." The other men supported Mr. Kaye and told of the things they knew he did for others, and all agreed that he was a "helpful person." I said that we certainly do get satisfaction from helping others, and I wondered if being on the other end, as they all would be if they decided to meet again, and work on plans for their future, wasn't a hard spot to be in. Mr. Hale denied there was anything hard in this and said that often he has had to ask strangers for help, and so he doesn't mind doing it now. Mr. Kaye, however, disagreed and said no matter how many times you have to be helped, you like to do things for yourself, and it was hard to ask someone to help you. Mr. Wells said that if he didn't absolutely have to do so, he wouldn't ask another person for help, but now he had to.

Between the fourth and fifth meeting of this group I invited each of the patient's relatives to the hospital to discuss with them the possibility of the patient's being paroled to their care. If the relatives refused, I tried to ease their guilt and enable them to free the patient so that he might move in another direction. During this time some patients left with relatives. Some left to use Foster Care; others were later to decide that if they could not leave with relatives, they did not want to leave at all.

January 6. Fifth Meeting

Everyone was buzzing at the same time. I said that a lot had happened during the past week, as they knew. Some of them had seen me with their relatives last Sunday. Some had had to face the disappointment of no relative showing up at all, and what this meant. Some had done really courageous things with their relatives in freeing themselves to move in one direction or another. At this, Mr. Vale, who had just begun to assert his difference from his mother and will go against her wishes in applying for Foster Care instead of returning to her, beamed, and seemed to draw real strength from my words. I continued that this was our fifth meeting and I wondered where each one of them was now. I told them when we began that we would have eight sessions at most. Were they any closer to where they wanted to go? If not, why not, and to what avail meeting with me?

What I had said hit the group with the force of a bombshell. Each man put a word in, almost all wanting to talk at once. Mr. Milner said that his family had been here, and he wondered when they would be coming to get him. I let him know that they would be coming on Sunday afternoon and that he would be going home for one week, after which he would be given an opportunity to speak with Dr. Green. He looked very happy at this and made a comment on the fact that things were moving for him, and he wouldn't be needing to come to the group anymore. Mr. Vale affirmed more strongly his desire to apply for Foster Care even against his mother's wishes, and he said he wanted a date set for him to come before Social Planning Staff. This was done. I gave him support and recognized how difficult this was for him—to ask for Foster Care against his family's wishes. Mr. West said he wanted to continue with his plans for coming before the Staff, and I indicated I had some real question about how I could bring anyone before the Staff from a closed Cottage. At this Mr. West wondered if I couldn't talk with Dr. Green and get him ground privileges and out of E Cottage. I wondered if there was anything he could do. Could he see Dr. Green about it? Mr. Kaye led the group in helping Mr. West see that he had a real part in this, and spurred by "God helps those who help themselves" Mr. West decided on a plan to see his doctor.

Before the next meeting several of the patients had come before the staff, passed it, and moved ahead and out of the group. At the following session, eight men were in the group, several for the first time.

January 13. Sixth Meeting

Most of the men arrived at approximately the same time. When Miss Gray (attendant) brought Mr. Roberts and Mr. Downs, she indicated that Mr. Downs had been asking for several days when he would be seeing "that man from Social Security." Mr. Downs, for the first time, looked pleased to see me and the group. The others laughed good naturedly at his error, explaining that I was the Social Service man not the Social Security man. To this Mr. Downs replied that he didn't care what they called me so long as they knew it was me he wanted to see—"the man who helped."

There was a loaded silence in the group, and there was a certain amount of looking around with wonder and surprise at the difference in the size and make-up of the group. Someone meekly commented about this. I picked it up, saying I guessed they were feeling the impact of some of the change, for the group was truly different and they might very well have some feeling about this one way or the other—perhaps they might be angry with me, thinking I had taken some of their friends out of the group. Mr. Hale, whose growth was very evident in the group this morning, in that he often caught himself interrupting others and would then say "pardon me" and let them go ahead (so different from his former overbearing way of shutting others out), commented that the group was different, but proceeded to say that he didn't have any feelings about it one way or the other. The group agreed with him, and I wondered then if they might have had some feeling, not at the difference but at being left behind, at not having proceeded as rapidly as some of the others. Mr. Adams said that he expected to be behind the others because he had started later than they had, but Mr. Kaye reminded him that he had begun, as several others had, at the same time. Now Mr. Hale, risking much, because he wanted to change and impress me and Staff with his different use of himself (without all the hostility which had characterized him) sparked the group into telling some of their discomfort at the change they found in the group. When each man (except Mr. Small, who was silent) had put some of this in, I said it was good they could share their feelings with me, even when they weren't the most pleasant ones. But then, wasn't life and weren't individuals made up of both kinds of feelings? Could they find something in this to help them move ahead?

Mr. Kaye said that he thought each one of them was different and they moved ahead at different rates of speed so some had to be behind others. Mr. Vale, whose ramblings had turned into real contributions to the group since he had found the courage to, with support, go against his mother's wishes and apply for Foster Care as a first big step in asserting his individuality, said they each had a part in deciding with me the dates to come to Staff, and he felt that his later date was his own choice. Now Mr. Adams, who had been showing his ambivalence toward life outside the hospital by procrastinating about setting a date for his staffing, said "Mr. C., aren't you forgetting something?" When I looked puzzled he said he was the only one now who didn't have a date, and he proceeded to move on and suggest a date. Mr. Hale said he knew that not everyone could come before Staff at the same time for there would be people from the Women's Group too, and he went on to tell a little of how he used the additional time to prepare further for his coming to Staff. From all this discussion the group arrived at the fact that some had to move more rapidly than others as was true for life on the outside, and they could live with it here as they would have to in the community, though they might not like it.

I wondered if they might find any difficulty in leaving the group or in leaving the hospital. Mr. Downs said, "Shucks no," he wanted to get out of this place and the sooner the better. The others, spurred by the momentum of their desire to leave and minimizing the fear at facing some of the problems in this move, quickly agreed with him. I asked if maybe there wasn't some problem whenever we left something. Mr. Hale said he never had any trouble with goodbyes. Mr. Kaye said if you had ever had to leave your family and home you knew how hard it is to leave, even though you had to do it to grow up. Mr. Vale, who is feeling this so deeply now, agreed and said that a person kind of got used to the group meetings and the people and the Social Worker. Mr. Adams told how you got into the routine of the hospital, the food, used to the nurses and attendants, and now the group let themselves feel some of the pain in ending with the group, the hospital, and me. I sat amazed at the real insight, the depth of feeling in this for each man, expressed in his own way. I wondered what I could do to help them with these endings. Mr. Kaye said if you could just keep with you the fact that you were leaving to get to a new and different life you could stand to do it. Mr. Roberts, who had been sitting stooped, silent, and red-eyed, said he was looking ahead to a Foster Home, though this had been second best for him. He hoped it would be better than the hospital.

Now a barrage of questions hit me about Staff. What should they wear? How should they talk? Mr. Hale put the meaning of what these questions were about nicley when he said that he was confident. He had faced many strangers in his life, and he'd be okay with the doctors and the Social Workers at Planning Staff. I asked how the others felt, for I wondered if some of their questions weren't the result of feeling a little anxious about coming to Staff. Mr. Adams said no matter how many times he went before Staff he was always scared until he had spoken for a while. Mr. Vale pointed out that he was a veteran at going before Staff and he was still nervous. The group laughed a nervous, relieved laugh. Mr. West looked at me, and his face seemed to carry an appeal for help. I wondered if there was anything in all of this that would be of help to them, not in doing away with the anxiety, for it was good that they could own to this, but that might help some so they wouldn't be immobilized by anxiety. Mr. Adams said he would tell the truth and know it was the truth, what more could be asked? Mr. Kaye said all he could tell the Staff was what he had done to get ready for it and now the others, each in his own way, told of what he had done to prepare for Staff, and said how this would help him live with the anxiety he had. Mr. West, seeing everybody move ahead so quickly, mobilized himself with a plan to see Dr. Green and set a date for Staff, too.

Mr. Hale again raised some questions (which he had expressed last week) about getting married, and the way and tone in which he did so expressed some of the difficulty he might find in taking help on the outside, for he knew the answers before he asked and he knew I was aware of that. I wondered if maybe he was asking this because it could be very restraining and hard to live within some of the regulations which they might have if their applications for Foster Care were accepted. I recognized too that it might be hard to continue to have a Social Worker in their lives. Mr. Kaye, who feels so abandoned by his relatives, told of how he thought he would be happy to have a Social Worker. It would be nice to have someone you could talk to who was interested in you, an aid in what you did. Mr. Vale said a Social Worker could help you to think more clearly on the outside, and he was all for it. Generally the group put out many positive feelings about how easy it would be for them to live within the rules of Foster Care and to work with a Social Worker. I could understand how hard it was to tell me of the problem in this, for all who were leaving for Foster Care wanted it badly, but I questioned some of the reality in this. Could they look at some of the problems, some of the hardness there might be in having a Social Worker in their lives? Mr. Adams said he thought sometimes they might be a little too personal. Mr. Hale told how he minded the fact that he would have to wait at least a year before he might get married; he minded the business of being "on parole." Mr. Downs said he was over seventy, and he thought he should be able to "fend for himself." All except Mr. Small put in a little of how hard it would be to take help, how much they would rather be discharged to themselves instead of paroled to the Social Service Department, as would be the case if they left to go to Foster Care.

I was glad that they could look at the problem, and I let them know it, wondering what they could do with it. Mr. Kaye said that much as he didn't like it, just that much he needed it, and he knew from working with me that he would be able to get along with his Foster Care worker. Several other men indicated that, hard as it might be, they needed and were asking for this help, and it was this that would make them use it. For they could not leave the hospital in any other way, and this is what they wanted to do.

It was now time for the group meeting to be over, and several of the attendants had come for the patients. Mr. Downs asked if he could see me later in the day, as he had something from his family that he wanted to talk with me about. I also talked a bit with Mr. Small about where he was in all this, and he mobilized himself to take a further step in getting his family involved in his planning, so that he would be free to move in one direction or the other.

PRINCIPLE I: *That diagnosis or understanding of the phenomenon served is most effective which is conceived as related to the use of service; which is developed, in part, in the course of giving the service, with the engagement and participation of the clientele served; which is recognized as being subject to continuous change as the phenomenon changes; and which is put out by the worker for the clientele to use, as appropriate, in the course of the service.*

RECORD I. A GROUP WORK SERVICE
FOR OLDER ADULTS

There is no indication that the worker sought or needed an individual life history for each of the group members in order to give the service helpfully. Rather the understanding of each of the women in the group, and of the group as a whole, that was sought and used is related to the service being offered, a leisure-time program with the social purpose (as it inheres both in the agency's purpose and the purpose of social work as a profession) of furthering an individually fulfilling and socially contributive use of the self for group members, and a socially contributive life for the group.

In the course of the meeting the worker's understanding of

each of the members is not only reflected in what she says and does but also grows and changes as, to some extent, individual capacity for socially productive participation in the group changes. Etta's feeling of being different from the others and her assertion of her difference as superiority (being more thoughtful, more concerned for ill and absent members, more interested in activities of greater social significance than card playing alone) appear to have been understood by the worker, not from the angle of what caused it in Etta's early life experience, but in its meaning to Etta and the group in the meeting. A search for cause would indeed have diverted both Etta and the group from the purpose and potential of the present experience. The worker might have given more recognition to what Etta has been carrying in the group and to her feeling of difference from the others. While this is not entirely missing, there may be some suggestion of mild irritation on the worker's part and of her "lining herself up" with group members in joint defense against Etta's "accusations." However, the group itself, through its own new awareness of Etta as a person, and following the worker's lead, suggests a channel for the expression of her uniqueness which can be contributive to the group and assure her a continuing place within it. The chairman, seconded by others, requested her to carry the duties she has stressed as important, as secretary.

The group's understanding of itself as wanting and valuing just being together in human relationships and interaction and as wanting, also, activities which could bring a widening of horizons, personal development, and social contribution is stimulated by Etta's questioning, the worker's encouragement of the question, the worker's suggestion of broadened activity for the group's consideration, and the worker's affirmation of the group's final choice of it. This group comes, too, to some further understanding of itself as made up of a majority of Jewish women, meeting under the auspice of a Jewish center, whose Jewish traditions need not be denied or minimized in order to maintain group life, but can be expressed and so bring enrichment to Jewish and non-Jewish members alike.

What may be indicated here is this particular worker's seemingly greater understanding of the group as a whole and greater skill in helping the group as a whole to understand and affirm itself as a particular kind of group, through its choice of program and the use it wishes to make of the worker in this very meeting, than her understanding of the individuals in the group, or her skill in helping them use it for their individual and social growth.

RECORD II. PRE-PAROLE SERVICE FOR A GROUP OF MENTALLY ILL MEN

Here the understanding recorded and used is not of the specific mental illness of each of the men, its dynamics, cause, or symptomatology. Rather, it is directed toward the kind of social functioning of which each individual is presently capable, as revealed in part, through what each is currently doing in the hospital, and specifically, in this group. There are references to an understanding of the group as a group, with note of the buzzing which introduced the session following the worker's seeing of relatives, the loaded silence in the group, the nervous laughing. The worker comments on how the group is, what the group is like, in other words gives back his understanding of it as a way of helping the individual patients work individually, yet in the group, on what their collective, group behavior is expressing. But there is considerable evidence also of the worker's awareness of each individual as an individual, and of his response to individuals in the group sessions in a way which furthers their productive use of the group experience. For example, the worker notes that Mr. Vale, who is moving toward a foster home on his release from the hospital rather than a return to his mother, expresses difficulty about leaving the hospital. The worker encourages not only Mr. Vale but also all the group members to experience and express both sides of their feeling, wanting to leave and fearing to leave, wanting a social worker's help after leaving (to Foster Care) and not wanting it. He puts out his understanding that both feelings are present and are being expressed, one way or another, as a help to each man's having a clearer understanding and a greater acceptance of himself as a whole person. Such dress-rehearsal weighing of both sides of the feeling about leaving facilitates choices being made and acted on responsibly rather than impulsively, with less chance that buried and denied feelings will later break through to obstruct forward movement.

Always the understanding sought and used is related to the specific purpose of the service: to see whether these patients are able to leave the hospital, and to the larger social work purpose, of which the specific purpose is an instance, of furthering the individually fulfilling and socially productive functioning of these long-hospitalized men to the extent possible for each.

It is significant that, in the use of social group work method, the worker's comprehension of the phenomenon served is drawn from many sources. In the above instance it derives, in part, from his understanding of human growth and capacity for growth, and of mental illness and mental health, as attained through his professional social work education. It draws as well on the hospital's records of these men, and on conferences with hospital personnel and with family members. It is augmented by what develops in the group experience. Individual members contribute to the worker's understanding of them and to their own understanding of themselves and of each other. The worker gives back his understanding, as it develops, and as it changes as group members and the group change, for the group to use and work with. For example, he notes their anxiety about coming to Staff and asks what they can do about it. Each patient contributes to a discussion of how to manage coming to Staff.

Certainly it is important for the worker to develop and use every bit of understanding he can get of the group members he serves. To recapitulate, part of his understanding comes from his store of knowledge about this kind of person, this kind of group, this kind of illness or problem or age period, as he has achieved that understanding through formal education for social work and subsequent experience. In the immediate instance he has resources for increasing his understanding of particular individuals and a particular group. What is being emphasized here is the additional rich source of understanding which lies in the immediate experience with the group and its members; the way group members contribute to the worker's and their own understanding of themselves as individuals and as a group; and the way the worker can give back his understanding or underline the understanding put forth by a group member, for the group, and the individuals who comprise it, to use for movement toward the realization of purpose.

PRINCIPLE II: *The effectiveness of any social work process, primary or secondary, is furthered by the worker's conscious, knowing use of time phases in the process (beginnings, middles, and endings) in order that the particular potential in each time phase may be fully exploited for the other's use.*

RECORD I. A GROUP WORK SERVICE
FOR OLDER ADULTS

In this single group meeting we miss the beginnings of the group's life, as served by this agency some three years earlier. We are involved in a "middle," and we must confine our consideration of time phases, of beginnings, middles, and endings, to the single session.

The casualness and relative separateness of the individuals as individuals are apparent as the women move about setting up card tables. The greeting of the worker, who had apparently returned after a short break, and the worker's warm response to their warmth help to move the group to greater cohesion and to a deepened relationship with her. Her comment that she had been thinking of them emphasized the group's continuity, as a group in its relation to their worker, and through her, the agency. The worker moves about greeting individuals and small groups, making suggestions for later activity for individuals in the group and for the group as a whole, but it is not until the meeting is under way that a growing intensity of shared feeling and thinking experience, so characteristic of a "middle" is possible.

As the meeting progresses the worker encourages the expression of difference, the hearing of various points of view, puts in comments and suggestions for the group to work with, and in these and other ways contributes to a deepening of individual and group experience, and to the group's sense of itself as a group. As the formal part of the meeting moves to a close there is some reluctance to have the free and warm exchange of feeling end. It is the worker's sense that this phase of the group's experience is coming to a close, which prompts her to suggest the ending of this part of the meeting and the beginning of card playing. A "tapering off" of intensity of feeling and experiencing, typical for endings, is evident.

A summary of what the group came to, in the way of the kind of program it wanted, the extent to which it chose to "carry" program itself, the use it chose to make of the worker, its plans for programs for subsequent meetings was made by the worker and affirmed by the group. It might have had even greater emphasis through a "pulling together" by the worker as a way of furthering the group's moving toward the conclusion of a particular phase of the meeting.

RECORD II. PRE-PAROLE SERVICE FOR
A GROUP OF MENTALLY ILL MEN

The actual beginning in this first session with the group is omitted from the recorded material, but some of its content and nature was available through conferences with the worker. Its recording would have had considerable value for this analysis. The men had been told about the meeting by the nurse on the ward, and those on the closed ward had been brought to the group by attendants. The relative isolation of each man from the others was marked in the early minutes of the first meeting. The worker's statement of the purpose of the meeting appeared to develop the beginning of a bond between the members and served, as well, to relate them to the worker, and to free them for some engagement with each other and with the worker.

The sessions are not recorded in full so that it is not possible to identify the beginning, middle, and ending phases of each of the sessions for which there is some recording. Furthermore, certain members leave the group, either out of their own choice not to continue or out of their readiness to leave it and go before Staff for a decision on their leaving the hospital. New members join the group. These factors constitute more attrition and change in group membership than is usual in the life of a different kind of group, meeting, for example, for a "leisure-time" purpose.

Nevertheless the life of the group, the interchange of thought and feeling, deepens in the course of the sessions with a climactic session occurring in the fifth meeting, here recorded. It is here that the members respond to the challenge of what they want to do with the time remaining. Individuals gain the courage of themselves through what happens in the group and what the worker puts in and take increasing responsibility for what they think and feel, what they want and fear. For example, Mr. Hale, in the following (sixth) session, "sparks" the group into putting into words some of the hurt and discomfort because some members have already gone to Staff.

The worker promotes movement by identifying, at the beginning, a series of eight meetings which will constitute the span for the work to be undertaken. He identifies the fifth meeting as being the fifth of the eight, as moving toward the end, and challenges the group with what they propose to do with the time remaining, whether it is worth while to come at all if they are no closer to where they want to go. It is this use of the time structure which results in the turning point for the group, as indicated above. This is a use of time which furthers engagement, mobilization of energy, finding and acting on purpose on the part of each man, and the group as a whole.

Since the record ends at the conclusion of the sixth session we do not have available the way the worker dealt with the final (eighth) ending session or how he arranged for continuity or beginning again on the ward, or with a caseworker, or with a new group, in accordance with what was indicated in the particular instance.

There is some summing up at the end of each session by the men themselves or by the worker, and perhaps there might have been more as a help in the group's capturing and possessing its movement in the particular session. At the end of each session, the worker sees briefly and individually each man who gives evidence of needing something from him which was not and could not have been met in the group.

The tentativeness of the beginning of each session, the intensification of feeling and engagement in the middle, the easing off and withdrawing into separateness at the end characterized each session.

PRINCIPLE III: *The use of agency function and function in professional role gives focus, content, and direction to social work process, assures accountability to society and to agency, and provides the partialization, the concreteness, the "difference," the "given" which further productive engagement.*

RECORD I. A GROUP WORK SERVICE
FOR OLDER ADULTS

Agency function, as was earlier stated, is not as clearly defined in the traditional group-serving agency whose general purpose is "recreation and informal education" as it is in agencies established to deal with some form of social problem or problems, and within which social casework has been the primary method used. The Jewish Community Center, from which the material being discussed was drawn, has the purpose of all such centers: to provide group association for persons seeking it and, in the course of doing so, to strengthen the significance of Jewish history and culture in the participants at the same time the participants are helped to take their place in the larger community, enriching it with their distinctive cultural contribution, and being enriched by different cultural influences and traditions within it. The agency, in employing social group workers to administer or supervise the program, affirms that it wants its purpose carried out in such a way that the social purposes of social group work are realized as well: (1) to help individuals use the group association for their own development as individuals who are social and (2) to help the group accomplish some constructive purpose as a group.

The worker's sense of function as Jewish Center group worker is implicit in what she does to further the satisfactions and opportunities in group association for all members during this particular meeting, and in her introduction of the possibility of the group's celebrating Purim, a Jewish festival. Her introduction of this possibility, first to individuals prior to the group meeting and specifically to the program chairman, Ruth Dubin, provided the opportunity for her to state one aspect of the agency's function very directly. "In response to Ruth's question I said that this is a Jewish-Christian group sponsored by a Jewish agency and I wondered if it might not be possible to celebrate each other's holidays naturally, instead of doing the unnatural thing of avoiding or ignoring them." Ruth replies: "Bring it up in the group and have the women vote." This is a concrete instance of the group's determining whether and how it will make use of agency function and so make agency purpose in serving them their own purpose for themselves. Other program ideas introduced by the worker and elicited from the group constitute additional ways for the group to achieve agency (and their own) purpose of opportunity for individual growth and development and increased self-valuing through group association. The suggestion that the group as group make a gift to a kindergarten or orphanage in the name of the group, rather than exchange gifts at the proposed Purim party, helps the group to take constructive social action as a group.

The worker's carrying of her function in role, as a social group worker, is exemplified throughout the session. She provides, or attempts to provide, for the participation of all members ("Let's hear from the quiet side" is addressed to some members who had not been participating.) She encourages the expression of different points of view and interjects both difference and affirmation herself to help the group move toward a decision as to the kind of group it wants to be, the kind of program it wants to have, and to experience group life in the course of it. In this group life the individual members are warmed and enriched by their association with each other and the group as a group makes a beginning of thinking of a constructive social purpose for the group. Agency function and the program suggestions which evolve from it, including the card playing, "just sitting around like this and talking," the Purim party, the dinner party, provide the concrete, the given, the content, which the members use for engagement with each other in human relationships. The worker's carrying of agency function, and her functional role, helps that engagement lead toward the group and each group member's own and the community's welfare. Such carrying of agency function, and functional role, assures accountability to agency and community in that agency purpose and community purpose in supporting it are being realized.

RECORD II. PRE-PAROLE SERVICE FOR A GROUP OF MENTALLY ILL MEN

Here the social work department's purpose in offering pre-parole service is defined in the department's manual. It forms a part of the larger purpose of the social work department within the hospital and of the still larger and encompassing purpose of the hospital itself: to help mentally ill persons make the recovery possible for them through the use of hospital care, to enter the hospital when that is the type of care they need, to leave the hospital when they no longer need that form of care, and to maintain or improve their mental health once they have left it. Within that encompassing purpose the social work department's purpose is to extend services to the patient and his family at every point of his relation to the hospital, prior to and upon entering, while hospitalized and prior to and following leaving—services which are designed to maximize the use he can make of the hospital's total resources, including social service itself.

Everything the worker puts into all the sessions has the clear focus for this "pre-parole group" of planning for the future, considering the possibility of living outside the hospital. The focus is on the patient's capacity to use and maximize the capacity for social functioning he presently has, whatever the nature of the illness which has resulted in his hospitalization. This clear purpose gives form, content, and direction to the group meetings. It provides the given with which the men can struggle and against which they can discover their own purpose in relation to the purpose of the hospital for them, and their own strength for realizing it. They are helped to experience and weigh the conflicting feelings which the pre-parole function introduces for them, the wanting to leave the hospital, not wanting to leave, wanting to use social work help in foster care, not wanting to, the hurt and the hope involved in what they and the worker are doing with relatives. At one point, as was earlier stated, the worker challenges the group on what they are doing, how they are moving toward a realization of the hospital's purpose in establishing the group, and questions their continuing if they are not using it constructively for themselves, as well as for the hospital, whether their decision is to be for or against leaving the hospital.

The purpose which inheres in the group work functional role is exemplified by the worker's evident skill in eliciting the kind of participation and interchange among the group members of which each is capable. It is exemplified further in his own participation, introduction of question, raising the "other side" for consideration, affirmation of what has been said, questioning what has been said or what is being expressed in nonverbal ways as he helps group members use the experience with each other and with him for surer possession and affirmation of themselves, their own wanting, and their own power for realizing their wants. Mr. West (fifth session) asks the worker to see the doctor for him. The worker's turning of this back to Mr. West is followed by group members' picking it up. "Mr. Kaye led the group in helping Mr. West see that he had a real part in this, and spurred on by 'God helps those who help themselves' Mr. West decided to plan to see his doctor." This is just one instance of the role of the group, as well as of the worker in his role as group worker, in furthering one member's realization of group work purpose, that is, use of the group for his own development and feeling of self worth. It realizes as well the specific agency purpose of helping patients discover and act on their readiness, or lack of readiness, to leave the hospital. Throughout all the sessions, the group's picking up and elaborating a point made by the worker, or the worker's underscoring what has been suggested by a single or several group members, carries an impact and significance for individual members not possible in an interview with the worker alone. Throughout, the experience of coming to the group, relating to each other and to the worker, learning to give consideration to ideas or feelings different from their own or to find strength through identification with others are themselves socializing experiences for these men, the heart of whose illness, whatever the specific psychiatric diagnosis, is incapacity to realize individual potential within society. The function of the group provides content for the experience of being together. Both the content of discussion of leaving the hospital (specific agency function in this instance) and the experience of group association for individual growth which is socially constructive (social group work function) conduce to a common end of individual and social welfare. As was earlier stated, the group has no purpose *as a group* since no life is projected for it other than the individual member's use of it. This makes it distinctive as a form of group work, but it does not rule out the opportunity to use group work skill as appropriate for this particular form of that social work process skill.

PRINCIPLE IV: *A conscious, knowing use of structure as it evolves from and is related to function and process introduces "form," which furthers the effectiveness of all the social work processes, primary and secondary.*

RECORD 1. A GROUP WORK SERVICE
FOR OLDER ADULTS

The worker's use of structure with this group includes her facilitating the group's determining the desirable frequency of meetings, length of meetings, content of meetings, proportion of time devoted to formal meeting and to card playing activity. It required, at the point of group formation, a consideration of group membership, basis for member selection, size of group, the place of the meetings "a recreation room in the apartment building where several of the members reside". Such selection of place both reflects the purpose of the group and is appropriate for carrying out purpose. Just as the structure of the group and the structure for group meetings evolved in process, and in relation to function or purpose, so structure or form in turn influences the social process, and specifically the social group work process, possible and desirable within it. The structure may be thought of as the bare bones which give form, assure continuity. It is the worker's investment of her human, professionally purposeful, knowledgeable, and skillful self which makes the structure work, which utilizes the structure for the accomplishment of a social purpose. When the women are reluctant to end that part of the meeting which preceded the card playing, the worker does not automatically cut off this activity with a stop-watch attitude, but she is sensitive to the lull that means the appropriate time is at hand to suggest the "other part" of the meeting. The group's wish to keep in touch with absent and ill members, introduced and championed by Etta, is given form, and so possibility of reliable realization, through the use of structure, the designation of such activity as the assigned responsibility of the secretary, Etta. Indeed the use of officers and the conduct of the meeting as through the traditional chairing of the meeting constitute a structure which furthers the participation of all and channels what transpires for subsequent action and realization: the suggestions for the Purim party, for giving a gift to the orphanage, for a dinner party. One interesting aspect of the structure of a group meeting, as one aspect of group work process, is the presence in the meeting of the group worker. The worker is part of the structure, with a different relation to the group from that the members bear to it. She is the server of the group; the group is served by her. Part of the content of this meeting was devoted to a consideration of the worker's role in this group. One of the members defined the relationship by saying "You are our employee." The worker rejected this and stated her function in a different way: "I am here to help the group help itself." What is missing in the member's remark is any sense of the worker as employee of an agency, the Jewish Center. The worker does introduce the agency and the group's connection with it when she refers to the "Jewish sponsoring agency." In general, the structure or form for this group's life, including the use of first names, reflects the kind of informality appropriate to the nature and purpose of this kind of group.

RECORD II. PRE-PAROLE SERVICE
FOR A GROUP OF MENTALLY ILL MEN

Here the structure takes the form of content for the discussions in group meetings, in fact for the use of discussion as the form of the group's activity; the use of meetings of a prescribed length and of a defined number (eight) as the maximum allotted for this particular group's life. As was stated in Chapter 8, the setting of an ending can serve as a means for promoting purposeful engagement and constructive use of what is limited and will not go on forever. The specific number of meetings or sessions appropriate in the particular instance grows out of experience with what seems the most productive span for the accomplishment of a particular purpose.

A piece of structure not referred to in this record material but used in this hospital, and presumably with this group, was the appointment card given to each man, carrying the date and place of the next meeting, together with the name of the worker. The concreteness of this piece of paper was found to have considerable meaning for the patients. It appeared to symbolize an individualization of them, as well as an expectation of a responsible kind of behavior, keeping an appointment in a specific place and at a specific time, which furthers such behavior and is characteristic of the kind of behavior that will be expected on the outside. The regularity of the meetings and the expectation of engagement within them constitute a form or structure which stimulates productive engagement. The meeting place, and always having the meeting place the same, could be thought of as holding a special meaning and carrying a certain expectation and symbolization which furthered what the men could do with the meetings. The holding of Social Planning Staff is a structure, a form, which channels the group's activities and gives purpose, direction, and substance to the group discussions. It is something to work towards. Within a hospital for the mentally ill, where time can be so endless and purpose and direction in living so lacking, it is particularly important to use time, defined periods of time (for example, eight group meetings) purposefully. The structure of time, in other words, assumes a particular importance, and its emphasis can be productive, as was the case in this work with a group of mentally ill men, long hospitalized. Because of the nature and purpose of this particular group, the form or structure was characterized by more formality than was true for the group of adult women.

PRINCIPLE V: *All social work processes, to be effective as processes in social work, require the use of relationship to engage the other in making and acting on choices or decisions as the core of working toward the accomplishment of a purpose identified as own purpose, within the purpose of the service being offered.*

RECORD I. A GROUP SERVICE
FOR OLDER ADULTS

The worker's activity is focused on engaging the group, and members of the group, from her beginning in the session, as when she "circulated saying something to each woman," and specifically when she raised the possibility of a Purim party with individual members, and later, in the group. The worker's intent is to see whether this group can engage in this activity through their own choice, after weighing both sides, as represented by individual members within the group, and by ambivalent feelings within individuals. Herein lies one of the complexities and differences in work with individuals and work with groups. For the caseworker in the individual interview, the task is to help an individual experience all sides of his feeling and thinking, and out of the conflict and tension thus engendered make what represents his fullest and truest choice of the moment; the group worker must help individuals within the group engage in the same kind of process with respect to some purpose for, or concern of, the group, but she has the further opportunity and responsibility to elicit the conflict which exists as between group members as a base for group decision.

The essential thread throughout all this session is the group's decision about the kind of group it will be as reflected in its choice of program, the kind of responsibility it will take for itself, and the kind of use it will make of the worker. Specifics of discussion, the Purim party, the giving of a gift to an orphanage, the theatre party, all represent choices to broaden the range of group activity and to bring its purpose closer to one particular aspect of the purpose of the sponsoring agency for it, without abandoning the equally important purpose of the agency for the group, and the group for itself, of card playing and "just sitting around like this and talking." This kind of provision of opportunity for human relationship in a group, and activity as a group, is an affirmed purpose of any group-serving agency in a democracy where life depends on the capacity of individuals to achieve responsible growth as individuals, capable of working together to achieve common and freely chosen goals. The content or substance of group activity, whether it is a hike to the park with children or card playing for a group of adult women, is relatively unimportant. The important consideration is that the program be appropriate for a given group at a given time, for a realization of the purpose of the sponsoring agency for it, and for the purpose of the profession (social work) through which the agency purpose is being discharged, as the group is able to make those purposes its own.

What gives the worker the right and responsibility to introduce program suggestions at all is her identification with the purposes of her profession and her professional process role (group work), as well as with the purpose of the specific agency she is representing. The *way* she introduces the suggestions, the *particular* suggestions she makes, and the way she helps the group and individuals within the group to work on them derive from her professional knowledge and skill. Difference or conflict arise: as between one member (Etta) with her concept of the kind of group this should be and the concept of the others; and as among Jewish members and between Jewish and Christian members of the group in respect to program choice; and in relation to the role of the worker, what it is and should be. In all instances, perhaps more skillfully carried out in the last two than the first, the worker's professional task is to elicit thoughts and feelings in the group in relation to the question, to recognize and respond to the feelings expressed and unexpressed, and to put in her own position when it is appropriate and helpful for that position to be introduced.

RECORD II. THE PRE-PAROLE SERVICE
FOR A GROUP OF MENTALLY ILL MEN

The same principle of the use of relationship, between the worker and the group, and between individual members within the group, to engage the group and its members in making and acting on choices or decisions, is clear in the second piece of material. Once again it is the purpose of the service being offered (pre-parole service of a mental hospital) which establishes the content of the choices to be made, the decisions to be reached: what to do in the face of the decisions of relatives with respect to the patient's planning, whether to continue with the pre-parole service through attending the group, how to get ready for Social Planning Staff where the hospital's decision will be reached, how to live within the hospital in such a way that the choice to leave has the best chance of being operative. Consistently the worker helps individual members face and deal with both sides of their thought and feeling, with respect to specific possibilities or actualities, just as he helps "both sides" to be represented through the participation of various group members who hold different points of view or express different feelings. When Mr. Downs says "Shucks he wants to get out of this place and the sooner the better" the worker does not let the ensuing one-sided agreement stand at that but frees the expression of the other side through raising the question of whether "there wasn't some problem whenever we left something." Mr. Hale's immediate denial is followed by Mr. Kaye's affirmation, "If you ever had to leave your family and home you would know how hard it is to leave." It is this kind of engagement, not just of intellectual processes, although that is of course part of it, but feeling engagement, the kind of engagement that derives from and leads to human relationships, which characterizes the decision-making processes in this (and all) group work practice. The depth and intensity of the feeling (relationship) involvement of members with each other and with the worker will be based on many factors: the emotional resources and capacity of the individuals concerned, the purpose of the group and consequent nature of the content of its meetings, the skill and the capacity for human relationship of the worker himself. But one of the characteristics of social work as a helping process as distinct from formal education is the conscious use of the worker's whole feeling, thinking self to engage the whole feeling, thinking self of the other to make and act on choices which involve something as total as a way of living or being, even though always in respect to some specific social situation or purpose.

The worker engages the group through introducing a purpose and keeping a focus which inheres in the reason for their being together; through eliciting and responding to thoughts and feelings on the part of the group members and the group with respect to that purpose as they discover whether they want to and can make it their own purpose for themselves; through utilizing the structure and form, the regularity of meetings and the time phases of the meetings as a whole and of each individual meeting; and through drawing on his knowledge and understanding of this kind of group, this kind of person and this specific person, this specific group, and of the elements in the group work helping process itself. Part of this worker's skill is the way he deals individually, in brief contact, following the meeting, or in ward interviews with group members whose behavior indicates the need for such help, in order to free them to use the group more fruitfully, or decide to leave it. As has been stated earlier, there is no attempt in this particular group to help the group as a group accomplish some social purpose, for that would be inappropriate. The nature of the program is also more controlled and circumscribed by the agency purpose than is true for the leisure time group, where there is more latitude for group decision on the specifics of content or program. The principle of the use of relationship for engagement of the group members and the group in making and acting on choices and decisions toward the accomplishment of a purpose identified as own purpose within the purpose of the service being offered remains the same. But the professional judgment of the individual worker is required to make appropriate application of the generic principle in the specific situation.

SUMMARY

The necessity, introduced at the end of the last chapter, which focused on social casework, to see the operation of all principles in relation to each other in order to apprehend the Gestalt of the helping process is obvious for these instances of social group work method. Perhaps it is clear as well that while the same generic principles operate for social group work as for social casework, they require a specific kind of application in the different social work process because of the different purpose of the process itself (within the encompassing purpose of any process in social work); the different configuration of relationships involved; and the different place of the worker in relation to the life and activity of the group as against the life and activity of an individual client, or even family members when seen "jointly." In the latter instance, the worker does not participate in the life of the family as an accepted part of it, and it would be false if he did, in the same way a worker participates and is part of the life of a group he serves. What has been suggested by the necessarily brief and somewhat fragmented discussion of two different illustrations of group work practice is that the generic principles as heretofore developed operate, but require an application specific for a particular process as well as for a particular agency function. It is further suggested that there are specifics of methodological knowledge and skill required as well, because of the nature of the specific process, its purpose, the configuration of relationships concerned, and the worker's role in relation to the persons served.

11 GENERIC PRINCIPLES OF SOCIAL WORK METHOD IN COMMUNITY ORGANIZATION

TO INTRODUCE a record which could be considered typical of community organization practice is even more formidable than was true for social casework or social group work. Although, as has been stated, of the three primary methods social casework was the first to be defined as *method,* followed by social group work, there is still controversy as to whether community organization can be identified as method or is, in fact, a distinctive method for social work practice. Recent years have seen a growing literature debate, discuss, and present various points of view about community organization as a field of practice and community organization as method. (See Chapters 3 and 5.) As a consequence, finding a record to show the use of community organization method to induce and sustain a community organization process has been difficult. Once again the record chosen is "typical" only in its use, or in its potential use, of generic principles of social work method.

The point of view of this book is that the generic principles of social work method, as previously developed, are as applicable to community organization method as they are to the two other primary methods and to all the secondary methods. As is true for all the methods, however, they both require a differential application and constitute a framework within which certain specifics of knowledge and skill must be further developed, refined, and applied, for the specific process to eventuate.

The record which is to be presented in this chapter is drawn from the files of a community council or welfare federation in a relatively large city. As auspice for community organization practice it could be considered common but not typical. The whole place and function of welfare councils is being reviewed in the light of the changing life in American cities, the changing nature of the community,* the multiplication of problems associated with urban living, and the introduction of programs, by the Federal government and by private foundations, to cope with them. Yet the record selected does present the opportunity to examine the five principles of generic social work method in respect to one area or auspice for practice currently using substantial numbers of social workers whose process concentration, in their formal educational, professional preparation, and subsequent experience, has been in community organization. Its "typical" elements *as method* derives from the nature of the professional social work skill required to engage and sustain the activity of citizens and organized groups within a community, toward community betterment, under the auspice of an organization whose purpose embraces both the goal of community betterment and the enlistment of community participation to achieve it.

THE LONGVIEW COMMUNITY COUNCIL

Late in August 1961 Mary Bates arrived at the Longview Community Council Office as the Area Field Worker of the Sterling Welfare Federation. Since 1945 the Welfare Federation of the Metropolis of Sterling has provided the services of social work trained community organization practitioners to numerous georgraphic areas within the city in order to help find solutions to health and welfare problems at the area level, thereby contributing to more effective and efficient social welfare planning within the community-at-large.

One of the twofold goals of the Federation's Field Service Program is:

To develop a quality of citizen participation which permits and encourages a sufficient degree of organizational collaboration for com-

* See Chapter 5, and particularly Warren's discussion of this point.

mon welfare within a specific geographic area and between members of an area and the wider community.

In order to implement this goal, Sterling's Welfare Federation Field Workers have traditionally assisted in the development and maintenance of an Area Council structure in twenty sections of the city through which all significant groups may become involved in community discussion, decision, and action on problems affecting their common welfare.

Longview, a community of 40,000 population, has long been known as the Italian section of town. It is a very stable area of primarily second and third generation Italian-Americans. Property ownership is about 70%, with parents passing on the home ownership to the children.

Most of the male employment is in the steel mills and related industries located throughout the community itself.

The Catholic Churches play an important role in the life of the residents, with many children attending the parochial schools, and adults active in church organizations.

ORGANIZATION OF THE LONGVIEW COUNCIL

For the last three years the activities of the Council have been concentrated in two areas: (1) attempting to get the major steel mill to install air pollution controls and (2) stimulating a voluntary community home conservation program.

Residents have considered the most acute problem in the area to be air pollution. Thick clouds of smoke, fumes, and odors are often spread over the community. Vigorous efforts on the part of the Council to get industries to control the pollution culminated in internal fighting within the Council, disbanding of its air pollution committee, and a sense of defeat.

The home conservation program represents a long-term education program, with intensive efforts being made throughout the first three years of its life. The Council encouraged the development of independent neighborhood associations which would have membership in the Council, and would carry out home conservation programs in specific neighborhoods in cooperation with the Council.

At the time of Mary Bates's arrival the Council had been without professional staff assistance for five months. The Council held its annual planning evaluation meeting in August just prior to the advent of Mary Bates.

In August the Longview Community Council Executive Committee consisted of twelve members, four officers elected by the total Council membership and the remainder appointed by the President.

The President, Bill Angelo, is a self-employed realtor who was reared in Longview. He served as Chairman of the Home Improvement Committee and as Vice-President of the Council before his election to the Presidency.

The Vice-President, the Reverend Harold Stark, is a Protestant minister who lives in a suburb adjacent to Longview, to which many of his parishioners have moved. His church is still in the area and he serves as president of a neighborhood club which organized around his church area.

The Secretary, Mrs. Ann DeLassandro, has been active with the Council since the death of her husband three years ago. She is employed as a receptionist at the local hospital.

The Treasurer, Mrs. Pat Reilly, recently moved away from the community. She has been active with the Council for about five years. A divorcee, she lives with her mother and three elementary school age children. She is Office Supervisor in an industrial firm. For the last two years she has served as Treasurer of the Larimer Neighborhood Club in the area where she used to live.

Membership Chairman, Charles Senza, the former President of the Larimer Neighborhood Club, served as Chairman of the Longview Council's Air Pollution Committee until it was disbanded earlier this year. He is a salesman for a candy company.

The Reverend Bob Long is a Protestant minister new to the area. He has been with the Council about two years, following in the footsteps of the former minister of his church. Although his parishioners are moving out to the suburbs he is actively recruiting new memberships from within the Longview community for the church and for participation in church activities, for example, a nursery school and a dramatics group.

Miss Betty Woodward, the local Neighborhood Center Director, has served on the Council Executive Committee for a number of years and has been active with the Council since its inception. She is well known and respected in the area, and a worker from the Center gives service to several of the neighborhood clubs.

Three new people were appointed to the Executive Committee during the summer by the President: Mrs. Pardone, Mr. Wills, and Mr. Banks. Mrs. Vera Pardone, appointed as Recreation Committee Chairman, is a housewife and the mother of four children. She is President of the Mayflower Neighborhood Club, which has been quite active in the Council. Mrs. Pardone has found much satisfaction in civic activity since it gives her the sense of being "a person in my own right." Fred Wills, bachelor, is the present Chairman of the Home Improvement Committee, and recently elected President of the Drake Neighborhood Club, which has not had good relationships with the Council over the last two years. Wills is a former housing inspector for the city. David Banks, high school teacher, in a suburb of Longview, is Chairman of the Schools Committee, and the local Ward Leader. He has a history of poor relationship with the Council and with former field workers around the Council's air pollution acitivities; and he has been accused of using the Council for political gains.

Mrs. Marie Taska resigned from the Executive Committee after attending the first committee meeting of the year without giving any reason in her letter of resignation. Mrs. Taska had been involved with the Council since the early 1950s; she was a leader in organizing the Council to fight air pollution and was very instrumental in getting the Home Improvement program started.

Father Michaels, immediate Past-President of the Longview Council, died the latter part of August. The President, Bill Angelo, told Mary Bates that the Father's death might mean the loss of some members of the Council; Father Michaels had been a very strong, idealized figure in the community; he had served as president of the Council for three years.

LONGVIEW COUNCIL EXECUTIVE COMMITTEE MEETS. The first executive Committee meeting of the Longview Community Council for the 1961–1962 program year was called in September by the President, Bill Angelo. All the members of the committee were present.

The Community Organization worker, Mary Bates, was shocked by the procedure which the President employed in conducting the meeting. He "told" the other members of the Executive Committee what the program at the general meeting for that month would include, without even the slightest attempt at soliciting comments from the committee. In a similar manner he moved through other items of business. Miss Bates had met with the President just prior to the meeting and knew what would come up for discussion, but she had not predicted the authoritarian manner in which it would be done.

At one point in the meeting Mr. Angelo called on Bates to make any comments she would like as the new field worker. Bates expressed her pleasure at being with the Longview Council and explained briefly what she saw as the function of the Welfare Federation's Field Service in Longview, using illustrations of the kinds of activities in which she might be engaging. Bates said that the worker would no longer be placing as much emphasis on work primarily with the Council, but would concern herself with the total Longview Community and work with health and welfare agencies and other groups and organizations in the community. Bates noted that the former worker with the Council had begun this approach of service to the community-at-large but that much of the program and operation of the Council, it appeared, had been carried by the field worker rather than by the Council itself. This was accepted by the members without any comments.

Another item which came up for discussion and involved Bates was the need for an editor for Longview Council's monthly newsletter. Bates explained that the former field worker and his office secretary had been getting out the newsletter in the past, but that if this was a citizen's newsletter it should be put out by the citizens of the community and not by professionals. The group did not seem aware of the great amount of time and effort the paid professionals had put into the production of the newsletter. Mrs. Reilly and Mrs. DeLassandro said that they had come into the office many times at the last moment to get the newsletter stapled and out in the mail. The committee agreed that an editor should be selected and workers obtained to work on the newsletter. The President said that he would see about getting someone to edit the newsletter.

Mrs. Reilly gave the Treasurer's report from the last meeting of the Executive Committee, but stated that she did not know what was presently in the treasury. She also said that a budget would have to be prepared for this year. Bates commented that as she had looked over the records in the field office there did not seem to be a clear record of past expenses and income. Mrs. Reilly commented that if the Field Worker was going to serve the entire community and not just the Council, that the Welfare Federation should be paying part of the operating expenses of the Council.

The Executive Committee agreed to the suggestion of the President that the Treasurer meet with Bates to set up a bookkeeping system and budget for the Council.

After the meeting, coffee was served by Bates, who felt that a social period following the meeting might help to develop relationships among the Executive Committee members.

BATES MEETS WITH ANGELO. Two days after the Executive Committee meeting, Bates called the President to arrange to talk with him about the meeting. He told Bates to come right over to his office. Bates said to him that she was puzzled as to why the members of the Executive Committee had not actively participated in the meeting. Angelo said that he knew that there would be some tenseness at the first meeting with his being new, and with a new worker and new members of the Executive Committee. Therefore, he said, he thought it would be best to restrict the discussion. Angelo said: "I was surprised and relieved that no one said anything about the appointment of David Banks. I thought there might be a blowup because he is not liked by some on the Executive Committee." Questioning by Bates revealed that Angelo had selected Banks as the School Committee Chairman in spite of knowing that there would be resistance to him and that he hadn't told any of the members of his action. Angelo seemed convinced that Banks could make a positive contribution to a School Committee because of his role as a teacher and his interest in the community.

Bates said that she felt sure that Angelo realized the importance of involving the Executive Committee in decision-making and that she could appreciate his apprehension about the first meeting. Bates did not say much more at this point in relation to the role of the Executive Committee or the President's appointment of Banks (and two others) to the Executive Committee because of her newness to the situation, her need to learn more about committee members' relationships to each other, and past modes of functioning of the Council. A telephone call to the Neighborhood Center Director, Miss Woodward, about the President's authoritarian manner brought the reply that if members of the committee had had something to say they would have said it.

BATES MEETS WITH REILLY. The following day Bates had arranged for herself and the Treasurer, Pat Reilly, to set up a system of bookkeeping. Bates said that she felt Mrs. Reilly was quite competent and capable of taking total responsibility for the Council's funds. Mrs. Reilly explained that in the past she had always received a financial statement from the worker the night of an executive or general meet-

ing, but that she had had no responsibility for payment of bills or anything else. She merely signed the checks; the worker's office secretary
handled the accounting of all finances. Mrs. Reilly expressed enthusiasm about setting up the new system and having responsibility for
keeping account of where money comes from and goes to.

While discussing the finances of the Council, Mrs. Reilly initiated a
conversation about how upset she was at the way the President ran
through a meeting and also how upset she was at finding David Banks
a chairman of any committee of the Council. She continued to state
that Angelo had not consulted with anyone on the Executive Committee with regard to new appointments. The other two new members are
not controversial figures as is Banks. With much heatedness, Reilly
told Bates of things which Banks had done against the interests of the
Council such as writing unauthorized letters on behalf of the Air Pollution Committee of the Council. She assured Bates that she has had
many years of experience with the Council and knows how executive
committees are supposed to operate. "And Bill Angelo knows too," she
said. She referred to the way Father Michaels used to do things, noting
that he was always very democratic. He would call members of the
Executive Committee about every important decision.

In between her negative comments, Mrs. Reilly said that she was not
blaming anything on Bates; that, of course, it was not Bates's fault. She
said she realized Bates had to listen to all sides of a story and that she
had to work closely with the President.

Picking up again, Reilly said that Mrs. Taska was going to quit.
"She and everyone else," said Reilly, "were surprised to see Banks sitting in the Council office that night. Banks had been a sore point with
the Council," Reilly emphasized, "and he has worked against the
Council rather than for it." She related Banks's comment during coffee
after the meeting the other night: "Why doesn't the Council pay for
the Executive Committee memberships out of the treasury, since others
seem to have been dipping into the treasury." Reilly said that he had
no right to make a comment like that. Bates agreed with her, and said
that she would help set the record straight about the treasury.

Bates suggested that Mrs. Reilly talk with the President about her
feelings. She also suggested some of the reasons which the President
had shared with her about his behavior. Mrs. Reilly said that the President was aware of what he was doing, and if he wanted to talk to her
he should get in touch with her.

The conference ended with Bates saying that she would attempt to see what could be worked out in the situation.

SECRETARY TAKES RESPONSIBILITY. After the October Executive Committee meeting (at which there was a bit more participation of committee members, but which was still held tightly in control by the President, with members not asked to make any decisions), Bates called the secretary, Mrs. DeLassandro, to ask if she would take the responsibility of sending out postcard notices to the Executive Committee members each month notifying them of the meeting. This responsibility had heretofore been carried by the field worker's office secretary. Bates considered this to be another step in the direction of making the Council as self-sufficient as possible and as independent of the Welfare Federation as possible. Mrs. DeLassandro beamed: "I'll be delighted to do it. I've thought that was something which I should have been doing, but the former field worker never said anything." And so it was agreed. "Shall I call you, Miss Bates, each month to confirm the date of the meeting?" Bates said that it would be better if she checked with the President.

A MEMBER RESIGNS. Bates arranged a meeting with Mrs. Taska to discuss the Health and Welfare Committee, of which she has been chairman. Mrs. Taska had not attended the September general meeting or the October Executive Committee meeting. As Bates approached the topic of Health and Welfare Committee, Mrs. Taska said that she did not feel she could actively participate in the Council anymore. "My health has not been good. I only continued on at the insistence of Father Michaels." In response to questions about the activities of the Health and Welfare Committee, Mrs. Taska said: "They created that committee just to keep me on the Executive Committee. There are nurses and a health center in the community to care for that. There is nothing we can do."

Mrs. Taska showed Bates around the hospital, where Mrs. Taska does volunteer work, and then took her home. She reminisced about the many meetings which had been held at her home and out of which was born the Home Improvement Program of the Council.

Bates thanked her for all the information about the past activities of the Council and suggested that if she were definitely convinced she no longer could participate on the Executive Committee that she let the President know by telephone or letter. Taska said she would do so within the next day or two.

After the November meeting, with still no word from Mrs. Taska to the Executive Committee, the President asked Bates if she would attempt to see what was what. Bates called Mrs. Taska and stated that the Council was asking what had happened to her; that they were not aware of her resignation since there had been no letter from her. Mrs. Taska remarked that she had thought Bates would tell the others. Bates said she had not, that she thought it better this come from her to the Executive Committee. Taska stated that she would get a letter off to Mrs. DeLassandro. A letter was received and read at the December Executive Committee meeting. The letter of resignation merely stated that she was offering her resignation from the Council.

At the December Executive meeting, David Banks moved, and it was unanimously approved, that a letter of appreciation be sent to Mrs. Taska for her devoted work with the Council over many years and that such a letter be published in the monthly newsletter.

CONTROVERSY BECOMES EVIDENT. Between November and January the tension among certain members of the Executive Committee heightened. Feelings of rejection, hostility, and distrust became evident to Bates and to other on the Executive Committee, who were not themselves directly involved in the personality conflicts which had been building up within the Council.

At a meeting of the Larimer Neighborhood Club, which Bates attended as part of her orientation to the community, Mrs. Reilly approached her and asked if there had been an Area Council Association meeting that month and whether or not she was still the delegate to the Association from the Longview Council. Bates said there had been a meeting, but she had not known that Mrs. Reilly was the delegate. She mentioned that Bill Angelo was present, and that he had asked about her absence. Mrs. Reilly laughed and said "I'll bet." She followed up this remark with such statements as "the President is trying to ease me out of the Council." These statements were made in front of the Larimer Neighborhood Club President and Chuck Senza, Longview Council's membership chairman.

Bates's later inquiry into the Area Council Association mailing list revealed that there had been a slip-up at the main office and that Mrs. Reilly's name had not been put on the mailing list as a delegate this year. This was remedied on the spot, and Bates called Mrs. Reilly to tell her of the error. Bates could not be sure whether or not Mrs. Reilly believed her.

After this incident, when Chuck Senza came into the field office to check on memberships, Bates took the opportunity to ask him what he could tell her about Mrs. Reilly's apparent attitude that she is not wanted by the President of the Council. Bates's inquiry set off a negative reaction. He stated gruffly that Bill Angelo knew what he was doing when he put David Banks on the Executive Committee. He commented in relation to the past meeting of the Executive Committee: "They were ready to create another air pollution committee the way they were talking." In response to Bates's query about whom he was referring to he said "Angelo and Banks." "They're in with each other." (At the meeting to which Senza was referring, the President reported on an article in the newspaper about the City Council's Air Pollution Committee. Banks made a few comments in relation to the article but gave no indication of the Longview Council's doing anything. And Bates was asked to report on the air pollution conference which she had attended at the Science Institute.) When Bates tried to encourage Senza to talk with the President about the situation, Senza laughed and said there was nothing to talk about.

AN EXPLOSIVE DECEMBER MEETING. The Secretary, Mrs. DeLassandro, was requested to read the letter which she had been authorized to send at the November general meeting. It was a letter commending a psychologist at a local State Hospital for volunteering her services when a cut-back was made in salaries. The motion to send such a letter had been made by David Banks.

Mrs. DeLassandro had called Bates several days prior to the December meeting, seeking Bates's reaction to her letter. In the conversation Mrs. DeLassandro commented that she wondered how many letters the Council was going to be writing to people, for every little thing. She didn't seem quite certain that she approved of sending the letter. Bates mentioned that this was a decision of the general body at the last meeting; that if she had some question perhaps it might be good to raise it with the President. "Well, I just don't know whether we ought to be sending this kind of letter." The following day she called Bates again, this time to inform her that she had checked at the hospital and found that the psychologist was not a doctor and that she had almost made a mistake and addressed her as "doctor." Bates mentioned that it was good thinking on her part to check on the name of the woman.

Immediately after Mrs. DeLassandro's reading of the letter, Chuck Senza asked gruffly: "How many of these letters are we going to be sending to people; there are lots of people whom we know in the Community who should get letters for the things they do. Our Secretary will spend all of her time writing letters." The President asked the Secretary how many letters she had written this year. She replied: "About three or four." Mr. Banks began to defend his position and stated that the Council had taken action to do this. Chuck Senza noted: "We were saved a great embarrassment because the Secretary looked into the situation and found that the woman was not a 'doctor' psychologist." Mr. Banks said that was not the issue; that regardless of what her title she had done a commendable thing and that it was appropriate for the Council to express this to her. Bates commented that Councils do engage in this type of letter-writing activity, some to a greater degree than others, but that this is an appropriate function for Councils to serve. She said also that discretion should be used with regard to whom and about what letters are written. Bates suggested that the Executive Committee might want to explore the policy of other Councils in this matter in order to help them reach some decision. The President, who had remained quiet throughout, stated that this was not necessary; that the Council had done this before, for example, with liquor legislation. Bates suggested, and it seemed agreed upon through silent consent, that the next occasion for letter writing be considered more carefully.

As the meeting progressed, Mr. Banks questioned whether or not the other letter to the state regarding the relief cuts had been written. Mrs. DeLassandro said that she did not have any such resolution recorded in her minutes. Tension continued to increase. Mrs. DeLassandro said that she had always taken correct minutes in the past, no one has ever questioned them, and that if the resolution had been passed she would have recorded it. Mr. Banks defended his position that a resolution had been passed, and he re-enacted in detail what was said at the general meeting. Bates asked if others on the Executive Committee could recall what had been decided. Mrs. Reilly and Chuck Senza had not been present at this meeting, the others were not clear on what had been decided because of the confusion that evening of carrying on business interrupted by the giving of awards for home improvements.

Bates suggested that perhaps this situation indicated the need for clearer procedures in the future with regard to motions. She suggested that after a motion is made the President request the Secretary to read it back to be certain that it is recorded correctly. "In this way," Bates said, "a slip-up would be less likely to occur." Bates herself had not been present at the general meeting when this discussion was taking place.

Two days later Mrs. DeLassandro called Bill Angelo to say that she wanted to resign. Mr. Banks had sent her a photostatic copy of the article appearing in the newspaper which, he said, supported his contention that he had not referred to the psychologist as "doctor" because it was nowhere in the article which he had used as reference at the general meeting. Implied, although not said, was that it was she who had made the error. Mr. Angelo reassured her that she was doing a good job as a secretary and that she should not let this upset her. However, in a conversation with Bates, Angelo said that he questions the minutes because sometimes in the past he has heard things read in the minutes that he knew had not taken place at a meeting.

To Angelo, Bates supported Mrs. DeLassandro's position that Banks should not have been so insensitive as to send a photostatic copy of the news article to everyone on the Executive Committee; that this kind of behavior could not help him to win acceptance on the committee. Angelo said that he would talk with Banks.

Mrs. DeLassandro had tried without success to get in touch with Bates on Friday of the newspaper incident. After the weekend Bates got in touch with Mrs. DeLassandro on another matter (Mrs. DeLassandro had told the office secretary not to let Bates know that she had tried to get in touch with her). Mrs. DeLassandro said to Bates that it was a good thing she had not been able to reach her on Friday as she would have resigned. Bates assured Mrs. DeLassandro of her value to the Council and tried to help her see what might be involved in Bank's behavior. Mrs. DeLassandro said that she felt the Council to be very important and that she wanted to stick with it, but that she wouldn't be able to take too much of Banks's behavior.

OPEN CONFLICT DEVELOPS. The precipitating factor in the Council's conflict revolved around a letterhead. Bill Angelo had got a letterhead for the organization without consulting with the Executive Committee, although he had talked with Bates about it. Mrs. DeLassandro commented at one of the Executive Committee meetings that she did not like the stationery. When the supply of letterhead stationery ran out, Angelo suggested that Bates look into other stationery which might be less costly. Bates continued to view as one of her goals to get the Council as independent of her as possible. Therefore, she suggested to the Treasurer, Mrs. Reilly, one day when she was in the office that she accept the responsibility for looking into the letterhead for the Council. She readily enough said she would.

Two days later when Bates was in Angelo's office discussing the business of the Council, she mentioned that in line with her philosophy she had asked the Treasurer to look into ordering the letterhead, and that she had accepted. Angelo said, "I want to see a copy of the letterhead before it goes through." Bates said that she specifically mentioned that to Mrs. Reilly, and that she wasn't sure whether or not Mrs. Reilly would go ahead and order some. Angelo said to be sure that she checks. Bates left word with her office secretary that when Mrs. Reilly called in, as she was expected to do that day, she relay the message that Bill Angelo wished to see a copy of the letterhead before she ordered any. This was done.

During this meeting between Bates and the President, the President said that he could no longer take the lack of cooperation which certain members of the Executive Committee were exhibiting. He said that Chuck Senza had not done a thing to get members other than to ask the office secretary to write some letters and to write membership appeals in the Council newsletter. "Chuck is really only interested in his Larimer Neighborhood Club and in the one problem of air pollution," said Angelo. "Now that the Council is not concerning itself with air pollution Chuck is no longer interested. Now that the Council is attempting to bring into its fold other neighborhood clubs in addition to Larimer, and people from different areas of the community, the 'clique' is losing interest." He stated repeatedly that some of the members of the Executive Committee did not really have the broad interest of the community at heart, that these people had "personal reasons" for being in the Council.

Bates discussed openly with Angelo the kinds of accusations which Pat Reilly and Chuck Senza had been making about him. Angelo said he was not behaving differently from the way the Council had operated in the past, but when Father Michaels and the former field worker were in the front seat no one objected. Now the story was different. He said that he realized he wasn't acting as a president should ideally behave, but that he didn't have around him the cooperative people necessary to make a Council run smoothly. On this occasion, as on others, Bates attempted to point out the importance of good operating practice on Angelo's part regardless of what went on under past leadership. Angelo said that he wanted to bring things out into the open at the January Executive Committee meeting. He wanted to know what Bates thought about this. She said to go ahead.

CHARGES AGAINST ANGELO. The following day Mrs. Reilly came to the office to work on the budget. She told Bates that she was very angry about the way the President handled the letterhead business. She wanted to know why it was all right for him to get a letterhead without anyone's approval, but that she had to get his. She said that she thought it was proper to submit a copy of the stationery to the total Executive Committee, but that he should have done that too. She was also annoyed that the Executive Committee meeting was delayed until the following week because the President was sick. "Couldn't the Vice-President have conducted the meeting? Why must *he* be at everything?" Bates told her that the Vice-President could not attend the meeting either.

Bates attempted to explain what had happened about the stationery: At a former Executive Committee meeting Mrs. DeLassandro had criticized the paper, and Angelo thought it would be best not to leave the responsibility to one person, so that no one person could be criticized if anyone did not like the paper. This Mrs. Reilly did not accept.

She asked Bates if it would not be possible to get someone from the downtown office of the Welfare Federation to come in as an objective person to look at the situation within the Council. Bates told her that the field worker is supposed to be the objective person. Mrs. Reilly said that Bates, of course, has to work with the President, that she has to listen to his story as well as to hers and the others, and that Bates could not help but be involved.

Bates told Mrs. Reilly that Angelo, likewise, was concerned about how the Executive Committee was functioning and that he was thinking of bringing it up for discussion. She said if he didn't that she intended to introduce the business about the paper at the January meeting. Bates encouraged her to do so. However, Bates also cautioned her about keeping the discussion out of the realm of "personalities," but rather on the function of Executive Committee members.

Mrs. Reilly repeated that this "situation" was not Bates's fault. She also brought out other factors that were disturbing her about the President.

First, she said that Bates had been hired on the president's okay with the downtown office: that the others on the Executive Committee had not been consulted after their interview with the worker. She said that they had wanted a man, but that they realized they needed to get somebody to work with them. She said, "We would have taken anyone." Bates mentioned that they had interviewed a man for the job. Mrs. Reilly said that he didn't want the job. Bates suggested that the Council would not want just anyone for the job; that the person should be competent regardless of whether a man or a woman. Mrs. Reilly said, "Of Course, anyone the Federation would send out to talk with us would have been professionally competent."

Second, the President had appointed new officers in August, but at the annual August planning meeting of the Executive Committee they were not told of this nor were the new officers present. She said that Angelo knew they would object to Mr. Banks.

She reiterated her objection to Angelo's not seeking the advice of the Executive Committee in developing the programs of the Council. She said, "This has become a one-man Council." She mentioned that at the first meeting of the year she and the Vice-President had arrived early and saw the President and field worker talking, and they waited in the outer office until the others came. Then when the meeting moved along without any soliciting of the opinions of the Executive Committee members she thought that the President and Bates had decided what the program was going to be and that was that. Bates explained to her that she and the President had been able to get together prior to the meeting and were discussing what should be on the agenda for the meeting. This, Bates explained, is the appropriate role for the field worker.

Mrs. Reilly said that she objected to Angelo's having to attend all meetings of a citywide nature, for example, the Area Councils' Association meetings; and she objected to his giving the publicity to the newspapers rather than appointing someone else to be in charge of publicity.

Bates attempted to indicate to Mrs. Reilly the number of changes taking place simultaneously in the Council and that it was expected that things might not run smoothly. Bates noted that it was unfortunate that the Council was unable to wait for the new worker to start before having the annual planning session in August. Mrs. Reilly said that they wanted to wait for the new worker to come before setting goals firmly—"We wanted to see what the worker's goals for the Council would be." She said that the former worker had emphasized publicity—getting the Council known. "We didn't know what you'd want to do," she said. Bates immediately said that the Council does not operate by the worker's goals but rather by goals which the members set for the Council. Reilly agreed, but said that each worker brought different goals to the group.

In further discussion with Mrs. Reilly about strategy for "clearing the air" at the January Executive Committee meeting, Bates emphasized that the group needed to clarify roles and also functions and responsibilities of different positions on the Executive Committee. Bates said that since she was new to the situation, she was unfortunately not in a position to be as helpful to the Council as she would be in time, also that the President was learning his role and needed Reilly's support and guidance since she had had considerable experience in the Council.

CONSULTATION WITH SUPERVISOR. The next day Bates consulted her supervisor about the conflict situation. Earlier in the year Bates had informed her supervisor that there was some internal conflict and that she would not be surprised should there be some turnover in Executive Committee members. Bates shared her analysis of what she thought was involved, which the supervisor considered to be a just evaluation of the situation. Bates's supervisor questioned the advisability of bringing this situation before the total Executive Committee in the light of what it might do to the morale of those members not directly involved in the conflict. The supervisor suggested that perhaps it might be better to have a meeting of those persons involved—President, Treasurer, Membership Chairman, and the worker, if desired. The Supervisor said that perhaps the situation could not be handled on any other than the "personal" level, but this should be avoided, if possible. The supervisor said that she would be available to talk with the Council about the functions, roles, and responsibilities of different officers should the Council desire; and that she has done this kind of thing with other Councils and it seemed to be helpful.

Bates talked with Mrs. Reilly after her conference with her supervisor and suggested to Reilly the idea of the small group meeting to discuss the difficulty. Reilly did not agree to this. She said that others on the Executive Committee were not happy, but they did not say anything directly. For example, she said, she had talked with Mr. Stark, who had mentioned a couple of things that concerned him. He was surprised when Mr. Banks passed out political literature at the Executive Committee meeting when it was known that the Council was to be nonpolitical (the literature was both Republican and Democratic). Also, Reilly said, Mr. Stark told her that the President should consult more with the Executive Committee members. She said that it is known that Mrs. Taska resigned from the Executive Committee because of Mr. Banks and for no other reason.

When Bates told Reilly that she had discussed the situation with her supervisor and that the supervisor had agreed to come and talk with the group if requested, Reilly seemed satisfied. Bates said she would talk further to the President about this.

MEETING WITH THE PRESIDENT. Later that day Bates called the President and suggested they meet that day to talk about the Executive Committee meeting, which was the following evening.

Bates shared with Angelo the suggestion of the supervisor; however, he did not think this would be the best way. He felt that it had to come out in the open. Bates emphasized to Angelo that he would be the controlling person at the meeting, that it would be up to him to set the tone in which the discussion would be conducted. Bates said that she thought this could be a very constructive discussion, but that it would depend on how the President handled it. She cautioned him to steer them away from discussing personalities and suggested that they look at the respective roles involved. Angelo said that he considered he had been conducting the meetings in an appropriate way, no different from the way they had been conducted in the past. At this point Angelo informed Bates how business used to be conducted: The "clique" (field worker, Father Michaels, Mrs. Reilly, and Chuck Senza) used to pass notes to each other during Executive Committee meetings; all plans were made outside the meetings. He said that everything was made into a big production, lots of publicity in his estimation. The Council had been composed of a clique from one part of the community, and it was concerned with only one problem, air pollution. The democratic process was not used at meetings. When Bates asked why Angelo never said anything to them about this, he asked, "Who was there to talk to"? He said, "Now the shoe is on the other foot and they don't like it."

Bates said that Reilly told her that she had been on the nominating committee which selected Angelo for the presidency; she had said that they wanted to see a businessman in the leadership rather than a clergyman. Angelo laughed and told the worker how the officers had been chosen. At the annual dinner a group met in the hallway. Father Michaels asked him if he would be President; he said he would if Father Michaels would be Vice-President. The decision was made before any nominating committee was appointed. Angelo said that had he known Father Michaels would die and not be with him at the Council he never would have accepted the presidency because, he said, "I knew that I would have difficulty working with some of the Executive Committee members."

He told Bates some personal things about the Treasurer and said that some community people had asked him why such a person could be on the executive Committee. Bates suggested that the Council should not be concerned with the personal lives of members except as Council business might be adversely affected. Angelo admitted to Bates that he did not trust Reilly and Senza and that he did not want to give responsibility or ask their opinion. He said that he hadn't liked the way they had worked in the past.

Also, during the conference, Angelo told Bates that he has repeatedly received calls from Banks, or Banks had stopped in his office to talk about the Council. "I have to hold his hand." Banks thinks that everyone on the Council is against him, including the field worker. Banks and the former field worker, according to Angelo, had several run-ins. One time Banks had said to Bates that the former field worker "was led by the nose by our Councilman." Angelo said that he was getting weary of trying to keep everyone happy; that so many of these people seemed to have personal interests at stake. Bates encouraged him to talk about this and tried to help him see that everyone has his reasons for belonging to an organization such as a Community Council—that this is normal. But, if a person's personal interests begin to be detrimental to the Council and the community, then it might be better if the person were helped to get out of the Council.

ATTEMPTS TO INFLUENCE THE COURSE OF CONTROVERSY. Bates had called the Vice-Chairman, Mr. Stark, a few days before the meeting to remind him of the change in meeting date. Bates took this opportunity to state that it looked as if there might be some difficulty at the Council Executive Committee meeting. She said that he had probably been aware of some friction between certain members of the Executive Committee and that some attempt was going to be made to resolve this friction. Bates suggested that he as a minister and highly respected person could be helpful in getting members to look at the situation in ɛ calm manner. Mr. Stark said that he would do whatever he could; that he felt certain everything could work out all right because "they are all good people with the community's interest at heart."

Bates suggested that he might offer constructive criticism to the President when he noticed something which could be improved upon. Mr. Stark said that any time Angelo wanted to call and ask for his advice he would be most willing to consult with him. Mr. Stark ended the conversation by saying that he felt that "the Council may be going through some rough times, but what is needed is a sense of love and brotherhood and concern about our community; with this we will be able to forget our differences."

Bates went to the Neighborhood Center to talk with Miss Woodward a few days before the meeting in order to tell her what might take place. Miss Woodward said she would be sure to be in attendance. They had a lengthy discussion about what was involved and how the meeting might go—and what Woodward's role might be in the meeting.

Woodward felt the conflict was due to the number of changes occurring in the Council at once: both a new president and a new field worker; jealousy of Bates by Reilly, who had had a close relationship with Father Michaels and the former field worker, a male; Reilly's ambiguous feelings about the need to sever her relationships with the Longview Community since taking up residence in another part of the city; and, in general, the struggle for power between the old guard and the new.

The day of the executive meeting Miss Woodward called Bates to tell her that Angelo had been to see her that day (the day after Bates had spent two hours with him); Woodward said that she did not want to get into a confusing relationship with Angelo since he is also a member of her Board. However, she felt she had served as a listening board. She reported that Angelo asked her, "Have I been doing anything wrong?" (To Bates he has always presented himself as sure of his position, although Bates has criticized him repeatedly for not involving the Executive Committee in decision-making.) Woodward said that she assured him that she thought he was doing an excellent job, but pointed out the changes which had taken place and might create some uneasiness among Executive Committee members. (Angelo has used Bates's office secretary in somewhat the same way—as a sounding board and to question what he is doing. To the office secretary he mentions problems he is having, such as the reluctance of the councilmen to appear on the same program with him or at the same meeting. The office secretary has been in the Longview field office for seven years.)

The afternoon of the Executive Committee meeting, Bates arranged to see Mr. Long, which was the first time he and the field worker had talked since Bates's coming to Longview. Bates told him she had to see him to seek his advice, that the Council was going through some rough times and would need his leadership. He arranged to see her. Earlier in the year Bates had called several times to arrange a meeting with Mr. Long, but he would put it off, saying he was busy and asking Bates to call another week. Angelo told Bates that there had been an unpleasant experience between the downtown office and Mr. Long some time last year because Mr. Long was "outspoken" at some meeting. The details of the situation were not clear; however, Angelo said that he thought the situation had some influence on the lack of active participation by Mr. Long at council meetings.

Bates discussed with Mr. Long the central figures involved in the conflict, relating her discussion with Angelo around raising the conflict situation at the Executive Committee meeting and her concern about the group getting into an argument based on personalities. Mr. Long said he would have to be late to the meeting because of a counseling appointment, but that he would get there as soon as possible (he has been consistently late for Executive Committee and general meetings). Bates could tell by his responses that she had convinced him of his importance to the group and the special role which he could play in the conflict situation. He was definitely going to come to the meeting to do whatever he could. Mr. Long mentioned that Chuck Senza and Mrs. DeLassandro had been dating; that they had attended a play at his church. (This shed considerable light on certain things which had been happening in the Executive Committee. It explained how Senza knew about the change of meeting date before Bates was able to be in touch with him; and the coincidence of his raising the letter-writing issue at the December Executive meeting, voicing almost the identical rationale that Mrs. DeLassandro had voiced to Bates over the telephone prior to the meeting.)

Twenty minutes before the Executive Committee meeting Bates called the recreation committee chairman, Mrs. Pardone, to let her know that there might be some difficulty at the meeting. Mrs. Pardone said she had been aware of some differences of opinion among the Executive Committee members. Bates said that she didn't want her to get upset over the conflict; that this kind of thing is bound to occur periodically, but could be healthy if handled properly. Mrs. Pardone did not seem concerned. (Persons who had *not* been contacted by Bates were Mrs. DeLassandro, Fred Wills, and Mr. Banks. Bates had tried to get in touch with Chuck Senza. He had called the office and told Bates's secretary he knew of the Executive Committee meeting and would be there.)

THE MEETING. (All were present except Mr. Banks, who was attending a political ward meeting; he arrived at the moment the meeting was finished.)

The President opened the meeting with several announcements, then asked for the Treasurer's report (since the Secretary was late her report was put off.) Mrs. Reilly's face appeared pale as she gave her report and reviewed the proposed budget for the year. The President asked for any comments on the budget or the Treasurer's report. When there was no comment, Mrs. Reilly said she had something she wanted to ask. She wanted to know why when she was asked to get the letterhead stationery for the Council it had to be checked with the President, but when the President got the first batch of letterhead it did not have to be checked. She told how she had been asked by Miss Bates to get paper and that the following day the office secretary called her to say the President would like to see a proof of the letterhead before ordering any. She asked why the President had not called her directly; why this had been decided when the field worker was in the President's office and it had been relayed to her through the office secretary.

There was silence. Angelo asked in a tense voice whether she had anything else to say. "No." "Does anyone else have anything to say," Angelo asked. Silence. Miss Woodward was the first to break the silence. She said she thought she could understand how Mrs. Reilly would feel when the office secretary called her. She said that she knows how put out she feels when one of her colleagues or a board member has his secretary call to give a message rather than do this himself.

Silence. Angelo asked again in a strained voice, "Does anyone else have something to say?" Silence. Miss Woodward again spoke and raised the question as to whether part of the difficulty arose because people on the Executive Committee were not clear as to their duties and responsibilities. Mrs. Reilly said that could be, but asked why the President had taken so much responsibility on himself. Miss Woodward mentioned that at the last meeting the Council secretary (who had come in by this time) had criticized the stationery and that perhaps the president had not wanted to put any one person in a position of being criticized. Mrs. DeLassandro said, "Yes, I certainly did say I didn't like the paper; and I don't." Mrs. Pardone confirmed this had occurred. Angelo agreed that this was the reason why he had requested to see a copy of the letterhead before proceeding to run off copies.

He then asked if there was anything further to discuss along this line, encouraging the bringing out of differences. Mrs. Reilly spoke again (when it seemed no one else would say anything further). She said that she had not been pleased with the way things had been going; that she did not know what went on within the Council. All she knew was that she came into the office and worked on the books. She said proudly, "We have an account of where every penny comes from and where it goes." But she said that except for her Treasurer's work she has no idea what goes on; she is never called to ask her opinion about any part of the program. She said that a "particular member" of the Executive Committee was appointed without any consultation with the Board when it was known that he had caused trouble for the Council in the past.

Angelo said that this was the place to express such concerns and asked if there were others who had something to say.

Chuck Senza said, "Since we're putting things on the table, who authorized you to say what you did in the newspaper about air pollution on behalf of the Council?" An argument ensued as to exactly what was said, with Angelo saying that he was careful about what he said and requested the paper put in quotes exactly what he said—"that the electrostatic precipitators were an *apparent* reality, but we would have to wait to see how effective they are in elimination of the red smog." Mrs. Pardone asked Senza what he thought the President had said that was wrong; she said she had read it and didn't see where it could have done any harm to the Council.

Miss Woodward said that perhaps she could help by comparing this situation to her own board. She said, "If I think it is some controversial issue I consult with my board before acting, otherwise I act." She said that a president has to take on certain responsibilities and sometimes move without consulting with the Board.

Senza said that the President knew of the trouble which the Council had had with Banks writing letters on behalf of the Council about air pollution. He asked, "What is to prevent his doing this kind of thing again; he should never have been put on the Executive Committee." Angelo said that he was well aware of the difficulty over air pollution, that he had given grave consideration to appointing Banks to the Executive Committee but that he felt it would be better to have this man on the side of the Council rather than working on the outside to the detriment of the Council. He said, also, that he felt Banks could make a contribution to the Council because of his role as a teacher. Senza made a dissenting facial expression to this. Angelo said that he had consulted with Father Michaels in the hospital about appointing Mr. Banks to the committee, that Father Michaels had felt there might be difficulty, but that the President should do what he thought best. Angelo asked if Banks had done anything out of order thus far. No. Angelo said that he has informed all committee chairmen that they are to consult him before any letters go out on behalf of the Council.

Mrs. Pardone said that she was not sure that she was welcome on the Executive Committee; she didn't know whether or not she had been passed by everyone; however, she said that she learned something. She related that after her first recreation committee meeting she had called the newspaper to give a story on what the recreation committee had decided. The reporter had told her that perhaps she ought to wait until the board of the Council approved the proposed program before putting anything in the paper about it. Mrs. Pardone said she hadn't thought about that, or that it might have created trouble.

Bates suggested that it appeared from what people had been saying that there was a need for the Executive Committee to spend time in clarifying the different roles, responsibilities, and duties of each office on the Executive Committee. She said that other Councils have in the past also felt the need to do this kind of thing, and that it would be possible to get some help from the Field Service Department of the Welfare Federation on this matter. Bates said that it might have been very embarrassing for Mrs. Pardone had she announced the recreation program, and that mistakes can be made out of ignorance of the correct procedure.

Mrs. DeLassandro nodded her head and said that she thought this would be good. Angelo added that the Area Councils' Association had reviewed the constitutions of the twenty-four member Councils and was recommending to Councils that they re-examine their constitutions since there were weaknesses in all of them. He then acknowledged that he was new in this role and naturally would make some mistakes. The group agreed to take a look at the constitution soon. Senza, who was sitting next to Bates and looking at the copy of the constitution, asked the President if the constitution gave him the right to appoint committee chairmen on his own. The President quoted from memory that part of the constitution which gave him the authority to appoint chairmen.

Miss Woodward asked Mr. Stark what had been his experience with his Board, asking if it had not been his experience that when people were not clear as to their roles disagreements could develop.

Mr. Stark gave a "sermon," which proved to have a quieting influence on the group. He said that "sometimes in our zealousness to do a good job we do not seek the advice of our helpers or move as slowly as we might." He talked of the love and the brotherhood of all the members of the Executive Committee, stating that he loved them all and that he felt sure that in their common interest, the community, they could work together.

Angelo thanked him for his words ("always so appropriate," he said) and asked Mr. Long if he had something to say. Long said that he felt the President had explained why he decided to appoint Mr. Banks to the Executive Committee and that "we must have faith and confidence in those we select as presidents. I must admit that even I was shocked that first night to find Banks on the Executive Committee." (This brought a chuckle from others.) "But our President has given us his reasons for his decision and perhaps he is right. We ought to give it our best in order to make it work out. Banks is on the Board now and hasn't done anything to warrant our asking him to leave." Mrs. Reilly nodded her head to this and agreed verbally that he is on the board and they may as well work with it.

Mrs. Reilly said that Banks was really the crux of the matter; that once the President had him put on the Executive Committee, anything from there on that the President did was not right.

Angelo asked if there was any further discussion around this issue, or could they go on to other business. There being nothing further, they went on.

Fred Wills was the only member of the group who had sat silent throughout the meeting. When it came his time to report on that month's program, of which he was in charge, Mrs. Reilly commented that he had been silent throughout. He said that being new he really didn't think he could say anything.

As the meeting closed, Banks came up the stairs to the meeting room. There was nervous laughter, and Banks received "hellos" from some Executive Committee members.

AFTER THE MEETING. Bates talked with Mrs. DeLassandro several weeks after the meeting. DeLassandro said that it was unfortunate that the January discussion ever had to take place, and that people had to pick on such petty things. She was sure that had a man of the "cloth" been the president this never would have happened. She remarked that the President had been doing a good job; that she thought he handled the January Executive Committee meeting very well. She mentioned that perhaps in the future only men of the cloth should be presidents so that this type of thing would not happen. Bates assured her that she thought the Council was over the "hump"; that relationships would improve; and that it was natural that it take a while for people to adjust to a businessman as president when the Council has had a number of clergymen as presidents in the past.

Bates called Mrs. Reilly several weeks later about the books and budget. Bates was told that Mrs. Reilly knew that members of the Executive Committee had been "primed" for the meeting. She had asked one of the men after the meeting if he had known anything was going to take place. "He, being a gentleman, told me that he had been told of the issue." Mrs. Reilly felt that it was not good for people to be "primed" because their true feelings may not come out in the open. She said that it was obvious from what Miss Woodward had said and how well versed Angelo was about the constitution that people had been prepared. Bates acknowledged that she had talked with some members of the Executive Committee in order to get their thinking on the matter; and said she felt this was appropriate to do. Mrs. Reilly said she would do as much work as was needed for the next two months (until her term of office was up) but that she knew she didn't need to say any more (inferring that she would not be in the Council after her term of office expired). She said it was very obvious that she got excluded from any committee work, citing the last Executive Committee meeting at which she was not asked to help on the committee to seek funds for the Council, something which, as Treasurer, she felt she should do. Bates said that perhaps Angelo was not aware that the

Treasurer was supposed to be a member of the Ways and Means Committee, but that she felt certain Mrs. Reilly would be welcome and helpful on such a committee. Reilly agreed to come into the office, work on the books, and get names of previous members to call about renewing membership in the Council.

FOLLOW-UP—JULY, 1962. The remaining months of the Council's program year saw some of the following actions on the part of the Executive Committee members:

Attendance at Executive Committee and general meetings by committee members was sporadic. There did not seem to be any pattern of either withdrawal from the Council or increased participation on the part of individual members. Mrs. Pardone continued throughout the year to attend all executive and general meetings. Mr. Long attended only one meeting.

Mrs. Taska, who had resigned from the Executive Committee, did attend a couple of the general meetings and was received warmly by other members of the Executive Committee and the Council at one of the general meetings.

The letterhead for the Council was not mentioned again, and no action was taken.

Mr. Angelo made direct contact with members of the Executive Committee as the occasion presented itself with respect to programming, rather than going through Mary Bates. In turn, committee chairmen consulted directly with Angelo about issues and called him for general consultation. Mary Bates was called for consultation by Angelo at least once a month, and she consulted with committee chairmen as they requested professional help with problem identification, program, and strategies for implementing program.

Angelo appointed, without Executive Committee consultation, a nominating committee for the June election of officers. Mary Bates initiated a conference with Angelo about this. She advised that it would be in the interest of good Executive Committee relations to ask the advice of the committee or at least of the officers. Angelo did not do this. He did select persons from the different Neighborhood Associations to serve on the Nominating Committee although this did include persons who had not been active with the Council and who were not in a position to know the present officers and those who had been active on committees. At the suggestion of Mary Bates, Angelo asked Miss Woodward to serve on the committee. Bates explained that she could serve as the objective, professional guide for the committee.

Mr. Angelo was nominated and unanimously elected President of the Council for a second term of office. Mrs. DeLassandro had told Angelo she did not want the Secretary's office again, and so she was not considered. The secretary of one of the Neighborhood Associations was elected to the position of secretary in the Council, and Mrs. Pardone was elected Vice-President.

The nominating committee reported that no one would accept the nomination for treasurer and, therefore, they were throwing this out on the floor to the general membership. David Banks got up and nominated Mrs. Pat Reilly for the position, commenting that she had been doing such an excellent job. Mrs. Reilly turned red and with a nervous laugh accepted the nomination, although murmuring, "I don't know why I do this." Mrs. Reilly was unanimously elected to the office of treasurer. (Absent from this meeting were Mrs. DeLassandro, Mr. Long, and Fred Wills.)

Mrs. Reilly was congratulated by people after the elections. She said to Mary Bates that she always gets herself into this job, that no one else ever seems to want the job of Treasurer. Mary Bates said to Reilly that she was certainly very competent as a treasurer, and that it was very good that she would be in this position for another year in order to continue setting up the new bookkeeping system so that at some point it would be simple for someone else to step into the job.

Also, Mrs. Reilly took one morning off from work in order to participate in an annual community luncheon sponsored by the Council for city recreation workers. At this meeting she was introduced as one of the parent representatives from the Larimer Neighborhood playgrounds.

And, finally, the Council agreed to schedule its annual summer planning-evaluation conference shortly. This had been delayed because Angelo had not completed his selection of committee chairmen to replace those who no longer wished to serve. Fred Wills had been undecided as to whether or not he wanted to continue as Neighborhood Conservation Committee chairman, and David Banks was not sure whether he would be able to continue as Schools chairman in the light of other responsibilities. Chuck Senza was not being considered by Angelo for membership chairman. Other committee chairmen remained the same. Angelo was to make contact with Mr. Long to determine his interest and ability to participate in the Council since his participation this year had been poor.

Angelo was making these decisions on his own. He had not, to date, consulted with Mary Bates about possible individuals to fill these positions. He felt that he knew the community and the potential chairmen better than Mary Bates, and that he did not need her guidance in this area of responsibility.

PRINCIPLE I. *That diagnosis, or understanding of the phenomenon served, is most effective for all the social work processes which is related to the use of the service; which is developed, in part, in the course of giving the service, with the engagement and participation of the clientele served; which is recognized as being subject to continuous modification as the phenomenon changes; and which is put out by the worker for the clientele to use, as appropriate, in the course of the service.*

The distinguishing characteristic of the understanding required of the community organization worker is that it is not primarily and essentially of a single person, a client (in his social situation, and of significant others in their relationship to him) or of a single group *and* of the individual members within a group, in a context of other groups served by the agency and of the community within which it functions. A third dimension is introduced. The understanding asked of the community organization worker is of (1) the community to be served, (2) the specific group using professional social work help to serve it (in this case the Longview Community Council), *and* (3) the individual persons who comprise the group, in this recorded material the Longview Council, and specifically the Executive Committee of the Council, to which the professional social work service is being given. In other words, the community organization worker, in distinction from the social group worker is not serving a group directly, for the benefit in self-value and social functioning which members can derive from their group association, with the task or activity being secondary. He is making primary the service to the community, through community participation and effort. The benefits in self-worth, for individuals concerned, and in their capacity to function as members of a group become the secondary and derived goals. The worker's "diagnosis," in this record, is of individuals who comprise the Executive Committee of the Council (see the brief descriptions at the record's beginning) of the Committee as a group, and the Council as a group, and of the community which the Council is seeking to serve and of which it is part. The diagnosis of each of the three client elements, individuals, group (Council), and community, is related to the purpose of the undertaking and the relationship of each to it.

The community to be served is geographically defined by the organization, that is, the Welfare Federation, which is providing the staff service and has made a division of the city into areas eligible to receive service from Federation staff. The Community is described in terms that are relevant for the kind of service a Welfare Federation is prepared to endorse, support, and staff. For example, an understanding of the make-up of the Community, its cultural and religious groups, its kinds of industry, the groups and agencies which function within it is relevant to a definition of problems which would be appropriate for a Community Council to work on, and the Welfare Federation to support through staff service. Such understanding is relevant as well to a delineation of certain factors which need to be taken into consideration in working on identified problems. Understanding of "communities in general" is required of the professional worker, as is understanding of this kind of community (urban, industrial) and understanding of this *particular* community in those characteristics which make it like no other.

Similarly an understanding of the service unit, the Community Council, is required which derives first from an understanding of community councils in general, the kinds of problems which may arise within them, and their possibilities for constructive functioning. It derives in the second place from an understanding of this kind of Community Council, an autonomous group to be staffed by a large city Welfare Federation; and third, from an understanding of the Longview Community Council in all its idiosyncratic features. Once again, the individuals who comprise the Council and, specifically, in the record under consideration, the members of the Council's Executive Committee, which is the unit being served, need to be understood as individuals but with special reference to the way they are carrying their functional roles within the Executive Committee.

The primary identification of certain members of the Longview Council's Executive Committee with other organizations, such as neighborhood houses or their places of employment, rather than with the Council, plus the fact that some members have moved out of the "Community" or represent agencies, some of whose clientele have moved out of the Community, constitute important elements to be "diagnosed" in examining this particular Council and its potential for vigorous functioning in service to the Longview Community.

Understanding of group process and of the way the Council and its Executive Committee function as "groups" is required as well. Part of this understanding the worker brings to her task, as a generalized body of knowledge, but part of it on all three levels develops and changes in the course of the service being given, and continuously modifies *what* she does in her professional capacity and *how* she does it. The community, the Longview Community Council, and the members of its Executive Committee undergo continuous change in the course of the service being offered. Members of the committee participate in developing the workers' and their own understanding of each other, themselves, the Longview Council and the community, always in respect to the tasks being carried within, for, and as the Council.

The worker expresses to individual members and to the Executive Committee her understanding or "diagnosis" as it seems to her appropriate to move the process forward. For example, she follows her oblique reference to the kind of chairman Mr. Angelo is being ("she was puzzled as to why members of the Executive Committee had not actively participated in the meeting") by a more direct sharing of her own understanding, of what she sees him doing as chairman, with him—something which might have been preferable in the first place. "She felt sure that Angelo realized the importance of involving the Executive Committee in the decision-making." At the same time she gives recognition to the feelings that might make it difficult for him to elicit participation. "She could appreciate his apprehension about the first meeting." Such understanding of individuals in relationship to the way they are carrying their roles, their relation to each other, and to the Council as a whole with its change in leadership both lay and professional is shared subsequently with increasing skill and sensitivity.

PRINCIPLE II. *The effectiveness of any social work process, primary or secondary, is furthered by the worker's conscious, knowing use of time phases in the process (beginnings, middles, and endings) in order that the particular potential in each time phase may be fully exploited for the other's use.*

While there is recognition of the meaning of this beginning, with the changed lay leadership, that is, the new president, and the changed professional staff service, that is, the new worker, and some acknowledgement and use of it with the Executive Committee and individual committee members, the record does not reveal as full and frank a use of that recognition as might have been helpful. There is something of the feeling of "walking on eggs" and "building up a relationship," as through the coffee hour, a relationship which can in fact be built only through frank and courageous sharing of what is involved in working together in the immediate moment, as well as through actually *working* in the immediate moment. The coffee hour can supplement, but not substitute for, such opportunity for relationship building. The deepening of the relationship between committee members, between individual members and the Executive Committee as a whole, and between the committee members and the committee as a whole and the worker, as well as the assumption of increased responsibility by committee members and by the committee as a whole, which might be expected to characterize a "middle," are indeed evident. They are fostered by the worker through her encouragement of members to carry responsibilities formerly carried by the professional workers, sometimes perhaps, with insufficient awareness of what this change in the role of a professional worker occasions for the members and the Committee as a whole, as in the case of the ordering of the letterhead. Bates's decision to pass on to the treasurer a responsibility the chairman had asked her (Bates) to carry (that is, to order the letterhead), without discussing that shift with the chairman might have weakened the chairman's confidence in her, and led to some tendency on his part to by-pass Bates in the future. Bates's relaying of a message to Mrs. Reilly, through a secretary, to show the letterhead to the chairman was not helpful. Undoubtedly resulting from an effort to save time, it was costly in intensifying feelings which interfered with the committee process.

The worker is increasingly able to take on herself the expression of feeling, particularly negative feeling, which is directed to her, and to facilitate a more frank sharing of thought and feeling among the members. Yet this does appear to continue to hold some problem for her since she apparently neither invites nor does anything with the sharp negative toward her put out both by Mrs. Reilly and by the chairman, Mr. Angelo.

The "middle" might have been more effectively introduced and sustained had her skill permitted a frank reception of Mrs. Reilly's preference for a man worker, her missing of the old leadership both lay and professional, and her resentment of the way the worker dealt with the "letterhead situation." How this function, for the worker, of furthering and deepening engagement and the increased motivation and capacity to carry responsibility in relation to own purpose extends from the Executive Committee to the Longview Community Council as a whole is not revealed in this record, since it was not the focus of the recording. The turning point or crisis for this series of Executive Committee meetings appears in the final meeting recorded.

Whether the ending of specific committee meetings and individual conferences was handled with the skill that could have increased a sense of accomplishment, both individual and group, for affirmation of what had been arrived at or done, and for possession of a new sense of competence, is not clear from the recording. In general, the process in respect to use of time phases may have been intuitively rather than knowingly and consciously carried as an element of professional skill. How a fuller and more skillful use of this principle might have affected the process can only be surmised.

PRINCIPLE III. *The use of agency function and function in professional role gives focus, content, and direction to social work processes, assures accountability to society and to agency, and provides the partialization, the concreteness, the "difference," the "given" which further productive engagement.*

The purpose or function of the organization making staff service available, the Sterling Welfare Federation, with specific reference to its Field Service Program, is defined in the opening of the record with respect to "one of its twofold goals."

To develop a quality of citizen participation which permits and encourages a sufficient degree of organizational collaboration for the common welfare within a specific geographic area and between members of an area of the wider community.

The other goal, defined by this Federation for its Field Service Program,* but not noted in the record is:

To bring about a more effective alignment of welfare and related services toward the alleviation, control and prevention of social problems in a geographic area of the wider community, by placing primary emphasis upon developing collaborative efforts among local institutional representatives and programs.

Both goals inform all the worker's activity. The purpose of collaboration between organizations for community welfare, of developing citizen participation toward this end, in short of the achievement of community welfare and betterment through coordinated activity of citizens and groups is not only the purpose of the worker's sponsoring agency but it constitutes also one of the purposes of the profession whose knowledge and skill she is employing to achieve her agency purpose, as well as one primary purpose of the specific professional method she is employing.

It should be noted that other patterns of community council-

---

* From a statement on Goals and Objectives of the Field Service Program, 9/18/1961, prepared by the Welfare Federation and submitted by the worker to the author.

federation relationship are operative in other cities and locales. Here the councils are considered autonomous groups with staff service being supplied by the welfare federation. This makes for some ambiguity about just what the power and prerogatives are, and indeed what the role of the worker is, with respect to the council. What does the council have a right to expect from the federation of service? To what extent can and should the federation worker affect the choice of problem on which the council works or its way of working on problem, if the council is really an autonomous body? In other settings and cities, area committees as they are sometimes called, or community councils, are frankly established and operated as arms of, parts of, the Welfare Federation or Health and Welfare Council, which thus becomes the parent organization. In these instances, the committees or community councils are staffed by a federation worker (a community organization worker it is true) with the title and responsibilities of director of the area committee. Such organization has greater functional clarity, which makes it easier for the community and its area committees or community councils to know the rules (policies and programs of the parent body) within which the community councils operate, as an integral part of the parent body. The functional role of the worker with respect to the local council can also be established with greater clarity. In any event it is important for the local council, the sponsoring organization, and the professional worker to be clear about what the functional relationships are so that they may know what rightfully can be expected, each of the other.

The focus of this record on the conflict between executive committee members minimizes, indeed practically eliminates, mention of the specific tasks to which the council is addressing itself. The names of some of the committees still active suggest what some of those activities may be. It is conceivable that a sharper sense of agency (federation) purpose, on the part of the worker, as expressed in the second goal for its field service program might have resulted in more help to the executive committee chairman in defining program appropriate for the council at this time, for executive committee and community council choice and decision.* This point is reminiscent of Warren's comment about the strengthening of the horizontal relationships (among community groups and members) as a possible primary focus for community work rather than concentration on the task to be accomplished.

The conflict between committee members might then have been worked out in relation to the concrete and externals of program, with less opportunity for getting bogged down in the personal and relationship aspects as such. This is not saying that the conflict which developed around the changing professional role of the worker, the changed make-up of the committee, and the new officer and professional leadership did not need to be worked on. It did and was, in individual conferences and in the climactic meeting with which the recording concludes. There is a possibility, however, that the worker focused on group participation per se *at the expense of* what the group was established to do, or participate in.

The participation might have been helped by a greater emphasis on tasks to be done, broad social goals, rather than so exclusively on internal housekeeping tasks, such as purchase of the letterhead, or on the roles of the committee members as such, unrelated to their engagement in carrying specific projects. A more whole, balanced, conscious, and knowing use of agency (federation) function, in the sense of the kind of activity the federation was prepared to support through the assignment of professional staff, might have provided content, substance for the meetings in a way that did not ignore the conflict but gave it some channel for being worked on in the course of group movement toward appropriate social goals of importance to the council, the community, and the federation.

The worker's carrying of her functional role as community organization worker reflects her concentration on the "involving citizen participation and coordinated activity" aspect of that role. This is indeed its heart and one of the strengths of this recorded

* See discussion of this point in Chapter 5.

process. Perhaps parts of the record not here available would reflect a stronger sense of the community as a whole, its concerns and aspirations, and the worker's responsibility to it through her service to the executive committee and the council. There is evidence of her concept of her role as different from that carried by the previous worker, in its emphasis on furthering increased individual and committee participation and carrying of responsibility, and on fostering in the committee a stronger sense of itself as executive committee for the council with responsibility for itself.

However, the worker introduces her concept of her role as different from her predecessor's in a way that can feel depriving and the taking of something away from the members without taking responsibility for dealing with the negative feelings inevitably aroused. The ambiguity, earlier referred to, involved in giving staff service to an operation that is "autonomous" undoubtedly operates here.

Through conferences with individual committee members, and in the meetings, the worker seeks to clarify her role, both in what she says about it and what she does and does not do. She even suggests that someone from the central office of the welfare federation meet with the committee to present the structure and role operation of other councils staffed by the federation. The functional role of the community organization worker as here exemplified, like the role of the group worker, requires continuous definition with the group served, since the worker is both in and of the group she serves, yet with a different relation to it and responsibility to it than is true for the members. There is the further complication for the community organization worker of being responsible to keep in mind some "community" as a whole which constitutes the target of a service he is helping individuals and groups to give, through coordinated activity. The complexity lies in the configuration of relationships involved, and in the nature of his role responsibility as inhering in his representing his sponsoring agency, and as being to a community as well as to a group which seeks not something for itself and its members (primarily!) but to give service. This complexity inevitably introduces specific requirements of knowledge and skill in method, in addition to calling for the use of the generic principles being described.

PRINCIPLE IV. *A conscious, knowing use of structure as it evolves from and is related to function and process introduces "form," which furthers the effectiveness of all the social work processes, both primary and secondary.*

As was true for the illustrative records of social casework and social group work method, the structure which furthers the effectiveness of any process evolves from it and should be modified as indicated in its course. The Longview Community Council operates rather autonomously with a not altogether clear relationship to the organization which provides its staff service, that is, the Welfare Federation. Its "form" of operation is comparable to the form employed by all the other units (Councils) staffed by this Federation, and to some extent by this kind of organization, or similar organization, wherever found. The worker is required to invest himself, his own person, in using the structure to further the process through which the purpose of his agency, his profession, and his professional method are realized. The structure of Council meetings and Executive Committee meetings, with the traditional officers carrying the traditional responsibilities, is used. The use of committees to discharge specific responsibilities, essential to the realization of the encompassing Council purpose, constitutes an additional structure. The timing of the meetings and the use of individual conferences between the professional worker and committee members are instances of use of form as is the designation and consistent use of a place for meeting. The fact that the meetings are undated, without specific reference to their spacing, may suggest that time as structure has not been accorded the value and place in furthering process which might have been true. The fact that some members of the Committee attended as representatives of specific organizations whereas others represent a much looser group such as "businessmen" or "the clergy" introduces yet another element of structure which the community organization worker takes into account and uses.

The keeping of minutes, the setting up of agenda, constitute additional instances of form or structure which serve useful purposes in the eventuation of the Committee's purposes as a Committee, and with reference to the Council as a whole. They act as well as content for group consideration, and for the worker's own activity in furthering the group's movement. The function of the sponsoring agency, the Welfare Federation, itself introduces the structure of content for Council activity and, as has been suggested, might have been used with more definitiveness and sharpness than it was to give focus, substance, and direction to what the Council and its Executive Committee were or might be working on. Finally, the structure which is useful for and used for the furtherance of process evolves from the purpose and nature of the process itself: community organization process, as it has been earlier identified in this writing.

PRINCIPLE V. *All social work processes, to be effective as processes in social work, require the use of relationship to engage the other in making and acting on choices or decisions as the core of working toward the accomplishment of a purpose identified as own purpose, within the purpose of the service being offered.*

What is somewhat shadowy here are the specific purposes within the general purpose of the Welfare Federation, in respect to which choices and decisions are being made and acted on by the Longview Community Council. It is the fact that these purposes fall within Federation purpose, which entitles the Council to receive Federation staff service. There is some reference to two previous primary activities which have enlisted the work of the Council: (1) attempting to get the major steel mill to install air pollution controls and (2) stimulating a home conservation program. The former activity had been abandoned without accomplishment, "due to failure to enlist industry cooperation, and internal Council fighting," and the second objective has apparently been largely allocated to independent neighborhood associations to carry out, in cooperation with the Council.

In the first meeting, when the Council had been without staff service for five months and when a new president was succeeding a beloved and apparently able president who had died, an effective means for engaging the Executive Committee and its members might have been to recognize the newness, and what could be hard in it, and then to find a focus for continued activity. In other words, they might have established a significant purpose or purposes within the overall Federation purpose which the group could make its own and move ahead to carry out if it wished staff service from the Federation. The very concreteness and purposiveness of such activity might well have facilitated a more vigorous and forward-moving engagement of the Council, in relation to goals newly chosen or rechosen. Instead, the focus appears to be on the worker's role, with an emphasis on what, in distinction from the previous worker, she would not do and what she expected the group and community to do for itself; and on her broader concern than "just the Council," that is, on the total Longview Community. However laudable these goals might be for the worker to keep in mind and implement as she went along, putting them out so abruptly and totally to this group, which had suffered twin losses in leadership both lay and professional, might well have seemed, as was earlier suggested, like refusal to help and lack of concern for the Council and what it was trying to do at a difficult period in its life. Mrs. Reilly's comment reflects what many might have been feeling in this connection. "If the Field Worker was going to serve the entire community and not just the Council . . . the Welfare Federation should be paying part of the Council's operating expenses." The social period which follows this meeting to "help develop relationships" could have been less effective for that purpose, as has been said, than working together in the meeting toward defining mutual goals. Had this been done, and a focus for Council activity in the year ahead agreed upon, or at least introduced for consideration, the coffee period could be an occasion for continuing and deepening an interaction which had begun through purposeful and functional engagement, rather than quite so purely "the relationship part" of the encounter. The worker's sensitivity to feelings of members toward each other, the group, and herself is apparent, and there are instances of skillful working with those feelings, as earlier suggested.

It is easy in situations of this kind for the purpose to seem to become to "keep the Council going and the members participating harmoniously with each other" rather than to accomplish a social goal through the Council structure and through the community organization method of engagement of the Council members, the Council, and the community as means to that end. True, the value is in the means as well as the end, when the social work method is involved, and the social purpose of the development of communities, groups, and citizens motivated and able to realize social purposes in concert is realized, but in community organization it is possible that that purpose is best achieved not as primary goal but as secondary to the accomplishment of social task or, to put it more clearly, *through* the accomplishment of social task.

The principle of engaging the other in doing for himself rather than "doing for" as a way of furthering responsible choice and action is evident here, in respect to helping the officers and members carry out their duties, as it was in the group work record in furthering Mr. Brown's seeing the doctor himself, in the other group work record as well, and, in the casework record, in helping Miss Devlin make her own living plan. In each instance the worker's help is available, but it consists of furthering what the other can do in his own behalf rather than in doing it for him.

Feelings directed toward the worker are dealt with differently in the casework situation, the group work situations, and the community organization situation, in accordance with what is appropriate to the different pocesses, but in each instance feelings are recognized and handled as an accepted part of the professional skill involved in carrying the process. It has been suggested that the worker for the Longview Community Council might have dealt even more directly than she did with angry feelings projected on her in order to free the individuals concerned to make a fuller use of her help.

SUMMARY

In this illustration of community organization practice each of the five principles has been found to be operative though with varying degrees of conscious skill employed in their use. There has been some suggestion that the full exploitation of all the principles in their relationship to each other, and as appropriate for the particular process involved, might have enhanced the effectiveness of the process, even though this record is presented as an illustration of skillful service in a field currently at work on a definition of purpose and the development and refinement of method and structure to carry the process through which purpose is realized.

Specifics of knowledge and skill have been recognized as being needed as well. This is necessary because of some special characteristics of the process of community organization method: its purpose; the configuration of relationships involved in all their complexity of individuals and groups concerned; the role of the worker in relation to the employing agency, the group served, and the wider community which is the ultimate recipient of the service offered.

12 SOME IMPLICATIONS FOR SOCIAL WORK EDUCATION

IN THE preceding chapters, method has been identified as being as significant as purpose for giving social work its distinctive character. It has been suggested further that the use of social work method, identifiable as such through its embodiment of certain generic principles, is necessary for the full realization of social work purpose. The core characteristic of any method in social work has been noted as being its engagement of the person or client system served in the realization of a social purpose, out of own motivation and choice, as that purpose finds congruence with the purpose of the social agency which constitutes the auspice for the service offered. Other professions, and endeavors other than social work, may and do make use of the principle of engagement to accomplish their distinctive purposes. As was earlier suggested, it is the constellation of values, purpose, social sanction, or auspice for a service *and* method for realization of purpose which makes the resulting endeavor social work.

Five principles have been proposed for use in all social work methods, primary and secondary. In each instance it has been appreciated that the nature of the phenomenon served (that is, the client or client system), the configuration of relationships involved, the purpose of the worker as it inheres in the specific method, and the consequent, in some respects distinctive, role of the worker require not only a differential application of the generic principles but certain specific knowledge and skill as well.

If the use of a characteristic method is accepted as an essential element in professional practice, the profession in question has the responsibility for the development of skill in use of method as a central task for its programs of professional education. In this chapter an attempt will be made to suggest some requirements of programs of professional education for social work if students are to be prepared to realize social work values and purposes through the use of social work method, that is, through a theoretically based skill in practice.

Because method is directed always to the accomplishment of social work purposes and the realization of social work values, social work is concerned in communicating a body of knowledge necessary for the student to make his own if he is to use method effectively, with skill, in the administration of today's social welfare programs, and to take a leadership role in shaping those programs, and the social policy from which they derive, in the future.

This body of knowledge will necessarily be concerned with these things: (1) What has been called "the terrain" within which social work is practiced—the configuration of social welfare programs and operations, social legislation, social policy, in their relation to the socio-economic-political scene, within which social work has traditionally made its contribution. (2) Human growth, human behavior, and the way individuals use and are affected by the environment and by social processes, and in turn affect that environment and those processes, as individuals and through group and community life. (3) Some fundamental principles of scientific inquiry which make possible raising and working effectively on significant questions related to social problems, social welfare organization, and social work practice. And (4) certain basic principles and characteristics of all social work methods in their similarity and in their differences. In addition to its responsibility for communicating a body of knowledge the school of social work has the responsibility for developing skill in the use of method to accomplish social work purpose. The objectives of all parts of the curriculum are realized through teaching and through student learning and experiencing in class and field, through a variety of class-field configurations.

It is through the selection and ordering of knowledge in all the curriculum areas and sequences and through the way it is taught in class and field that social work purposes and values are communicated. The purpose of social work education is to give the student the opportunity both to understand social work purposes and values and to deepen his commitment to them, even as he becomes knowledgeable and skillful about ways of working toward their realization within the purview of his profession and through the use of its distinctive methods. The development, ordering, and continuous review and modification of a body of knowledge to be required of all students is a task of great magnitude for any profession and for all of that profession's schools. This is particularly true for social work, which draws on knowledge from other fields and disciplines as well as on what it has developed out of its own history and experience. The rapid change in the society it seeks to serve, its own rapidly changing ways of serving society, new knowledge being developed indigenously within the profession and within the disciplines on which it draws—all put formidable demands on social work educators for continuous examination and decision with respect to curriculum content, curriculum organization and structure, and educational processes best suited to prepare for social work practice. Always, the intent is to prepare for practice which shall be at once responsible to the society it serves and contributive to the shaping of that society and social work's own role within it, in the direction of the realization of social work's values.

The 1962 Curriculum Policy Statement of the Council on Social Work Education,[1] to which reference has been made, represented a giant step in ordering knowledge through identifying sequences which constitute the broad areas of knowledge requisite for social work education. That statement put additional flesh on the bones of the Council's earlier curriculum policy statements, and incorporated suggestions for knowledge content, derived, in significant part, from the Curriculum Study[2] which had just been completed under Council auspice. The conception of social work education as a continuum, beginning in the undergraduate years, is receiving considerable attention at the time of this writing. The specific place and nature of field work in social work education have been given extensive and intensive consideration in the 1950s and 1960s by the Council on Social Work Education and its constituent bodies and member schools.[3]

Some brief consideration of the purpose and province of each of the curriculum areas and sequences as they are presently defined and of the place of the field in the total program may be useful before considering how the generic principles of social work method, developed earlier, may be applied to the conduct of a school of social work toward its own more effective realization of purpose.

To the Social Welfare Services and Policy sequence falls the responsibility for developing an historical perspective for viewing the field of social welfare as the locus for social work practice; for identifying changing patterns of social welfare programs over the centuries and throughout the world, and the personalities and movements which helped to shape them; for placing social welfare in its relation to the socio-economic-political scene, in the past and in the present; for examining present programs and operations through which social work functions, the social policies which guide them, the values they express, in all their contradiction and complexity. It is within such a context that the student must grasp the development of social work as a profession, the profession he has chosen as his own, and learn to grapple as the profession must grapple with the problem of how social work can make its best contribution to a changing society which it seeks to serve with its own changing knowledge and skill. It is within this sequence that the student discovers some of the meaning of functioning as a member of a profession which is institutionalized, of functioning not as a private practioner but as a member of a social agency. As he internalizes social work's essential values of respect for the dignity of the individual, commitment to each individual's having the fullest possible opportunity for the realization of himself as an individually fulfilled, socially contributive person, and the development of the kind of society which makes such individual-social self-realization most possible, he is at work on how social policies and programs presently in operation, including the one in which he is placed for field work, further or fail to further those values, realize or fail to realize both the broad purposes of social welfare and social work, and the specific purpose embodied in his particular (field work) agency. So he is both acquiring knowledge and having experiences which fit him to participate in making social work values and purposes more sure of realization through social policy and social welfare organization.

Within the sequence currently identified as the Human Behavior and Social Environment sequence, as in the Social Welfare Services and Policy and in all the sequences, the student both tests and further develops his commitment to social work values. Here he makes his own a sense of the individual as carrier of the life force as it has persisted since life began, as product of his own particular inheritance genetic, cultural, ancestral, as "germ" for his own continuing development as a unique person. He comes to appreciate the way the individual from conception and fetal life forward experiences orderly progressive development, how purpose moves in him, how he expresses purpose as he acts upon and makes use of his environment just as it acts upon and helps to shape him. He gains respect, through following the individual throughout his life cycle, for what he brings to his own growth and for the significance of the "outside" as well, from the first outside of the womb to his relationship with the mother, the family, the neighborhood, the community, the world, the ever-widening "outsides" to which he relates as they affect him and he affects them throughout his life. He learns some of the common ills the flesh is heir to, both physical and psychological, of ways individuals and groups of individuals deal with stress, both physical and social.

As he is developing a deeper understanding of the individual in his infinite variety, physical, intellectual, and emotional, within cultures and as between cultures, he is experiencing more deeply within himself what it is to be human, what it is to be his own highly developed individual self, both as he further develops that self and becomes responsible for its use as a social worker. It is this sequence which carries the responsibility for helping the student become better able to serve individuals and groups and communities of individuals through his understanding of the human being's capacity to make use of relationship to attain personal development and growth in the course of working toward a social purpose. It is in this sequence that a psychological base is laid for Method, rooted in the use of relationship to help another find and work on his own purpose. It is this sequence which contributes so centrally to the student's becoming able, through increased self-awareness and self-discipline, to put himself responsibly and helpfully at the service of another, whether individual, group, or community, in respect to whatever social problem, directed toward whatever specific social purpose.

Within the Methods sequence which constitutes his concentration, the student makes his own the theory underlying his use of a particular social work method to attain some social work purpose, whether of an individual, a group, or a community, as that purpose is congruent with the purpose of some social agency or program. It has been the practice for the three primary methods to be taught separately in the basic professional Master's degree program. There has been a sequence of courses in social casework for the student whose concentration was social casework, a sequence of courses in social group work for the student whose concentration was in social group work, and a sequence of courses in community organization for the student whose process concentration was in community organization. In every instance the student's field placement has been in the process which constituted his practice course, or more accurately, the Methods or practice course has been in the method which constituted the student's field placement.

For students whose process concentration was in one of the secondary processes, for example, supervision, administration, research, or teaching (usually at a post-Master's level) a process course or practice course accompanying the field placement in the process has been made available, uniformly in some schools, not in others.

Discussion of record material, both the student's own drawn from his concurrent (or block) field experience and as introduced by the instructor, has constituted the method of choice for teaching in this sequence. But the emphasis, more marked in some schools than in others, perhaps, has been on the identification and teaching of principles of practice, as they found expression or failed to find expression in the material under discussion. The intent has been to build a theoretical base for the use of a method in social work. Such drawing of the principles from examples of actual practice has been accompanied, in some schools, by a presentation of the principles themselves with illustrative record material serving as the base for discussion of the principles.

Various patterns of experimentation in preparing the student to use more than one method, or to use some principles of a method other than his own, have been in effect for many years. There has been increasing recognition that all social workers work with individuals, groups, and community, and require something other than, or at least in addition to, concentration in one method alone if they are to be effective in meeting the changing requirements of the field. This problem has been met and is being met in a variety of ways. Some schools offer a course at some point in the curriculum which presents the three primary methods in their likenesses and differences. Courses such as Use of Group Process, for students whose concentration is in social casework, or Work with the Individual, for students whose concentration is in social group work are rather common. More rare is the practice of making available one year of concentration, class and field, in one process, for example, Social Casework, and a second year (of the Master's program) in another, for example, Community Organization or Group Work. Some schools are currently experimenting with teaching a single Methods course for students, some of whose placements are in social casework and others in social group work. In yet others the field placement itself is being designed to offer, for certain students, supervised experience in two of the primary processes with the accompanying Methods course encompassing both processes. For some time, the third year or the first year of the doctoral program in one school,* has included a required course in Social Work Processes which presents a generic base in theory for all social work processes, as well as a base for the several processes, primary and secondary, in their differences. The field placements of students in this course cover the range of all the processes, primary and secondary. More recently this course has been accompanied by a Methods course for each student, or group of students, in the particular process which constitutes the focus in his field placement.

It has been stated as the thesis of this book that, as generic principles of practice are developed, as has here been attempted, it is increasingly possible for a student whose concentration has been in one method to learn to use another or to make suitable adaptation of another in the course of his practice. But it should also be clear that sufficient difference has been identified for each of the methods to suggest that a two-year process concentration in one method, class and field, would ordinarily be necessary to produce even a beginning practice skill. To attempt to prepare students in a "generic social work method" for "generic social work practice" seems to this writer to ignore the complexities and the differences of the several methods and to run counter to the way learning of skill in social work practice most surely takes place. At the same time, all schools have the obligation to develop imaginative ways of using the field experience and organizing courses and classes to prepare students with an appreciation and understanding of all Methods, and a capacity for a flexible use of method, without sacrifice of depth of knowledge and skill in one. The point being made here is that what is generic to all social work method can be learned and can *best* be

* The School of Social Work of the University of Pennsylvania.

learned in a single method, mastered in some depth, rather than through exposure to, or a more superficial experience in, several.

Administration as a Method in social work is ordinarily reserved, in its executive sense, for process concentration at the doctoral level of social work education, although there has been some experimentation with its use at the Master's level. However the experience of every student requires an understanding of the principles of administration as they have relevance for social agency practice generally, and specifically, for his own performance as a member of an agency staff as experienced in his field placement. Each student requires the development of some skill, as well, in the administrative aspects of his own performance as a social worker, whatever his primary process concentration.

The Research requirement of all students seeks to assure that students develop the capacity to formulate a question, make an appropriate design for its study, and develop some beginning skill as well in undertaking a study. In other words, the social work student is expected to be helped, not just to be a "consumer of research" but an active participant in research as a member of an agency staff or as individual enterprise. The research attitude, the spirit of questioning what is, including the very bases and premises on which he works, the motivation to extend knowledge should permeate all areas of the curriculum so that the student becomes a doubter and questioner and seeker at the same time he becomes a doer. The learning-teaching problem is not small in helping students develop the confidence to act and at one and the same time the capacity to question as a base for continuing development of their profession and themselves as professional persons. The research sequence or unit has an important part in accomplishing this educational objective but, as has been suggested, it is possible of accomplishment only as the "spirit of inquiry" permeates as objective, and as appropriate to each of its parts, the curricula as a whole, both class and field.

The field placement has appeared by indirection, as each of the curriculum areas has been considered, as a central part of a total curriculum in social work education. A lively state of ferment characterizes this part of curricula in social work at the present time. Because the early schools of social work developed outside of universities as attempts of social agencies to prepare workers to give improved service of a specific (agency) kind, the label of "apprenticeship" was early ascribed to "field work" as part of social work education. As schools moved into and originated within universities, and particularly as they drew increasingly heavily on social science content in addition to social work knowledge, vigorous attempts have been made to "make field work more educational." Too often this objective involves muddy thinking about the purpose of field learning in relation to the total learning experience, and about what is truly educational for the kind of learning there required.

Social work education still accepts, and must always accept if it continues to be professional education, a primary obligation to prepare for practice. That practice, as has been suggested, requires some beginning skill for engaging in research as part of practice. It includes as well, at the doctoral level, opportunity to prepare for research, administration, or teaching as the form of practice for which preparation is given. But for the great bulk of students in the Master's program the preparation is for practice in making available some social service through one of the primary methods of social work, with such appropriate adaptation or use of other methods as the situation may require.

It is the field placement which must always constitute not the locus for the student to apply his knowledge, but the opportunity to develop skill in giving a service. The difference is crucial. In the first instances, the clients, the agency, the community are means to the student's end of becoming a professional social worker. In the second instance, they remain ends in themselves. It is through serving them as ends in themselves and learning to serve them with helpfulness, skill, and accountability that the student becomes a social worker.

The problem of the field unit, with the field instructor a member of the School of Social Work faculty placed in the agency to serve a unit of students from the School, is that the instructor is not "agency." She and the students are an island within the agency without the same kind of necessity and accountability for service that is true for the agency-employed supervisor, who is helping students become professional social workers through giving an agency service. There are advantages in school unit field learning, in the supervisor's closer relation to the school and its total curricula, and often in her greater facility in the teaching aspects of supervision. But such field experience is most effective if it perceives and acknowledges the problem as well as the special advantages in that particular kind of field learning and as school, agency, and field supervisor work to minimize the problem and exploit the promise.

Conversely, the field as locus for learning of one or two or three students supervised by an agency-employed supervisor has the very real advantage of constituting for the student an experience in "playing for real." His supervisor's obligation is to see that agency service reaches the clientele helpfully, skillfully, and with accountability to the supporting society. This administrative requirement constitutes a powerful impetus which the student feels and incorporates as "agency responsibility for service." It is the requirement to give service which motivates him to acquire the knowledge and develop the skill necessary to do it rather than to rely solely on the motivation of his own professional development for his learning. Similarly, as he feels a responsibility (as it inheres in the agency) to serve an individual or group or community he views them, not with the dispassion of observing how they react as it may increase his store of knowledge about people but with a commitment to try to understand in order to help.

There is problem in this kind of field learning too. The agency requirement to give service may bear so heavily on the supervisor that she fails to relate that requirement to what is possible for the student to do at this time, what is *educational* for him to do at this time, and to keep her focus on the student rather than the "case." Her relatedness to the school's total curricula and objectives and her skill in the teaching aspect of her responsibility may be less than the school-employed unit supervisor's. Here too, the task is to face and work with the problem, in imaginative and responsible ways, as developed by the school in conjunction with the agency, and at the same time to exploit the promise or opportunity in this special kind of field learning.

It should be clear that the field placement constitutes the primary opportunity for the student to develop skill in the use of social work method, although classroom learning contributes also in important ways which have been suggested. But the opportunity and the requirement of field learning is broader than that. It is here that the student is functioning as a social worker. The field supervisor's responsibility is to help him understand the purpose of the agency, the values its purpose embodies, its organization for realization of purpose, the administrative process through which its purpose is achieved, and to take responsibility for contributing to the agency's smooth and efficient operation as agency, in addition to developing skill in serving the client, group, or client system assigned to him.

The supervisor's task is to help him place the agency historically in its own growth as part of social welfare effort, and as it is related to a present configuration of agencies and to the social scene. It is in the field placement that the student has the opportunity to question as well as to do, and the supervisor's task is to help him find the balance that is in his own interest as learner, in raising and working on question, and in working from tested knowledge and what presently is. Should his field agency be the locus for his research project, as it is in some schools, the student has the opportunity to work on some question, however limited, in a purposeful, responsible way and to develop skill in "inquiring" through making an inquiry.

For students to develop skill in the use of social work method characterized by the generic principles which have been identified, and by the knowledge and skill which remain specific to them, as well, it is necessary, first of all, for the school as a whole, faculty, class, and field, to be in accord: (1) that the development of skill in method is an important, indeed a focal concern for a professional school of social work, and (2) that all social work method is characterized by the generic principles, which have been identified. When these two conditions obtain, classes in all the curriculum areas are taught in such a way that the student is best able to make use of them, not only for the affirmation of social work values, recommitment to social work purpose, and the acquisition and assimilation of relevant knowledge but also for the development of skill in method as well.

For the Methods teachers themselves, agreement on and full comprehension of the generic principles result in their teaching within a common conceptual frame of reference, and in their use of a teaching method designed to help the student master the theory he is learning. This calls for small classes for the Methods courses, case discussion method, even though principles are presented, extracted, and discussed; liberal use of student's own practice records; intensive use of faculty advising by the faculty member most closely related to the student's practice, that is, his Methods or practice teacher. It calls for the development of structure for keeping the field supervisors closely related to the student's learning in all his classes, and specifically to the principles of practice being developed in the Methods courses. The conferences between advisers and field supervisors, the content required in the periodic field work evaluations of student performance, the theme of supervisors' meetings over the academic year, all reflect the school's endorsement of the generic principles of Method which the student is expected to incorporate in practice skill.

It is suggested further that students are best helped to develop skill in social work method which leads to a social work process of the kind described in those schools which not only value that process and know how to teach it but also use the principles characterizing it in the operation of the total educational program.

"Diagnosis" of the applicant to the school is related not to the student as a total person and not to an assessment of his personality with an attempt to conclude whether that "kind of person" can make a social worker. Rather, the entire application process if focused on the service being offered, a program of professional education for social work. The student is asked to respond in writing and in the application interview to questions related not to his early life and family relationships but to his interest in becoming a professional social worker, and entering on an educational process to that end. Whether or not he appears to be suited for graduate social work education is discovered, by both school and applicant (although the school makes the final decision!), in the course of the application process, on the basis of the way the applicant presents himself and uses the application experience, as well as on the content of what he says about the development of his interest in social work education, life experiences that seem to him related to his interest, his family's relation to his planning, and like matters. Similarly, how he is appearing to the interviewer is put out for the applicant to use in the course of the application interview if that would seem to serve a useful purpose in the school's coming to a conclusion about his suitability for social work education. "You are so guarded in everything you are saying to me, giving so very little of yourself, I wonder whether that is characteristic of you. Would that make it hard for you to share in classes in a way you would be expected to in this school?"

Data other than those derived through the interview with the applicant are used also in the school's coming to its decision on admission: the undergraduate record and quality point average, any available test scores including the result of the graduate record examination, health reports, reference letters, the usual data which have been found significant. Any or all of these data may serve as content for discussion in the application interview, as applicant and interviewer work together to determine both his interest in and suitability for admission to the school of social work. Central in the application process is the engagement of the student in his own diagnosis of himself as a suitable candidate for this particular school, the relating of the diagnosis to the service being offered, and the sharing of the school's understanding of him as a potential candidate as that understanding is being developed and clarified, and as appropriate to the situation.

The principle of relating to the use of time phases as characterizing a process has relevance for every aspect of the student's experience in the school. From the time his inquiry is received by the school, through his application, admission, entering on first year program, ending it, moving to second year, and graduation, the student's experience in the school is regarded as a process. The school takes responsibility for understanding and exploiting what is involved in each time phase to facilitate student engagement in and use of it. Suitable structure is devised to carry the process: meetings with advisers on registration day to facilitate a beginning, student assembly at the opening of the school year, the attention to "beginning" given in each of the classes and in the field. As the year moves along the student is encouraged to deepen his experience as he takes increased responsibility and chooses again and again, each time at a new depth of commitment, to do what he must in order to become what he wants to be.

As the school year and then the two-year program move to conclusion, again suitable structures are devised and used to carry the ending movement: ending conferences of students with advisers, evaluation conferences with field supervisors, class meetings, and all the ceremonies attendant upon graduation.

The school administration is responsible for conceiving of the educational program as a process in which students are engaged, with opportunity provided for all of its time phases to be exploited in their interest as learners. It is responsible as well to conceive of the total operation of the school, in all of its parts, as a process requiring the devising and use of structure to carry that process, with advisory board and like groups, with field supervisors and agencies, with faculty, secretarial staff, library staff. The development and use of appropriate structure to carry the process of an educational program in social work require their own book for development in depth.

The concept of function of agency (professional school of social work) and function of role (whether faculty, secretary, librarian, board member, school administrator) is useful at every step of the process as each party to the process is expected and encouraged and facilitated in carrying his own role fully, with a realization of his own stake in the operation, as it relates to the purpose or function of the undertaking as a whole— the professional education of social work students.

Central to the entire undertaking is the concept of engagement of the other toward realization of an own purpose. Key here is the student himself whose stake in becoming a social worker is recognized and related to in everything the school does, and in the way it is done, from responding to the first inquiry through to graduation. There is open recognition with the student that the choice is his and his alone as to whether he will become a social worker. The school makes available a body of knowledge and teachers to teach it. All the school's resources, class and field, library, secretarial and office, are there for the student, at his disposal, and each part is held accountable for its part in the common undertaking. But whether a student will learn and how deeply he will learn remain his own responsibility.

Dedication to and use of the principle of engagement of the other as the surest way of freeing him to accomplish his own purpose call for examination of the structure necessary to further such engagement. What is the optimum size of class in a particular content area to ensure the most fruitful engagement? How frequently should classes be held? Over how long a time? What is the nature of assignments most conducive of engagement of the student as a learner? What kind of teacher response to assignment is most productive of engagement? What are the nature and structure of the field experience if it is to engage the student in becoming a social worker most fully, in all aspects of what is required of a social worker, and not in any narrow sense of development of skill in method alone? The principle of engagement is true for the school administrators working with faculty and staff no less than for the faculty working with students. It holds for the school's way of working with its field agencies, with individual supervisors, as well as with its board and committees.

What has been presented is suggestive only, but perhaps it is enough to establish that a consistent theoretical base underlying the practice of social work in all its methods has its own relevance for the operation of a program of social work education. Such a base does not by any means constitute the substance of that program. Nor does it by any means constitute all that needs to be known of teaching method or the method of administration of a school of social work. It *can* serve as a frame of reference within which a rich and vital program of education for social work may develop and thrive.

In conclusion, any school of social work which values the development of skill in method and specifically in the kind of method here described, as an important, even focal, concern, is constrained to help its students not only (1) to assimilate appropriate knowledge and develop the motivation and skill to continue to assimilate it and to extend it, (2) to achieve a skill in use of a method characterized by the application of known principles, but (3) to become as well the kind of person capable of functioning effectively as a social worker within the frame of reference affirmed by the school as a whole. The methodological frame of reference developed in this book asks that the student become creative within a pattern, that he achieve his own development as a unique person, and the motivation to continue that development, but that he discipline himself to use his uniqueness within the pattern of his institutionalized profession. This requires that he learn to function contributively as part of some agency staff or operation "whole." It asks further that he achieve what is necessary in his own growth in order that he may consistently, compassionately, generously put himself at the service of some other for its own achievement of its own purposes through the use of the relationship skill and social resources which he is able, and responsible, to extend.

SUMMARY

The purpose and focus of this writing have been recapitulated. Some implications have been suggested for the conduct of those programs of professional education for social work which identify the development of skill in method, and in the particular kind of method here developed, as not only significant but also central in their operation. Relevance of such an identification and commitment have been established for the selection and ordering of knowledge, and for the development of teaching method within the curriculum as a whole, class and field, as well as within the Methods sequences. There has been some consideration of how the affirmation and use of the principles developed as generic for all social work methods can be used in the conduct of an educational program in social work, as a whole and in all of its parts. These principles can be used for the enrichment and progressive development of an educational program as an instrument designed to prepare for a profession which makes heavy demands of its practitioners in knowledge, personal development, and theory-based skill but offers rare reward, too, not only for its members but also for the society they seek to serve.

NOTES

Chapter 1. PURPOSE AND PURVIEW FOR SOCIAL WORK
PRACTICE

1. Kenneth L. M. Pray, "The Role of Professional Social Work in the
World Today," *Social Work in a Revolutionary Age,* pp. 33, 34.

2. Werner Boehm, "Objectives for the Social Work Curriculum of the
Future," *Social Work Curriculum Study,* Vol. I; and Werner Boehm, "The
Social Work Profession," *Society and the Schools.*

3. Helen Witmer, *Social Work,* p. 121.

4. Quoted by permission of Karl de Schweinitz.

5. Grace Marcus, "The Necessity for Understanding Agency Function,"
mimeographed paper in the Library, of the School of Social Work, University of Pennsylvania.

6. See *Proceedings,* First Conference of Charities and Corrections, New
York, 1874, and subsequent *Proceedings* in that decade, especially 1878.

7. *Social Casework, Generic and Specific,* a Report of the Milford Conference, 1929.

8. Central in the contribution of the Council in this respect was the direction given by its first Executive Director, Ernest Witte, and its former
Associate and present Executive Director, Katherine Kendall.

9. Notably the American Association of Medical Social Workers and the
American Association of Psychiatric Social Workers. For the history of
specialization in social work education, see Ruth E. Smalley, *Specialization in Social Work Education,* 1956.

10. By-laws, National Association of Social Workers, 1955.

11. *Ibid.*

12. Ruth E. Smalley, *Specialization in Social Work Education.*

13. By-Laws, National Association of Social Workers, 1962.

14. It will be noted that community organization as a social work process had by this time "joined" casework and group work as a primary method in social work.

15. See "A Working Definition of Social Work Practice," *Social Work,* Vol. III, No. 2(1958), pp. 5–8.

Chapter 2. SOCIAL WORK PROCESSES

1. Funk & Wagnall's *Standard Dictionary of the English Language,* International Edition.

2. *Ibid.*

3. *Ibid.* For a penetrating analysis of *skill* in social casework, see Virginia Robinson, "The Meaning of Skill," in *Training for Skill in Social Casework, Journal of Social Work Process,* Vol. IV (1942).

4. Official Statement of Curriculum Policy for the Master's Degree Program in Graduate Professional Schools of Social Work, *Council on Social Work Education,* 1962.

5. Jessie Taft, "Introduction," and Robert Gomberg, "The Specific Nature of Family Casework," in *A Functional Approach to Family Casework, Journal of Social Work Process,* Vol. V(1944). Reprinted in *Family Casework and Counselling, Journal of Social Work Process,* Vol. VI(1948), IX, X, pp. 82–132.

6. Mary Richmond, *Friendly Visiting among the Poor* (1889), p. 180.

7. Mary Richmond, *What is Social Casework?*

8. *Ibid.,* p. 259.   9. *Ibid.,* p. 255.   10. *Ibid.,* p. 260.   11. *Ibid.,* p. 258.

12. Mary Richmond, *What Is Social Casework,* pp. 98, 99.

13. *Social Casework, Generic and Specific,* a Report of the Milford Conference, 1929.

14. Almena Dawley, "The Essential Similarities in All Fields of Casework," *Proceedings of National Conference of Social Work,* Memphis (1928), pp. 358–60.

15. Virginia P. Robinson, *A Changing Psychology in Social Casework.*

16. *Ibid.,* p. 185.

17. Jessie Taft, "The Relation of Function to Process," *Journal of Social Work Process,* Vol. I, No. 1(1937). Reprinted in Virginia P. Robinson (ed.), *Training for Skill in Social Casework* (Social Work Process Series), 1942, and in Virginia P. Robinson (ed.), *Jessie Taft, Therapist and Social Work Educator,* 1962.

18. *Ibid.,* pp. 3, 5.   19. *Ibid.,* p. 8.

20. Anita Faatz, *The Nature of Choice in Social Casework.*

21. Gordon Hamilton, *Theory and Practice of Social Casework,* pp. 12, 370.

22. Florence Hollis, *Social Casework, a Psycho-Social Therapy.*

23. *Ibid.,* p. 1.

24. Helen Perlman, *Social Casework, A Problem Solving Process,* p. 4.

25. *Ibid.,* p. 203.

26. Felix P. Biestek, S. J., *The Casework Relationship.*

27. Wilber I. Newstetter and Research Associates, *Group Adjustment, a Study in Experimental Sociology.*

28. Grace L. Coyle, *Social Science in the Professional Education of Social Workers,* p. 31.

29. Grace L. Coyle, *Group Work with American Youth,* p. 25.

30. Grace L. Coyle, *Social Science in the Professional Education of Social Workers,* p. 46.

31. Gertrude Wilson and Gladys Ryland, *Social Group Work Practice,* p. 61.

32. *Ibid.* The worker's role is developed particularly in Chapter III, "The Social Group Work Method."

33. Helen U. Phillips, *Essentials of Social Group Work Skill,* pp. 42, 43.

34. C. F. NcNeil, "Community Organization for Social Welfare," *Social Work Year Book* (1954), p. 121.

35. Eleanor Ryder, Essence of a statement prepared for use of the School of Social Work, University of Pennsylvania, 1964.

36. Donald Howard (ed.), "Three Papers on Community Organization," in *Community Organization: Its Nature and Setting.*

37. Harry L. Lurie, "The Community Organization Method in Social Work Education, and appendices, *Social Work Curriculum Study,* Vol. IV.

38. Kenneth L. M. Pray, "What Makes Community Organization Social Work," *Social Work in a Revolutionary Age,* p. 276.

39. *Ibid.,* p. 286, 287.

40. Harold Lewis, "Toward a Working Definition of Community Organization."

41. See, for example, Jack Rothman in *Social Work,* Vol. IX, No. 2, April 1964, and subsequent letters to the Editor, *Social Work,* Vol. IX, No. 3, July 1964, evoked by Rothman's article.

42. Kenneth L. M. Pray, *Social Work in a Revolutionary Age,* p. 277.

43. Harriet Bartlett, "Toward Clarification and Improvement of Social Work Practice, A Working Definition of Social Work Practice," *Social Work,* Vol. III, No. 2.

Chapter 3. SECONDARY SOCIAL WORK PROCESSES

1. Sidney Eisenberg, *Supervision in the Changing Field of Social Work*.
2. Virginia P. Robinson, *The Dynamics of Supervision under Functional Controls*.
3. *Ibid.*, and Virginia P. Robinson, *Supervision in Social Casework*.
4. Virginia P. Robinson, *The Dynamics of Supervision under Functional Controls*, pp. 34, 35.
5. Grace Marcus, "The Need and Value of Supervision," *Journal of Social Work Process*, Vol. X(1959), p. 56.
6. Charlotte Towle, "The Place of Help in Supervision," *Social Service Review*, Vol. XXXVII, No. 4(1963).
7. Sue Spencer, "The Administrative Method in Social Work Education," *Social Work Curriculum Study*, Vol. III, p. 17.
8. Kenneth L. M. Pray, *Social Work in a Revolutionary Age*, p. 285.
9. Lewis Merriam, *Public Service and Special Training*, pp. 1, 2.
10. Virginia P. Robinson, "The Administrative Function in Social Work," in *Four Papers on Professional Function*, p. 30 f.
11. Samuel Mencher, "The Research Method in Social Work Education," *Social Work Curriculum Study*, Vol. IX, pp. 20, 21.
12. Harold Lewis, "Research Analysis as an Agency Function," *Journal of Social Work Process*, Vol. XIII (1962), p. 73 f.
13. E. V. Hollis and A. L. Taylor, *Social Work Education in the United States*, the Report of a Study made for the National Council on Social Work Education.
14. Werner W. Boehm, *Social Work Curriculum Study*.
15. Ruth E. Smalley, "Freedom and Necessity in Social Work Education", *Education for Social Work*, Proceedings, Eleventh Annual Program Meeting, Council on Social Work Education. "Today's Frontiers in Social Work Education," *Frontiers for Social Work*. "Education of Social Workers," *Society and the Schools*.

Chapter 4. A PSYCHOLOGICAL BASE FOR SOCIAL WORK PRACTICE, I

1. George Corner, *Ourselves Unborn.*
2. *Ibid.*, p. 122.   3. *Ibid.*, p. 175.
4. Edmund W. Sinnot, *Cell and Psyche*.

5. *Ibid.,* p. 111.　　6. *Ibid.,* p. 70

7. Edmund W. Sinnot, *The Biology of the Spirit,* pp. 52, 53.

8. For a development of this point, see particularly *The Biology of the Spirit,* Chapter VI.

9. Gordon W. Allport, *Becoming,* pp. 100, 101.

10. Clark Moustakas, *The Self.*

11. Helen Merrell Lynd, *On Shame and the Search for Identity.*

12. *Ibid.,* p. 141.

13. For other writers who express a similar understanding of human nature, see Frondizi, Frankl, Krutch, Dewey, Whitehead, among others.

14. Otto Rank, *The Trauma of Birth.*

15. Marie Jahoda, "Toward a Social Psychology of Mental Health" in *Symposium of the Healthy Personality,* Supplement I, *Problems of Infancy and Childhood,* Transactions of Fourth Conference, 1950.

16. Erik H. Erikson, "Identity and the Life Cycle," Papers by Erik H. Erikson, in *Psychological Issues,* Vol. I, No. 1 (1959).

17. Frederick Allen, "Dilemma of Growth," Reprinted in Frederick Allen, *Positive Aspects of Child Psychiatry,* pp. 63, 64.

18. *Ibid.,* p. 64.

19. Otto Rank, *Will Therapy and Truth and Reality,* especially Chapter XXI, "Creation and Guilt."

20. Erik Erikson, "Identity and the Life Cycle."

21. Dorothy Hankins, "Mental Hygiene Problems of the Adolescent Period," *The Annals* (1944), pp. 128–35. The points which follow are developed in depth in this article.

22. Frederick Allen, "Dilemma of Growth."

23. Erik Erikson, "Identity and the Life Cycle."

24. Clara Thompson, "Cultural Pressures in the "Psychology of Women" and "The Role of Women in this Culture", in Patrick Mullahy (ed.), *A Study of Intra-personal Relations.*

25. For a development of this point, see Erich Fromm, *The Art of Loving.*

26. For a review of some of the literature in this field, see Blenkner, Jahn, Wasser, *Serving the Aging,* Part II, Review of the Literature.

27. *Ibid.,* p. 215.

28. R. J. Havighurst, *Human Development and Education.*

29. Otto Pollak, "Social Adjustment in Old Age: Research Planning Report," *Social Science Research Council Bulletin* 59 (1948). Reference made in *Serving the Aging* (1964), p. 220.

30. J.A.M. Merloo, "Some Psychologic Problems of the Aged Patient", *New York State Journal of Medicine,* Vol. 58. Reference made in *Serving The Aging,* p. 220.

31. Robert Louis Stevenson, "Requiem."

32. Webster's *Dictionary,* unabridged, Third Edition.

33. Jessie Taft, "A Conception of the Growth Process Underlying Social Casework Practice", *Proceedings, National Conference on Social Welfare* (1950), Part II, *Social Work in the Current Scene,* p. 294. Reprinted in *Jessie Taft, Therapist and Social Work Educator,* p. 330.

34. Otto Rank, see particularly *Will Therapy and Truth and Reality.*

35. *Ibid.,* pp. 72, 73.   36. *Ibid.,* p. 73.

37. *Ibid.,* p. 213.

38. Jessie Taft, "Living and Feeling," *Child Study,* Vol. X., No. 4 (1935) p. 105; reprinted in *Jessie Taft, Therapist and Social Work Educator,* p. 153.

Chapter 5. A PSYCHOLOGICAL BASE FOR SOCIAL WORK PRACTICE, II

1. Michael S. Olmsted, *The Small Group; see also* Cartwright and Zander (eds.), *Group Dynamics,* for significant articles in this field.

2. *Ibid.,* p. 144.   3. *Ibid.,* p. 21.

4. *Ibid.,* p. 23, footnote.

5. Ronald Lippit and Ralph K. White, "An Experimental Study of Leadership and Group Life."

6. J. L. Moreno as reported in Michael S. Olmsted, *The Small Group,* pp. 96, 97.

7. Fritz Redl, "Group Emotion and Leadership."

8. Alex Bavelas, "Communication Patterns in Task Oriented Groups."

9. George Homans, *The Human Group.*

10. Michael S. Olmsted, *The Small Group,* p. 112.

11. Robert F. Bales, *Interaction Process Analysis.*

12. Michael S. Olmsted, *The Small Group,* pp. 117, 118.

13. Michael S. Olmsted, *The Small Group,* p. 126.

14. For a full development of this point, see Helen U. Phillips, *Essentials of Social Group Work Skill.*

15. For an analysis of older and newer approaches to a definition of community, see Roland L. Warren, *The Community in America.* This is a book of unusual merit in its presentation of a theoretical conception of community phenomena and of the community as a phenomenon.

16. Louis Wirth, *Community Life and Social Policy,* p. 10.

17. Werner E. Gettys, "The Field and Problem of Community Study" in *The Fields and Methods of Sociology,* edited by L. L. Bernard, p. 74.

18. George A. Hillery, Jr., "Definitions of a Community: Areas of Agreement," p. 118.

19. Roland L. Warren, *The Community in America,* p. 9.

20. *Ibid.,* p. 9.   21. *Ibid.,* Chapter VI.

22. *Ibid.,* see especially Chapter III.

23. *Ibid.,* p. 237.   24. *Ibid.,* Chapter X.

25. *Ibid.,* p. 311.

26. Harold Lewis, Outline statement in response to a draft statement, "Toward a Working Definition of Community Organization Practice," circulated to member graduate schools of the Council on Social Work Education, mimeographed, Library, School of Social Work, University of Pennsylvania, April 1961.

27. Ronald Lippit et al., *The Dynamics of Planned Change.*

28. Herman Stein, "Social Work and the Behavioral and Social Sciences," *Journal of Jewish Communal Service,* Vol. XLI, No. 1 (1964).

29. Hans Selye, *The Stress of Life,* pp. 299, 300.

30. Jessie Taft, "A Conception of the Growth Process Underlying Social Casework Practice," p. 336.

Chapter 6. *A SOCIAL BASE FOR SOCIAL WORK PRACTICE*

1. Grace Marcus, "The Necessity for Understanding Agency Function."

2. This point is developed in the article noted above.

3. Jessie Taft, "The Relation of Function to Process in Social Casework."

4. For some of the specific writings in which contributions to functional theory have been made for the several social work processes, see, among others:

   a. Herbert Aptekar, *Basic Concepts in Social Case Work.*

   b. Anita Faatz, *The Nature of Choice in Social Casework.*

   c. Goldie B. Faith and Rosa Wessel, *Professional Education Based in Practice.*

   d. Harold Lewis, "Research Analysis as an Agency Function"; "Toward a Working Definition of Community Organization Practice"; Functional Theory in Social Work, a Review of the Literature"; "The Significance for Social Work Education of the Student's Approach to the Formulation of a Research Question."

e. Helen U. Phillips, *Essentials of Social Group Work Skill.*

f. Kenneth L. M. Pray, *Social Work in a Revolutionary Age* (particularly for the processes of community organization and administration).

g. Virginia P. Robinson, *Supervision in Social Casework; The Dynamics of Supervision under Functional Controls; Training for Skill in Social Casework; The Administrative Function in Social Work.*

h. Ruth E. Smalley, "The Significance of Believing for School Counsellors"; "Mobilization of Resources within the Individual"; "Helping the Troubled School Child"; "Inner and Outer Resources That Support the Choice of Life and Growth"; "Freedom and Necessity in Social Work Education."

i. *Jessie Taft, Therapist and Social Work Educator,* ed. Virginia P. Robinson (editor), Chap. II. See articles by Taft reprinted in this book.

j. Rosa Wessel, "Family Service in the Public Welfare Agency—Focus or Shift"; "Implications of the Choice to work for Mothers on ADC."

k. See also *Journal of Social Work Process,* Vols. I–XV (1937–1966).

5. Jessie Taft, "The Relation of Function to Process in Social Casework", pp. 13, 14.

6. *Ibid.,* p. 5.   7. *Ibid.,* p. 6.

8. *Ibid.,* pp. 7, 8.   9. *Ibid.,* p. 18.

10. For a particularly fine-grained development of this point, see Anita Faatz, *The Nature of Choice in Social Casework.*

Chapter 7. *A PROCESS BASE FOR SOCIAL WORK PRACTICE*

1. Saul Hofstein, "The Nature of Process: the Implications for Social Work," *Journal of Social Work Process* (1964), p. 17. This original and penetrating article should be read in its entirety for a point of view on the development of process theory in its relevance for social work. The author is indebted to it for much of the thinking here developed.

2. Helen Merrell Lynd, *On Shame and the Search for Identity,* p. 83.

3. *Ibid.,* p. 83

4. Britannica World Language Edition of Funk and Wagnall's *Standard Dictionary.*

5. Webster's *Third New International Dictionary.*

6. Saul Hofstein, "The Nature of Process: the Implications for Social Work."

7. F. C. S. Northrup, *Man, Nature and God.*

8. Banesh Hoffmann, *The Strange Story of the Quantum,* pp. 14–15.

9. Peter Drucker, "The New Philosophy Comes to Life," *Harper's Magazine* (August, 1957), pp. 4–5.

10. *Ibid.* p. 5.

11. See Chapter 4 for some references which support this statement.

12. Julian Huxley, *Evolution in Action,* p. 2.

13. Saul Hofstein, "The Nature of Process: the Implications for Social Work," p. 27.

14. Otto Rank, *see* particularly *Will Therapy and Truth and Reality, Art and Artist,* and *Beyond Psychology.*

15. Jessie Taft, "The Relation of Function to Process."

16. Jessie Taft (ed.), "Introduction," *Journal of Social Work Process,* Vol. I, No. 1 (1939), p. 4.

17. *Ibid.,* p. 3.

18. See particularly the references noted at the end of Chapter 6, Item 4.

19. Roland L. Warren, *The American Community,* p. 147.

Chapter 8. FIVE PRINCIPLES GENERIC FOR SOCIAL WORK PRACTICE

1. For a development of this point, see Otto Rank, *The Trauma of Birth.*

2. Jessie Taft, *Time as the Medium of The Helping Process,* a penetrating presentation of the utilization of time for social work helping, *Jewish Social Service Quarterly* (1949).

3. For a discussion of the meaning of life fear and death fear, see Otto Rank, *Will Therapy and Truth and Reality.*

4. Algernon Swinburne, "The Garden of Proserpine."

5. Webster's Third *New International Dictionary.*

6. The Economic Opportunity Act of 1964, Senate 2642 Public Law 88–452, August 20, 1964, Title II, Sec. 202(3).

7. Ruth E. Smalley, "Inner and Outer Resources That Support the Choice of Life and Growth," *Proceedings,* Conference on Social Crippling, Baltimore, Maryland, 1959.

8. Lewis Merriam, "Public Service and Special Training."

9. Bertha Capen Reynolds, "Between Client and Community," *Smith College Studies,* 1934.

10. Virginia P. Robinson, *The Dynamics of Supervision under Functional Controls.* This point is developed particularly in the final chapter.

Chapter 12. SOME IMPLICATIONS FOR SOCIAL WORK EDUCATION

1. Official Statement of Curriculum Policy for the Master's Degree Program on Graduate Professional Schools of Social Work, *Council in Social Work Education* (1962).

2. *Social Work Curriculum Study,* Vols. I–XIII, Werner Boehm (ed.), Council in Social Work Education.

3. See publications of the Council on Social Work Education since its organization in 1952, including the *Proceedings of Annual Program Meetings.*

BIBLIOGRAPHY

Allen, Frederick, M. D. "Dilemma of Growth," *Archives of Neurology and Psychiatry,* Vol. 37 (1937). Reprinted in Frederick Allen, Positive Aspects of Child Psychiatry, New York, W. W. Norton and Co., 1963.

Allport, Gordon W. Becoming. New Haven, Yale University Press, 1955.

Aptekar, Herbert H. Basic Concepts in Social Case Work. Chapel Hill, University of North Carolina Press, 1941.

Bales, Robert F. Interaction Process Analysis. Reading, Mass., Addison-Wesley Publishing Co., 1950.

Bartlett, Harriet. "Toward Clarification and Improvement of Social Work Practice—A Working Definition of Social Work Practice," *Social Work,* Vol. III, No. 2 (1958).

Bavelas, Alex. "Communication Patterns in Task Oriented Groups," in Group Dynamics, Dorwin Cartwright and Alvin Zander (editors), Evanston, Ill., Row, Peterson and Co., 1953.

Bernard, Luther Lee. (editor). The Fields and Methods of Sociology, Second Edition. New York, Farrar and Rinehart, 1934.

Biestek, Felix P., S.J. The Casework Relationship. Chicago, Loyola University Press, 1957.

Blenkner, Jahn, Wasser. Serving the Aging. New York, Community Service Society of New York, Institute of Welfare Research, 1964.

Boehm, Werner W. "Objectives for the Social Work Curriculum of the Future," Werner Boehm (editor), Social Work Curriculum Study, Vol. I. New York, Council on Social Work Education, 1959.

—— (editor). Social Work Curriculum Study, 13 volumes. New York, Council on Social Work Education, 1959.

—— "The Social Work Profession," in Society and the Schools. New York, National Association of Social Workers, 1965.

Cartwright, D., and A. Zander (editors). Group Dynamics, Research and Theory. Evanston, Ill., Row, Peterson and Co., 1953.

Conference of Charities and Corrections, *Proceedings, 1874–1884,* Vols. I and XI. Boston, Press of George H. Ellis, 1885. Vol. II–X, a variety of publishers.

Corner, George. Ourselves Unborn. New Haven, Yale University Press, 1944.

Coyle, Grace L. Social Science in the Professional Education of Social Workers. New York, Council on Social Work Education, 1958.

—— Group Work with American Youth. New York, Harper and Brothers, 1948.

Curriculum Policy Statement for the Master's Degree Program in Graduate Professional Schools of Social Work, New York, Council on Social Work Education, 1962.

Dawley, Almena. "The Essential Similarities in All Fields of Casework," in *Proceedings,* National Conference of Social Work, Memphis, 1928. New York, Columbia University Press, 1929.

Drucker, Peter. "The New Philosophy Comes to Life," *Harper's Magazine* (1957).

Economic Opportunity Act of 1964. Senate 2642. Public Law 88-452, August 20, 1964. Title II.

Eisenberg, Sidney. Supervision in the Changing Field of Social Work. Philadelphia, Jewish Family Service Society of Philadelphia in association with the School of Social Work, University of Pennsylvania, 1956.

Erikson, Erik H. "Identity and the Life Cycle," in papers by Erik H. Erikson, *Psychological Issues,* Vol. I, No. 1 (1959).

Faatz, Anita. The Nature of Choice in Social Casework. Chapel Hill, University of North Carolina Press, 1953.

Faith, Goldie B., and Rosa Wessel. Professional Education Based in Practice. Philadelphia, School of Social Work, University of Pennsylvania Press, 1953.

Frank, Jerome D., M.D. Persuasion and Healing. Baltimore, John Hopkins Press, 1961.

Fromm, Erich. The Art of Loving. New York, Harper and Brothers, 1956.

Funk & Wagnall's Standard Dictionary of the English Language, International Edition.

Gettys, Werner E. "The Field and Problem of Community Study," in L. L.

Bernard Luther (editor), The Fields and Methods of Sociology. New York, Farrar and Rinehart, 1934.

Gomberg, Robert. "The Specific Nature of Family Casework," in Jessie Taft (editor), Family Casework and Counselling, a Functional Approach, *Journal of Social Work Process,* Vol. V. Philadelphia, University of Pennsylvania Press, 1944. Reprinted in Jessie Taft (editor), Family Casework and Counselling, *Journal of Social Work Process,* Vol. VI. Philadelphia, University of Pennsylvania Press, 1948.

Hamilton, Gordon. Theory and Practice of Social Casework. New York, Columbia University Press, 1940.

Hankins, Dorothy. "Mental Hygiene Problems of the Adolescent Period," *The Annals* (1944).

Havighurst, R. J. Human Development and Education. London, Longmans, Green and Co., 1953.

Hillery, George A., Jr. "Definitions of a Community: Areas of agreement," *Rural Sociology,* XX, No. 2 (June 1955), 118.

Hoffmann, Banesh. The Strange Story of the Quantum, Second Edition. New York, Dover Publications, 1959.

Hofstein, Saul. "The Nature of Process: the Implications for Social Work." Rosa Wessel (editor), *Journal of Social Work Process,* Vol. XIV. Philadelphia, University of Pennsylvania Press, 1964.

Hollis, E. V., and A. L. Taylor. Social Work Education in the United States, the Report of a Study Made for the National Council on Social Work Education. New York, Columbia University Press, 1951.

Hollis, Florence. Social Casework, a Psycho-Social Therapy. New York, Random House, 1964.

Homans, George. The Human Group. New York, Harcourt, Brace and Co., 1950.

Howard, Donald (editor). "Three Papers on Community Organization," in Community Organization: Its Nature and Setting. New York, American Association of Social Workers, 1947.

Huxley, Julian. Evolution in Action. New York, Harper and Brothers, 1953.

Jahoda, Marie. "Toward a Social Psychology of Mental Health," in M. J. E. Senn (editor), Symposium of the Healthy Personality, Supplement I, Problems of Infancy and Childhood, *Transactions of Fourth Conference.* New York, Josiah Macy, Jr. Foundation, 1950.

Journal of Social Work Process. Philadelphia, University of Pennsylvania Press, Volumes I–XV (1937–1966).

Lee, Porter. Social Work as Cause and Function and Other Papers. New York, Columbia University Press, 1937.

Lewis, Harold. Statement in Response to Draft Statement, "Toward a Working Definition of Community Organization Practice," Philadelphia, 1961. Unpublished.

—— "Research Analysis as an Agency Function," in Marie Ganister (editor), *Journal of Social Work Process*, Vol. XIII. Philadelphia, University of Pennsylvania Press, 1962.

—— "Functional Theory in Social Work—a Review of the Literature," in Rosa Wessel (editor), *Journal of Social Work Process*, Vol. XV. Philadelphia, University of Pennsylvania Press, 1965.

—— "The Significance for Social Work Education of the Student's Approach to the Formulation of a Research Question," Social Work Education, Supplement. New York Council on Social Work Education, 1961.

Lippit, Ronald, and Ralph K. White. "An Experimental Study of Leadership and Group Life," Readings in Social Psychology, Revised Edition, Guy Swanson, Theodore Newcomb, and Eugene Hartley (editors). New York, Henry Holt and Co., 1952.

Lippit, Ronald, et al., in William B. Spalding (editor), The Dynamics of Planned Change. New York, Harcourt, Brace and Co., 1958.

Lurie, Harry L. "The Community Organization Method in Social Work Education" and appendices, in Werner Boehm (editor), Social Work Curriculum Study, Vol. IV. New York, Council on Social Work Education, 1959.

Lynd, Helen Merrell. On Shame and the Search for Identity. New York, Harcourt, Brace, and World, 1961.

McNeil, C. F. "Community Organization for Social Welfare," in Social Work Year Book. New York, American Association of Social Workers, 1954.

Marcus, Grace. "The Necessity for Understanding Agency Function." Philadelphia. Unpublished.

——. "The Need and Value of Supervision for the Experienced Case Worker," Dorothy Hankins (editor), *Journal of Social Work Process*, Vol. X. Philadelphia, University of Pennsylvania Press, 1959.

Mencher, Samuel. "The Research Method in Social Work Education," in Werner Boehm (editor), Social Work Curriculum Study, Vol. IX. New York, Council on Social Work Education, 1959.

Merloo, J. A. M. "Some Psychologic Problems of the Aged Patient," *New York State Journal of Medicine*, 58 (1958), 3810–14.

Merriam, Lewis. Public Service and Special Training. Chicago University of Chicago Press, 1936. Copyright 1936 by the University of Chicago.

Moustakas, Clark (editor). The Self. New York, Harper and Brothers, 1956.

National Association of Social Workers, By-Laws. New York, NASW, 1955 and 1962.

Newstetter, Wilber I., and Research Associates. Group Adjustment, a Study in Experimental Sociology. Cleveland, School of Applied Social Sciences, Western Reserve University, 1938.

Northrup, F. C. S. Man, Nature and God. New York, Trident Press, 1963.

Olmsted, Michael S. The Small Group. New York, Random House, 1959.

Perlman, Helen. Social Casework, A Problem Solving Process. Chicago, University of Chicago Press, 1957.

Phillips, Helen U. Essentials of Social Group Work Skill. New York, Association Press, 1957.

Pollack, Otto. "Social Adjustment in Old Age: a Research Planning Report," *Social Science Research Bulletin* 59 (1948).

Pray, Kenneth L. M. Social Work in a Revolutionary Age. Philadelphia, University of Pennsylvania Press, 1949.

Rank, Otto. The Trauma of Birth. London, Paul, Trench, Truber & Co. and Harcourt, Brace, 1929. No translator given.

—— Beyond Psychology. (Published privately, 1941.) New York, Dover, 1958.

—— Will Therapy and Truth and Reality. Translated by Jessie Taft. New York, Alfred A. Knopf, 1947.

—— Art and Artist. Translated by Charles Francis Atkinson. New York, Alfred A. Knopf, 1932.

Redl, Fritz. "Group motion and Leadership", *Psychiatry,* Vol. V, 4 (1942).

Reynolds, Bertha Capen. "Between Client and Community," Smith College Studies, Vol. V, No. 1. Northampton, Smith College School of Social Work, 1934.

Richmond, Mary. Social Diagnosis. New York, Russell Sage Foundation, 1917.

Richmond, Mary. Friendly Visiting among the Poor. New York, The Macmillan Co., 1899.

Richmond, Mary. What Is Social Casework? New York, Russell Sage Foundation, 1922.

Robinson, Virginia P. "The Meaning of Skill," in Virginia P. Robinson (editor), Training for Skill in Social Casework. *Journal of Social Work Process,* Vol. IV. Philadelphia, University of Pennsylvania Press, 1942.

—— (editor). Jessie Taft, Therapist and Social Work Educator. Philadelphia, University of Pennsylvania Press, 1962.

—— A Changing Psychology in Social Casework. Philadelphia, University of Pennsylvania Press, 1930.

—— "The Administrative Function in Social Work," in Four Papers on Professional Function. New York, American Association of Social Workers, 1937.

—— The Dynamics of Supervision under Functional Controls. Philadelphia, University of Pennsylvania Press, 1950.

—— Supervision in Social Casework. Chapel Hill, University of North Carolina Press, 1936.

Rothman, Jack. "An Analysis of Goals and Roles in Community Organization Practice," *Social Work,* Vol. IX, No. 2 (1964).

Ryder, Eleanor. A Statement on Community Development and Community Organization. Philadelphia, 1965. Unpublished.

Selye, Hans. The Stress of Life. New York, McGraw-Hill Book Co., 1956.

Sinnot, Edmund W. Cell and Psyche. Chapel Hill, University of North Carolina Press, 1950.

—— The Biology of the Spirit. New York, The Viking Press, 1961.

Smalley, Ruth E. "Helping the Troubled School Child," *Social Work,* Vol. I, No. 1 (1956).

—— "The Significance of Believing for School Counsellors," *The Bulletin,* National Association of School Social Workers (1952).

—— "Mobilization of Resources within the Individual," *The Social Service Review,* Vol. XXVII, No. 3 (September, 1953).

—— "Inner and Outer Resources That Support the Choice of Life and Growth," in *Proceedings,* Conference on Social Crippling, Baltimore, Maryland, State Department of Mental Health and the National Institute of Mental Health, 1958.

—— "Today's Frontiers in Social Work Education," in W. Wallace Weaver (editor), Frontiers for Social Work. Philadelphia, University of Pennsylvania Press, 1960.

—— "Education of Social Workers," in Society and the Schools. New York, National Association of Social Workers, 1965.

—— "Freedom and Necessity in Social Work Education," *Proceedings,* Eleventh Annual Program Meeting, Council on Social Work Education. New York, Council on Social Work Education, 1963.

—— Specialization in Social Work Education. New York, Council on Social Work Education, 1956.

Social Casework—Generic and Specific: An Outline (A Report of the Milford Conference). New York, American Association of Social Workers, 1929.

Spencer, Sue. "The Administrative Method in Social Work Education," in Werner Boehm (editor), Social Work Curriculum Study, Vol. III. New York, Council on Social Work Education, 1959.

Stein, Herman. "Social Work and the Behavioral and Social Sciences, *Journal of Jewish Communal Service,* Vol. XLI, No. 1 (1964)

Stevenson, Robert Louis. "Requiem."

Swinburne, Algernon Charles, "The Garden of Proserpine."

Taft, Jessie. "Time as the Medium of Helping Process," *Jewish Social Service Quarterly,* Vol. XXVI, No. 2 (1949).

—— "The Relation of Function to Process in Social Casework," in Jessie Taft (editor), *Journal of Social Work Process,* Vol. I, No. 1 (1937).

—— "Introduction," in Jessie Taft (editor), A Functional Approach to Family Casework, *Journal of Social Work Processes,* Vol. V. Philadelphia, University of Pennsylvania Press, 1944. Reprinted in Jessie Taft (editor), Family Casework and Counselling, *Journal of Social Work Process,* Vol. VI. Philadelphia, University of Pennsylvania Press, 1948.

—— "Living and Feeling," *Child Study,* Vol. X, No. 4 (1933). Reprinted in Virginia P. Robinson (editor), Jessie Taft, Therapist and Social Work Educator. Philadelphia, University of Pennsylvania Press, 1962.

—— "A Conception of the Growth Process Underlying Social Casework Practice," in *Proceedings,* National Conference of Social Work, Atlantic City, 1950, Part II, Social Work in the Current Scene. New York, Columbia University Press, 1950. Reprinted in Virginia P. Robinson (editor), Jessie Taft, Therapist and Social Work Educator. Philadelphia, University of Pennsylvania Press, 1962.

Thompson, Clara, "Cultural Pressures in the Psychology of Women" and "The Role of Women in This Culture," in Patrick Mullahy (editor), A Study of Interpersonal Relations. New York, Hermitage Press, 1949.

Towle, Charlotte. "The Place of Help in Supervision," *Social Service Review,* Vol. XXXVII, No. 4. Chicago, University of Chicago Press, 1963.

Warren, Roland L. The Community in America. Chicago, Rand McNally & Co., 1963.

Wessel, Rosa. "Family Service in the Public Welfare Agency—Focus or Shift," *Public Welfare,* Vol. XXI, No. 1 (1963).

—— "Implications of the Choice to Work for Mothers on ADC," in Training for Services in Public Assistance, Social Security Administration, Bureau of Public Assistance, Department of Health, Education and Welfare, 1961.

Wilson, Gertrude, and Gladys Ryland. Social Group Work Practice. Boston, Houghton Mifflin Co., 1949.

Wirth, Louis. Community Life and Social Policy. Chicago, University of Chicago Press, 1956.

Witmer, Helen Leland. Social Work. New York, Farrar and Rinehart, 1942.

INDEX

Administration, as secondary process in social work, 49–52; as "posdcorb," 50, 51; use of generic principles of social work method in, 139, 140; 145, 150; 160, 161; 165–67; 170, 171; as process concentration in social work education, 292, 293, 295

Adolescence, 74–76

Agency function, values in use of, 103 ff.; resistance to use of, 116–17; use of as generic principle of social work method, 151 ff.; *see also* Function; Functional social work

Allen, Frederick, quoted, 41, 71, 72; 76

Allport, Gordon, quoted, 64, 65

Bales, Robert, 91, 92

Bartlett, Harriet, 42

Bavelas, Alex, 91

Beginnings, significance of, 142–46; *see also* Time, use of

Beistek, Felix, 28

Birth, significance of, 68, 69; rank on, 69

Boehm, Werner, 2, 57

Choice, significance of making and acting on, 167, 172; *see also* Faatz, Anita

Community, nature of, 94–98; difficulties for change agent in working with, 96, 97; as process, 128, 129; *see also* Warren, Roland

Community organization, development as primary method and process, 35 ff.; differentiated from community development, 35 ff.; defined as method, 42; use of generic principles in, 134 ff.; illustrative record of, 249 ff.; analysis of use of generic principles in cited record, 273 ff.; as methods concentration in social work education, 292, 294

Conflict and stress, ways of dealing with, 99

Corner, George W., 62; quoted, 63

Council on Social Work Education, role in social work education, 7; significance in laying base for unity, 8; role in establishing fields for practice, 9, 10; role in identifying process concentration in social work education, 10; aegis for curriculum study, 57; curriculum policy, statement of, 289; concern with field work, 290

Coyle, Grace, quoted, 31, 32, 33

Curriculum areas in social work education, 290 ff.

Curriculum policy statement, 18, 289; *see also* Council on Social Work Education

Curriculum study, 54, 289; *see also* Council on Social Work Education

Dawley, Almena, 22

Death, 80

de Schweinitz, Karl, definitions of *social welfare, social services, social work,* 3, 4

Diagnosis, use of as generic principle of social work method, 134–41; use of in social work education, 299–300